# Christian Faith Perspectives in Leadership and Business

Series Editors
Doris Gomez
Regent University
Virginia Beach, VA, USA

Kathleen Patterson
School of Global Leadership and Entrepreneurship
Regent University
Virginia Beach, VA, USA

Bruce E. Winston
Regent University
Virginia Beach, VA, USA

Gary Oster
Regent University
Virginia Beach, VA, USA

This book series is designed to integrate Christian faith-based perspectives into the field of leadership and business, widening its influence by taking a deeper look at its foundational roots. It is led by a team of experts from Regent University, recognized by the Coalition of Christian Colleges and Universities as the leader in servant leadership research and the first Christian University to integrate innovation, design thinking, and entrepreneurship courses in its Masters and Doctoral programs. Stemming from Regent's hallmark values of innovation and Christian faith-based perspectives, the series aims to put forth top-notch scholarship from current faculty, students, and alumni of Regent's School of Business & Leadership, allowing for both scholarly and practical aspects to be addressed while providing robust content and relevant material to readers. Each volume in the series will contribute to filling the void of a scholarly Christian-faith perspective on key aspects of organizational leadership and business such as Business and Innovation, Biblical Perspectives in Business and Leadership, and Servant Leadership. The series takes a unique approach to such broad-based and well-trodden disciplines as leadership, business, innovation, and entrepreneurship, positioning itself as a much-needed resource for students, academics, and leaders rooted in Christian-faith traditions.

More information about this series at
http://www.palgrave.com/gp/series/15425

Bruce E. Winston
Editor

# Transparent and Authentic Leadership

## From Biblical Principles to Contemporary Practices

palgrave
macmillan

*Editor*
Bruce E. Winston
Regent University
Chesapeake, VA, USA

Christian Faith Perspectives in Leadership and Business
ISBN 978-3-030-61995-4 ISBN 978-3-030-61996-1 (eBook)
https://doi.org/10.1007/978-3-030-61996-1



This Palgrave Macmillan imprint is published by the registered company Springer Nature Switzerland AG
The registered company address is: Gewerbestrasse 11, 6330 Cham, Switzerland

# Copyright Notices

# Preface

From public interest commercials addressing corporate malfeasance to institutes on the future of humanity, a clarion call has been issued for transparent and authentic leaders. This book examines and consolidates the many principles and scriptural foundations on what being a transparent or authentic leader truly means. Pertinent questions are addressed such as: How might ancient biblical leaders have principles of transparent and authentic conduct to share with today's leaders? How might openness, honesty, and other variables relate to building trust with followers? Do certain situations influence different levels of prudence in transparency? Might greater levels of transparency prevent organizational crises and contribute to greater organizational success? What characteristics of professional identity and social identity are associated with authentic leadership and followership? What factors contribute to the development of these characteristics? How is self-awareness and self-actualization beneficial as a leader? How does authentic leadership relate to ethical development and organizational culture? Most importantly, what can we learn from the sacred scriptures about transparency and authenticity in leadership for the twenty-first century? How do advanced technologies, social media, and other modes of rapid communication impact transparency and authenticity in leadership? From the exploration of biblical codes to contemporary best practices, readers will have a well-informed and biblical approach to cultivating transparent and authentic leadership in their organizations.

To address the purpose of this book, the authors divided the chapters into three units: (a) Unit One—Genuine Self-Concepts, (b) Unit Two—Honest Roles and (c) Unit Three—Ethical Leadership.

## Unit One—Genuine Self-Concepts

Kristan Price Mason's chapter takes readers on a journey to gain a deeper more profound understanding of Self-Awareness and Self-Actualization as elements of Authentic Leadership.

Danica Myers then addresses how Web 2.0 communication technologies impact leaders' communication. Danica makes the case that stakeholders request organizational leaders to demonstrate high levels of authenticity and transparency in all aspects of organizational communication.

E. Ashley Newcomb focuses on women leader and how they can draw guidance from Biblical values that focus on doing what is right and good rather than seeking the approval of others.

Tim Gregory examines the leadership practices of King Josiah that enabled him to lead his nation in what could be considered one of the greatest reform movements to ever be successfully undertaken. Eight leadership principles are identified and examined

Julie Headley reviewed the lives of ancient Biblical leaders. Daniel, Joseph, and David as three exemplary leaders in the Old Testament that demonstrated the four components of authentic leadership: self-awareness, relational transparency, balanced processing, and internalized moral perspective. By applying the lives of these men to lessons of modern-day authentic leadership, current leaders can further develop their authentic leadership skills.

## Unit Two—Honest Roles

Unit two begins with Patrick Millsap's discussion of Balaam and his donkey, which is a story that reveals both authentic leadership and followership and inauthentic leadership and followership. The chapter includes applications for authentic leadership, authentic followership, and the possibility of authentic organizational context, or culture.

Daniel Holmquist presents a new model of judicious transparency. Judicious transparency refers to the wise, discerning, astute, and sensible use of transparency that seeks to build trust within organizations. This approach to transparency offers a more refined and robust understanding of the nature of transparency, as well as, a potentially stronger and more productive way of practicing transparency.

Andrew Morgan presents accounts of the disciple Peter's life from an intrapersonal and interpersonal perspective of authentic leadership. Peter's account offers an example of authentic and transparent leadership.

## Unit Three—Ethical Leadership

Alicia Peltier continues with the communication theme and discuses leaders use of social media and how transparency and authenticity should be demonstrated. Values-based leadership supports how leaders cultivate authentic relationships with stakeholders

Emmanuel Mamaril examined the Prophet Nathan's rebuke of King David which offers contemporary leaders and followers the power of effective followership and its impact in improving leader transparency.

Sharon Hathaway Forest examines what transparent leadership behaviors are most likely to ensure ethically aligned design and use of AI, the Internet of Things (IoT), blockchain, and cloud services. Her chapter looks at how the rapidity of advanced communications and pervasiveness of social media influence a new digital transparency in leadership along with heightened concerns for privacy and security. Leaders who desire to guide their organizations in the ethical design, development, and use of artificial intelligence and other advanced technologies will find the chapter highlights illuminative strategies for transparent actions and communications.

Amy S. Hamilton examined Rahab's traits and authentic leadership behaviors through a socio-rhetorical analysis of the book of Joshua. Hamilton's chapter explores the question of whether a person who behaves in ways that align with his/her culture but are not aligned with other cultures can be authentic.

Chesapeake, USA — Bruce E. Winston

# Contents

# Editor and Contributors

## About the Editor

**Bruce E. Winston** is Professor of Business and Leadership at Regent University, USA. He previously served as Dean of the School of Leadership Studies. He is co-editor of *Leading an African Renaissance: Opportunities* and *Challenges; as well as Ethics: The Old Testament, The New Testament, and Contemporary Application.* He is the author of *Biblical Principles of Hiring and Developing Employees*, *Biblical Principles of Leading and Managing Employees*, and *Biblical Principles of Being an Employee in Contemporary Organizations.* He is a co-author of *Evaluating Employee Performance through Christian Virtues.*

## Contributors

**E. Ashley Newcomb** is the Director of Training and Curriculum for a government contactor. She completed her Ph.D. in Organizational Leadership at Regent University. Her dissertation was The Role of Leadership in the Social Resilience of Alabama Churches Impacted by Natural Disaster.

**Sharon Hathaway Forrest** is a practitioner in information technology with an emphasis on the mathematics of data science. Her current research focuses on the impact of the Christian faith on the design, development, and use of artificial intelligence and quantum algorithms through a new measurement scale for transparent entrepreneurial leadership with application to more effective and efficient multi-sector collaboration in information technology globally. She is a member of the Association of Women in Mathematics.

**Tim Gregory** is the senior pastor of Family Worship Center in Santa Fe, Texas. He has a Ph.D. in organizational leadership with a concentration in ecclesial leadership. Tim has led multiple mission teams around the world preaching the Gospel and training pastors and church leaders.

**Amy S. Hamilton** is a Ph.D. candidate at Regent University in organizational leadership in the School of Business and Leadership. She presented on the "The Secret to Life from a PMP" at TEDxStuttgart and published "The Project Manager: Life is a Project" in May 2017. Her research focuses on leadership in the modern world.

**Julie Headley** is a third-year Ph.D. student at Regent University studying Organizational Leadership with a focus on Human Resource Development. She has an interest in leadership lessons from the Bible, and as such, has studied the Bible at the undergraduate, graduate, and doctoral levels

**Daniel Holmquist** is President of Church Assistance Ministry, a consulting group that provides leadership development assistance to Christian nonprofits globally. His research focuses on managing and correcting destructive forms of leadership.

**Emmanuel Mamaril** is currently a Doctoral candidate at Regent University's School of Business and Leadership and is pursuing a doctorate in Organizational Leadership with a concentration in Human Resources Development. His research interests include examining ethical leadership and followership, and his dissertation explores the impact of toxic leadership and its impact in organizations specifically within the United States military. In his professional life, Emmanuel Mamaril is serving in the United States Navy as a Human Resources Officer.

**Patrick S. Millsap** has been a global lecturer and trainer as a Vice President and the North American Director of sales for Nikken, Inc., a multinational corporation. He completed his master's degree at Fuller Theological Seminary in global leadership and has taught as an adjunct since 2005. Currently, he is teaching at the University of California—Extension to international students in San Diego and Riverside, California, and in the Fermanian School of Business at Point Loma Nazarene University. He has been the Entrepreneurial module coordinator for the master's program at Mount Saint Mary's University since its inception in 2008. He is currently completing his Ph.D. at Regent University in organizational leadership.

**Major Andrew Morgan** is a Salvation Army Officer serving as the Principal of The Salvation Army College for Officer Training in Winnipeg, Canada. Andrew holds a B.A. in Biblical and Theological Studies and an M.B.A. He is a Ph.D. student studying Organizational Leadership, His research interests include organizational communication.

**Danica Myers** is a doctoral student in the school of business and leadership at Regent University, whose work explores toxic followership and social identity. She is the Chief Operations officer and a staff minister for Damascus Roads, a non-traditional Christian church organization. She is an inspirational speaker and author of the book *Exodus: There is a Way Out* (2015).

**Alicia L. Peltier** teaches in the College of Arts and Science at Regent University, the graduate program at University of Maryland Global Campus, and in the College of Online and Continuing Education at Southern New Hampshire University. She teaches both undergraduate and graduate courses in information systems, computer programming, cyber law and ethics, human factors in cybersecurity, and leadership. She is a Ph.D. student at Regent University where her work explores the intersection of job satisfaction and person–job fit as they relate to motivational gifts for minority populations.

**Kristan Price Mason** a postdoctoral scholar who completed her studies through Regent University's Business and Leadership School, earned a Ph.D. in Organizational Leadership, Human Resource Development. She currently serves as an instructor at Blueridge Community and Technical

College in the Business and Professional Studies department. Scholarly research includes topics such as; authentic leadership, professionals identity, and the concept of flow as it relates to professionals in higher educations.

# List of Tables

CHAPTER 1

# Leveraging Self-Awareness & Self Actualization to Maximize Outcomes

*Kristan Price Mason*

## Introduction

> On the Sabbath (sic) we went outside the city gate to the river, where we expected to find a place of prayer. We sat down and began to speak to the women who had gathered there. 14 One of those listening was a woman from the city of Thyatira named Lydia, a dealer in purple cloth. She was a worshiper of God. The Lord opened her heart to respond to Paul's message. 15 When she and the members of her household were baptized, she invited us to her home. "If you consider me a believer in the Lord," she said, "come and stay at my house." And she persuaded us. (Act 16: 13–15, NIV)

This chapter is geared towards addressing the question; how is self-awareness and self-actualization beneficial to a leader? In order to address

K. Price Mason (✉)
School of Business and Leadership, Regent University, Virginia Beach, VA, USA

Bunker Hill, WV, USA



B. E. Winston (eds.), *Transparent and Authentic Leadership*, Christian Faith Perspectives in Leadership and Business,
https://doi.org/10.1007/978-3-030-61996-1_1

this question, we will take a journey through the ends and outs of what it means to be an authentic leader in order to show how self-awareness, and self-actualization are key elements of authentic leadership. The benefits are addressed from the perspective of the leader and the follower (members of the organization) and the greater good of society. This chapter will open with a biblical reference of a leader.

## Lydia a Trail Blazer and Faithful Believer

Lydia from the city of Thyatira, today known as Turkey, is referenced in Acts 16:1–15, 40 and Philippians 1:1–10. Lydia is a businesswoman, a merchant of purple, a precious commodity in the city of Thyatira (Pascuzzi, 2018). She was spiritual and faithful, a successful businesswoman, influential, a trailblazer and hospitable. Her home was a place of worship.

The purple cloth was unique to the city of Thyatira, in that no other area could produce the cloth, in turn, the city become known and respected for the purple cloth. Therefore, Lydia a woman in an era of patriarchal hierarchy was a well-known, respected seller of purple in a renowned city. She is believed to have been associated with the elite and in highly regarded Roman social circle. Lydia's success was evident in the home she owned which was large enough to accommodate worshipers upward of 35 people, and her comfortable lifestyle which included servants to care for her and her home. Although committed to her work, she always made time to worship and prioritized her spiritual journey.

In Act 16: 12-15 and 16: 40, Lydia is referenced not only as a merchant of purple but also as a worshiper of God. In this passage, Lydia worships with other women of the community, and after Paul baptized her, she invites Paul to stay at her home during his travels.

Lydia was baptized, and it is believed she influenced others to do the same. Lydia is believed to be Paul's first European convert. She played a significant role in ensuring the success of Paul's mission to spread the gospel and convert the people of Europe. Lydia does not have a story of needing to escape a difficult or oppressed past but a story of triumph and early success as a woman whose spirituality was awakened and refined through Paul's preaching's.

After being baptized when Lydia invited Paul to her home, it is believed she was an assertive headstrong woman and unlikely to be one who would take no for an answer. There is no mention of a male in

Lydia's life; therefore, she did not appear to answer to the male hierarchal system that was typical of the era. She appeared to be operating independently in her life.

Lydia took on the role of leadership in leading the first church in the community as entrusted by Paul. Her home was a proseuchē, a prayer-house and served as the first church in Philippi.

Lydia's story reflects a confident and self-assure woman. Her actions represented a level of self-awareness and social awareness. She acted not out of selfishness but seemed to have a deep concern for others. While the biblical details regarding Lydia's life are sparse, the information that is available one could argue defines her as a self-aware, authentic leader. Her commitment beyond work alludes to her achieving the lower needs of Maslow's Hierarchy of Needs; physical, safety, love and esteem and one might presume she was motivated by self-actualization considering her concern for others and greater purpose represented by her devotion to her religious practice.

As we delve deeper into authentic leadership and the elements of self-awareness, and self-actualization allow Lydia's story to be a potential point of a reference.

The complexity of leadership continues to increase due to the complexity of society, in fact, "evolutions and revolutions in technology, globalization, business consolidation, and marketplace fragmentation have fundamentally changed the nature of organizations" (Stum, 2001, p. 4). Additionally, "a workforce has emerged that is more educated, mobile, diverse and discerning in work and life choices than ever before" (Stum, 2001, p. 4). Statistically speaking women are well represented in comparison to men in obtaining degrees of higher education including advanced degrees. Therefore, it would only be expected that women are in the workplace and potentially seeking leadership positions (Levitt, 2010). These facts demand response and leadership that will accommodate these shifts and future shifts. This requires "building a new employee/employer social contract that enables organizations to improve employee commitment and retention, it is a challenge of blending some well- established truths with innovative approaches that fit new circumstances" (Stum, 2001, p. 9). Understanding and leveraging the social exchange theory can be used to strengthen the leader follower relationship and positively effect factors such as organization communication, employee satisfaction and employee engagement (Jiang & Men, 2017).

Leaders are expected to exercise moral judgment and be accountable for their members and outcomes (Branson, 2007). Therefore, a leader's moral conscious is significant. The leaders moral conscious is rooted in a desire to make the world a better place, exercise passionate determination and make sound moral decisions (Branson, 2007, p. 471). This requires reflection of SELF; self-concept, self-esteems, motives and values (Branson, 2007). Structured self - reflection is a key element of moral development in that it nurtures moral consciousness (Branson, 2007, p. 473). Moral consciousness aids in the leader's growth, living a more fulfilling meaningful life and gaining self-knowledge (Branson, 2007, p. 473). Therefore, moral consciousness can be associated with self-actualization. The leader "through the gaining of self-knowledge, the person is more able to transcend both their mind and their body and thus can be aware of them as objects in awareness, as experiences" (Branson, 2007, p. 475). Likewise, strong leader- member relationships are important as well as fostering an environment of trust is pivotal.

Authentic leadership has been conceptualized as pattern of leadership behaviors which include strong self-awareness, internalized high moral standards, balanced processing of information as it relates to ethical decision making and transparency in cultivating interpersonal relationships between leader and follower (Walumbwa, Avolio, Gardner, Wensing, & Peterson, 2008). In fact, Jiang and Men (2017), state "Employees who are managed by authentic leaders tend to perceive the organization, communication as transparent" (p. 238). According to Walumbwa et al. leaders' self-awareness is a personal reflection of their personal strengths, weaknesses, and how one's multifaceted self is contracted through the interaction with others. The social exchange theory, which is centrally focused on the reciprocation of benefit between two mutually dependent parties, can be used to help understand the relationship between these factors and employee engagement. For example, when employees perceive personal enrichment in their life from their work experience, they are more likely to be more engaged in their work (Jiang & Men). These factors can work together to build honest relationships built on the foundation of a mutually beneficial relationship between leader and follower. Jiang and Men summarize this very well, "organizations should build a transparent communication culture or climate that ensures the free flow of truthful, complete, relevant, and substantial information in a timely manner, facilitates upward communication and listening, and welcomes employee participation and comments regardless of whether they are commending, criticizing, or complaining" (pg. 240).

## The Authentic Leader

Authentic leadership can be defined as one deploying his or her true self in daily enterprises (Kinsler, 2014). Key qualities of Authentic Leadership are high self-awareness and self-regulation (Kinsler, 2014). Authentic leadership is associated with positive organizational behavior and member success. Historically speaking authenticity dates back to the Greek philosophy, "Know Thyself" (Duncan, Green, Gergen, & Ecung, 2017).

Therefore, research advocates for Authentic Leadership Development which supports leaders as well as the entire organization including front line staff. Kinsler (2014) posits "the notion of cultivating an 'authentic organization' is suggested as a way of realigning what a company claims they value with what followers and customers experience" (p. 92).

As it relates to Authentic leadership and Authentic Leadership Development the following has been gathered from the research. Authentic leaders have the following (Kinsler, 2014).

- A high level of self-awareness.
- Ability to objectively know one's strengths and weaknesses.
- Ability to exercise objective decision making.
- Ability to interact honestly with others.
- Ability to act based on one's personal beliefs and values.
- Exercise self-regulation.
- Strong ethics and positive moral values.
- A since interest in the development and success of others.

Authentic leadership embodies four dimensions; self-awareness, balanced processing, internalized moral perspective and relational transparency (Kinsler, 2014).

- Self-awareness refers to an individual understanding and how he or she makes sense of the world. This is an awareness of strengths, limitation and other perception.
- Balance processing is exercising objectivity and taking into account multiple perspectives and the options of others.

- Internalized moral perspective refers to an individual's ability to be guided by his or her high moral standard and ethical conduct and not by the external pressures.
- Relational transparency is a leader's ability to present one's true self. This requires openness and sharing information and expressing one's feelings.

Self-awareness as an element of Authentic leadership is the objective and selective processing of information about oneself. The components of self-awareness are as follows; values, identity, emotions, and motives/goals (Kinsler, 2014). The key components of self-regulation as it relates to Authentic Leadership, include; internalized regulation, balanced processing of information, authentic behavior and relational transparency.

Authentic leaders have a high level of Emotional Intelligence (EI). EI can be defined as an individual's ability to reason based on accurate emotions and use emotional knowledge to enhance thought (Duncan et al., 2017). Bar- On is the mixed model approach to approaching EI. This method is a cross between the interrelations of emotional and social competencies. The is an approach to understanding how well individuals understand themselves, others and manage daily demands (Duncan et al., 2017).

Authentic leadership has also been linked to high self-esteem and life satisfaction (Kinsler, 2014). Authentic leaders typically have high self-esteem and sense of self-worth and therefore less likely to conform to others which is all positively associated with positive work outcomes (Kinsler, 2014). Authentic leaders also have a positive effect on followers, fostering a sense of hope, trust, and optimism all associated with positive well- being for followers as well.

While the data is limited there is empirical evidence which shows a relationship between authentic leadership and employee turnover and retention. This is based on the notion that authentic leaders' have the ability to create optimal work environments and foster strong relationships will increase employee engagement and therefore increase the likelihood of the retention (Azanza, Moriano, Molero, & Mangin, 2015). The study conducted by Azanza et al. (2015), supports that there is a negative relationship between authentic leadership and turnover but a positive relationship with engagement. In turn, suggesting that an authentic leaders' ability to engage members and encourage and support member development increases the members commitment to their work (Azanza et al. 2015). The impact that authentic leaders have on members can also be discussed in reference to elements such as Positive Organizational Behavior, trust, emotions, and identity theories (Liu, Fuller, Hester, Bennett, & Dickerson, 2018, p. 219). Additionally, authentic leadership encourages positive behaviors amongst members through cognitive and motivational processes such as supervisor–member trust (Liu et al., 2018).

Liu et al.'s (2018) study supported that authentic leadership is positively associated with supervisor identification, psychological safety, and job engagement. Furthermore, supporting authentic leaders can positively influence members' creating hope, increasing optimism, and building self-efficacy. The findings also support the significant role authentic leadership can play in empowering members and building high-quality relationships.

There is limited research which posits that authentic leadership has a positive relationship with creativity. This is because authentic leadership has been acknowledged as increasing positive emotions amongst members and creating a positive, transparent interaction which are all positively associated with creativity (Xu, Zhao, Li, & Lin, 2017).

Research also supports that authentic leadership and LMX (Leader-Member Exchange) are positively associated. Leaders who are able to have high-quality LMX relationships are also more likely to encourage creativity amongst members. Likewise, authentic leadership, high level of LMX relationships are also associated with a sense of psychological safety and individuals' thriving. These factors also contribute to individual creativity (Xu et al., 2017).

To further explore what thriving at work means it refers to positive connections and relationships with members at work including leaders. Authentic leaders' level of self-awareness and mindfulness, along with their respect for others allows him or her to be transparent and encouraging to members. This fosters an environment where members feel a sense of achievement, are encouraged to learn and be positive (Xu et al., 2017). In a study conducted by Xu et al. (2017), it was concluded: "LMX and employee thriving at work sequentially mediated the positive relationship between authentic leadership and individual creativity" (p. 490).

Authentic leadership is believed to be at the root of other leadership styles and processes. The elements of authentic leadership which overlap between other leadership styles and theories serve as an opportunity to provide validity to these leadership styles including but not limited to transformational leadership with authentic leadership and employee performance (Liu et al., 2018).

While there are key characteristics and qualifying elements of authentic leadership it is also important to acknowledge Authentic Leadership is unique because it is contingent on the individual leaders' skills and personal approach (Kinsler, 2014). Considering the ever-changing and the complexity of the economy, authentic leadership can have a significant impact. Authentic leadership can aid in restoring organizational confidence, hope, optimism, resilience and meaningfulness (Liu et al., 2018).

## Self-Awareness

Self-awareness as a key element of authentic leadership offers an opportunity to explore the definition and implication of self-awareness. Mindfulness is a construct of authentic leadership but also a component of self-awareness. Mindfulness is defined as attentive awareness of what is taking place. Mindfulness is positively associated with the following:

- lower levels of emotional disturbance,
- high levels of subjective well- being,
- greater awareness,
- understanding and acceptance of emotion,
- individual flourishing,
- optimistic wellbeing, and
- less defensive reaction when threatened (Kinsler, 2014, p. 100).

Mindfulness requires one to silence internal noise and be in a space with one's thoughts, emotions and body sensations. Practicing authenticity allows a leader to be him or herself and experience clarity. Exercising mindfulness can enrich self -awareness (Kinsler, 2014). Practicing mindfulness and being in the moment may encourage the leader to be more aware and receptive to information he or she may not have been willing to receive if not being mindful. Additionally, aiding in the leader removing bias when processing information (Kinsler, 2014). Mindfulness is also associated with self-regulation (Kinsler, 2014). The leader's awareness promotes flexibility and discourages the somewhat natural reactive response but instead allows the leader to be more intentional and thoughtful in his or her decision making. The reactive or the automatic response is acting from a place of mindlessness, and while it may be based on previous lived experience, it may not accurately account for the present.

Operating from mindfulness versus mindlessness provides the leader an opportunity to recognize the moment of automatic response and make a choice "consciously align behavior with inner values and needs" (Kinsler, 2014, p. 100). To approach the situation without bias and objectively. The approach of mindfulness since it does remove bias and requires the leader to be objective and consider multiple perspectives the leader is less likely to be acting from a selfish-space, or in one's self-interest. Therefore an "authentic leaders' perspective, the opportunity arises for more intentional, proactive and purposeful action that is aligned to their authentic self" (Kinsler, 2014, p. 101)

## Self-Actualization

"Leaders with high emotional intelligence can establish psychological contracts with employees to ensure their lower level needs are met and help them achieve the higher order needs on Maslow's model, especially high self-esteem and self-actualizing behavior" (Decker and Cangemi, 2018, p. 30). Self-Actualization is where an individual reaches his or her full potential (Decker and Cangemi, 2018). This is an on-going state, and one will continue to be motivated by the need for self-actualization as he or she grows and set new goals. The self-actualized person has a problem—centered approach to life, increased creativity, and high frequency of peak experience (Thornton, Privette, & Bundrick, 1999).

Self-actualization can also be defined as the process of one maximizing their full potential "creativity, autonomy, spontaneity, and a vibrant understanding of what one's desires and wishes" (Tripathi and Moakumla, 2018, p. 499). Authentic leadership is associated with factors which define self-actualizations, psychological wellbeing, and life satisfaction. Research has drawn a parallel between authentic leadership and emotional intelligence. Likewise, there is an existing relationship between EI and self-actualization. This is important and relevant because business has shifted and the demand for leadership skills are beyond cognitive intelligence and technical knowledge. A strong leader should possess EI as well. Be reminded EI is defined as an individual's ability to reason based on accurate emotions and use emotional knowledge to enhance thought.

The components associated with EI are; self-awareness, self-regulation, motivation, empathy and social skills.

Maslow's Hierarchy of needs explores the factors that motivate people. This is often is depicted in a pyramid and include physical needs, security and safety, love and belonging, self-esteem, and self-actualizing. The focal point here is the later, self-actualizing. Based on Maslow's Hierarchy of Needs there is an interdependency on each of the five motivating levels and one cannot achieve a higher level without first achieving the lower (Decker and Cangemi, 2018). Therefore, in order for one to achieve self-actualization or be motivated to achieve self-actualization one must have already achieved the four lower levels. Leaders who have high EI are believed to have achieved the first three needs and moving past self-esteem to now be motivated by achieving self-actualization. According to Decker and Cangemi (2018) "Leaders high in emotional intelligence achieve self-actualizing behavior through utilization of the four skills described by Bradberry and Greaves (2009): self-awareness, self-management, social awareness, and relationship management" (p. 28).

Those striving towards self-actualizing are highly creative and strive towards self-mastery. Those who are motivated by self-actualization and embody EI have; Self-awareness, exercise self-management, social awareness and relationship management (Decker and Cangemi, 2018). Based on Maslow's research on self-actualization, leaders with EI, have an "efficient perception of reality and are comfortable in their own'(sic) skin" (Decker and Cangemi, 2018, p. 28). In addition to perception, impeccable sense of self these leaders have an awareness of how their actions affect others (Decker and Cangemi, 2018). "Emotionally intelligent leaders practice humility and respect others, thus creating a democratic character structure...... They also resist enculturation by understanding cultural norms and differences" (Decker and Cangemi, 2018, p. 30).

An emotionally intelligent authentic leader, motivated by self - actualization will operate in a state of mindfulness and have an awareness of how their actions will affect others, having empathy for others. An emotionally intelligent, authentic leader motivated by self - actualization will invest in and make time for personal development.

Self-Management is where:

- "Self-regulated leaders can control their emotions and avoid the temptation to over-react in stressful situations" (Decker and Cangemi, 2018, p. 29).

- "They understand their values and do not compromise them and are personally responsible for their actions; they hold themselves accountable rather than blame others, and practice being calm" (Decker and Cangemi, 2018, p. 29).
- "They are problem-centered as opposed to ego- centered and integrate their talents towards finding solutions to address the problem at hand" (Decker and Cangemi, 2018, p. 29).

Social awareness allows this leader to have empathy, organizational awareness and be service oriented (Decker and Cangemi, 2018). There is a level of sensitivity to environmental factors and a natural ability to build rapport and relationships with other. Per Decker and Cangemi (2018) "self-actualizing behaviors occur through a feeling of kinship with others, or what Maslow (1970) referred to as *gemeinschaftsgefühl* and through deeper, more profound interpersonal relationships" (p. 30).

Relationship management as it relates to the self-actualized, emotionally intelligent leader refers to the leader's strong sense of self-confidence and ability to enhance positive relationships. Their confidence in service as a sense of security and allows this leader not to feel threatened by others (Decker and Cangemi, 2018). Leaders with EI are self-motivated and do not see limits. The characteristics of EI aligns with those who someone who is motivated by self-actualization.

Peak performance and optimal experience parallel with self-actualization (Thornton et al., 1999). Peak performance refers to a high level of functioning and superior behavior exceeding one's average performance. It is a state of efficiency, creativity, and productivity (Thornton et al. 1999). A peak experience and peak performances often coincide. Maslow (1971) described the peak experience as a state of "pure success" (p. 122). Peak experience is essential to the achievement of self-actualization (Maslow, 1971). Additionally, it is believed that peak performance occurs in what can be described in an altered state in which one does not have control over and therefore does not occur intentionally (Thornton et al. 1999).

Peak performance occurs when one is in a state of FLOW, this is where there is just the right balance between challenge and personal skill. Thornton et al. (1999), posits this an intrinsically rewarding experience. Peak performers much like emotional intelligence and self-actualization are described as self-managers and also have an innate desire for meaningful achievement (Thornton et al. 1999). This desire for meaningful achievement is on-going and accompanied by an innate desire to learn and grow (Thornton et al. 1999). Peak experiences are associated with the feeling of fulfillment, significance and joy (Thornton et al. 1999).

Per Thornton et al. (1999). "If self-actualization can be operationally defined as the frequent occurrence of peak performance and peak experience, further avenues are opened for application of self-actualization theory in business." (p. 262).

16 Distinguishing Characteristics of Self-Actualizing People:

- Realistically Oriented,
- Acceptance and realism,
- Spontaneity,
- Autonomy and Solitude,
- Confidential and privacy,
- Autonomy and Independence,
- Sustained newness/appreciation,
- The Peak Experiences,
- They identify with mankind,
- Interpersonal relations,
- Values and Attitudes,
- Discriminating between means and ends,
- Philosophical and unhostile sense of humor,
- Creativeness,
- Resistance enculturation, and
- Imperfections, (Tripathi and Moakumla 2018).

## Outcomes

> People want leaders with moral codes that are deep, innate, and instinctive so that they will not lose direction in the face of uncertainty or pressures. (Branson, 2007, p. 471)

Considering the importance of Authentic Leadership and the significant impact in which Authentic Leadership could have on business this is an opportunity further explore how to scale. The Authentic Leadership Questionnaire (ALQ) cab be used to measure authentic leadership. The ALQ measures four dimensions: relational transparency, internal moral perspective, balances processing and self -awareness. The ALQ attempts to incorporate EI and elements of self-awareness (Duncan et al., 2017).

Based on the data presented in this chapter the following are all outcomes of Authentic Leadership;

- Associated with Emotional Intelligence,
- Cultivating Authentic Organizations,
- Leading Ethically,
- Influencing an Ethical culture,
- Reinforce follower trust,
- Associated with personal development,
- Associated with perspectives,
- Increased creativity,
- Positive LMX,
- EI and Self-Actualization,
- Peak Performance and Peak Experiences,
- Increased member engagement,
- Decrease turnover intent,
- Develop and foster meaning relationships, and
- Summarize the Benefits.

## Conclusion

> People want their leaders to act morally (sic) whereby they will not produce harm but rather will show the virtues of doing good, of honoring others, of taking positive stands, and of behaving in ways that clearly show that their own (sic) self-interests are not the driving motivation behind their leadership. (Branson, 2007, p. 471)

Authentic leaders in all that has been discussed are exemplary examples of leaders with GRIT. GRIT per Stoltz (2015), "is your capacity to dig deep and do whatever it takes—even sacrifice, struggle and suffer—to achieve your most worthy goals in the best ways." (p. 5). Leadership GRIT is defined as "your capacity to get your team, or followers in general, to dig deep and do whatever it takes—even sacrifice, struggle, and suffer—to achieve their most worthy goals in the best ways" (Stoltz, 2015, p. 50). Not only does the Authentic leader display GRIT but their ability to practice mindfulness, be self-aware as well as socially aware and their desire to help others allows Leadership GRIT to be a natural aspect of their leadership style. The four dimensions of GRIT are; resilience, instinct, tenacity, and robustness (Stoltz, 2015).

We opened with the story of Lydia, as a virtuous example of a women in leadership during a time where this was uncommon. Through Lydia's story she was transformed by god after meeting Paul and committed herself to Jesus and encouraged those who followed her to do the same. The New King James Version of the bible reads in Philippians 1:6, being confident of this very thing that He who has begun a good work in you will complete it until the day of Jesus Christ. Wesley's teaching on Philippians 1:6 focus on three themes; justification, sanctification, and glorification. In one sense Wesley discuss persuasion as it relates to "he who hath begin a good work in you, will perfect it until the day of Christ" (Griffin, 2018, p. 127). Here is a slight deviation in the NKJV of the text from "complete it until the day of Jesus Christ" to read instead "perfect it until the day of Christ." Griffin suggest while this deviation may have been an attempt to bring the text closer to the original it may have also been intentional by Wesley to place emphasis on the idea of working towards perfection over time. Potentially in the sense of perfecting oneself, constantly working to improve, to be a better version of one's self each day. Wesley, to support the idea of holiness of the heart and life, and Christian perfection in his work suggests that the good work of god in the believer starts at the point of justification when forgiven of their sins and then continues with growth and maturity within the believer. The transformation of the believer to God's new creation creates a state of great holiness and happiness.

## References

Azanza, G., Moriano, J. A., Molero, F., & Mangin, J. P. L. (2015). The effects of authentic leadership on turnover intention. *Leadership & Organization Development Journal, 36*(8), 955–971. https://doi.org/10.1108/LODJ-03-2014-0056.

Branson, C. M. (2007). Improving leadership by nurturing moral consciousness through structured self-reflection. *Journal of Educational Administration, 45*(4), 71–495. https://doi.org/10.1108/09578230710762463.

Decker, P., & Cangemi, J. (2018). Emotionally intelligent leaders and self-actualizing behaviors: Any relationship? *Ife Psycholgia, 26*(2), 27–30.

Duncan, P., Green, M., Gergen, E., & Ecung, W. (2017). Authentic Leadership—Is it more than emotional intelligence? *Administrative Issues Journal: Connecting Education, Practice, and Research, 7*(2). https://doi.org/10.5929/2017.7.2.2.

Griffin, R. K. (2018). The good work of justification, sanctification, and glorification: John Wesley's soteriological explanation of Philippians 1:6. *The Asbury Journal, 73*(1) 121–137. https://doi.org/10.7252/journal.01.2018s.06.

Jiang, H., & Men, R. L. (2017). Creating an engaged workforce: The impact of authentic leadership, transparent organizational communication, and work-life enrichment. *Communication Research, 44*(2), 225–243.

Kinsler, L. (2014). Born to be me… who am I again? The development of Authentic Leadership using evidence-based leadership coaching and mindfulness. *International Coaching Psychology Review, 9*(1), 92–105.

Levitt, H. (2010). Woman and leadership: A developmental paradox. *Adultspan Journal, 9*(2), 66–75.

Liu, Y., Fuller, B., Hester, K., Bennett, R. J., & Dickerson, M. S. (2018). Linking authentic leadership to subordinate behaviors. *Leadership & Organization Development Journal, 39*(2), 218–233. https://doi.org/10.1108/LODJ-12-2016-0327.

Maslow, A. (1971). *The further reaches of human nature*. New York: Viking.

Pascuzzi, M. (2018). Lydia: Leader of the first house church in Philippi. *L'osservatore Roman*. Retrieved from http://www.osservatoreromano.va/en/news/lydia-leader-first-house-church-philippi.

Stoltz, P. (2015). Leadership GRIT: What new research reveals. *Executive Forum, 78*, 49–55.

Stum, D. L. (2001). Maslow revisited: Building the employee commitment pyramid. *Strategy & Leadership, 29*(4), 4–9. https://doi.org/10.1108/10878570110400053.

Thornton, F., Privette, G., & Bundrick, C. (1999). Peak performance of business leaders: An experience parallel to self-actualization theory. *Journal of Business and Psychology, 14*(2), 253–264.

Tripathi, N., & Moakumla. (2018). A valuation of Abraham's Maslow's theory of self-actualization for the enhancement of quality of life. *Indian Journal of Health and Well-being, 9*(3), 499–544.

Walumbwa, F. O., Avolio, B. J., Gardner, W. L., Wernsing, T. S., & Peterson, S. J. (2008). Authentic leadership: Development and validation of a theory-based measure. *Journal of Management, 34*, 89–126.

Xu, B. S., Zhao, S. K., Li, C. R., & Lin, C. J. (2017). Authentic leadership and employee creativity: Testing the multilevel mediation model. *Leadership & Organization Development Journal, 38*(3), 482–498. https://doi.org/10.1108/LODJ-09-2015-0194.

CHAPTER 2

# Authentic Leadership in a Digital World

*Danica Myers*

## Introduction

The virtual business world has become an even more critical component in the sphere of business due to the shift in the business environment, because of the global pandemic. The current business environment abounds with turbulence, and there is a need for new technologies as traditional business operations face disruption. As organizations face disruption, organizations must adapt their business strategies to address the revolution that is taking place. New business models are emerging, and some organizations have embraced new technologies to conduct operations in a more significant digital context. With business models changing, the demands of leadership must change as well. Leaders need to adapt to leading in a digital context.

The shift to digital technologies through the "digital revolution" crucially changed the way leaders lead (Schwarzmüller, Brosi, Duman,

D. Myers (✉)
School of Business and Leadership, Regent University, Virginia Beach, VA, USA

Steele, AL, USA



B. E. Winston (eds.), *Transparent and Authentic Leadership*, Christian Faith Perspectives in Leadership and Business,
https://doi.org/10.1007/978-3-030-61996-1_2

& Welpe, 2018). Leadership is vital, in the shift to a digital business environment, as organizations seek their footing (Kane, Phillips, Copulsky, & Andrus, 2019). During this time of disruption, organizations require influential leaders at the helm (Kane et al., 2019). In a digital world, organizational leaders must not only articulate a vision people can rally around, but also create the conditions that enable digital maturity as well as attracting the best talent and bringing out the best in the talent they attract (Kane et al., 2019).

## Advanced Technology

Technology has transformed how people access, connect with and construct information (Gardner, 2013). Technology has advanced rapidly, with its functionality available on different platforms (cell phones, personal digital assistants [PDAs], and laptops) and networks (Internet protocol, wireless fidelity, etc.) (Denstadli, Julsrud, & Hjorthol, 2012). With advanced technologies and modes of rapid communication, individuals across the world possess instant access to information. People are no longer compelled to wait to send and receive information. Information is emitted and disseminated, with the capability to reach thousands of people in a matter of minutes.

Advances in communication technology emerged into what is known as Web 2.0. Web 2.0 technology, such as the Internet, provides a higher measure of communication and collaboration (Andriole, 2012), as the Internet has become an essential tool (Montague, Gazal, Wiedenbeck, & Shepherd, 2016). The Internet affects how individuals and organizations communicate. As organizations evolved to use Web 2.0 technology, the use of Web 2.0 technology spread into the business sector with the rise of Enterprise 2.0. Enterprise 2.0 offers a new approach to the management of knowledge (Gardner, 2013). Enterprise 2.0 enables new forms of communication, collaboration, and innovation (Gardner, 2013).

Enterprise 2.0 organizations adapted to create and maintain an online presence through e-commerce, where E-commerce is a form of e-business. E-commerce constitutes serving customers and collaborating with business partners and implementing electronic transactions in an organization (Darwis, 2013). New technologies can facilitate work not possible previously (McAfee, 2006). Along with other technological advances and the advance of Web 2.0 and Enterprise 2.0, these advances brought forth what some call the “digital revolution.”

## The "Digital Revolution"

The shift of organizations to a digital context began first with the rise of the Internet. The rise of the Internet, along with the "digital revolution," impacted organizations, where specific industries, including entertainment (books, music, and movies), have physical stores as a secondary method (Montague et al., 2016). The "digital revolution" shocked many once-prominent organizations. So much so that the forces of the digital revolution have shaken company after company. Industries have been transformed. Entire media and product forms have vanished (Michelman, 2019). The landscape of the business world is continuing to adapt and change as organizations are forced to change business models to survive.

The "Retail Armageddon" and "digital revolution" are taking place due to changes in the way that people communicate and interact with the advent of advanced technologies, modes of rapid communication, and the shift in the way businesses operate. Advanced technologies, rapid modes of communication, and economic crises have acted as catalysts for change from face-to-face operations to a digital world. This digital world expanded the reach of individuals and organizations alike.

## Web 2.0

Web 2.0 technology processes include such things as blogs, sharing sites, interactive webinars, crowdsourcing, virtual worlds, telepresence, voice and video over IP, and really simple syndication (RSS) (London, 2012). Other technologies include computer conferencing systems, online bulletin boards, e-mail, group support systems, voice mail, intranets, video conferencing, virtual collaboration, texting, mobile phones, and social media (Rice et al., 2017). Web 2.0 technology exists on various levels, as Web 2.0 technology exists both inside and outside corporate firewalls. Its structured and unstructured data is created by anyone and everyone (Andriole, 2012).

Web 2.0 technology allows for the capability of technology to exist in either a channel or a platform. Channels exist where digital information can be created and distributed by anyone. Still, the degree of commonality of this information is low (McAfee, 2006), Platforms function as intranets, corporate Web sites, and information portals (McAfee, 2006). Platforms are the opposite of channels as the content is generated, or approved, by a small group, but then is widely visible with centralized production. The commonality is high (McAfee, 2006).

In the Web 2.0 era, one of the popular tools that emerged as a result of the rise of the digital market is social media (Montague et al., 2016). Wagner, Baccarella, and Voigt (2017) posited while there are many forms of social media, social networking sites (SNS), such as Twitter, Facebook, Instagram, and LinkedIn, are pre-eminent measured, by users. Social media and networking sites offer an array of features and grew into a mainstream part of the culture.

Once viewed as tools for young people, social networking sites are now mainstream tools of communication for individuals in all age groups (Cardon & Marshall, 2015). Social media encompasses a broad reach with a multi-cultural and multi-generational audience. There are no age limits for individuals conducting online activities and social media. Adults, college students, teens, and even preteens are online (Ahlquist, 2014).

## Enterprise 2.0

Advanced communication technologies that include Web 2.0 technologies shifted how individuals communicate. Web 2.0 beget shifts in the ways individuals communicate, along with changes in how organizations communicate as well. Communication changed not just in organizations, externally, but organizational communication shifted internally in addition to the external shifts. Enterprise 2.0 impacted the business world, where the phenomenon of the Internet and information technology have opened a new medium of communication for individuals and businesses and provided opportunities to communicate and get information in an entirely different way (Khrais, 2017).

Enterprise 2.0 employs social media tools at a higher level of enterprise, along with process-oriented software that breaks the traditional departmental silos (Trimi & Galanxhi, 2014). Enterprise 2.0 brings a competitive advantage and new opportunities for organizations (Trimi & Galanxhi, 2014). New opportunities for organizations include engagement with stakeholders, innovation in the way that groups interact, and group collaboration. Enterprise 2.0 evolved to include the usage of social software, to engage stakeholders better and to allow for more organizational creativity, agility, and productivity (Christidis, Mentzas, & Apostolou, 2011).

### *Stakeholder Engagement*

New opportunities for organizations include higher levels of stakeholder engagement. As social media usage increases so too does the potential for organizations to connect with stakeholders not conventionally accessible through traditional communication channels (Men & Tsai, 2016). Previously, the limits of time and space reduced barriers to exchange and engagement. Today, organizations possess the ability to reach stakeholders that are not in the same geographic regions, that do not speak the same language, nor share the same cultural beliefs.

#### *Group Interaction*

Another new opportunity for organizations is increased levels of group interactions. Group interaction and teamwork is critical in organizations. Meetings confirm participants' values and identities and strengthen their relationships with others (Denstadli et al., 2012). Organizational communities have mechanisms that create and connect relationships between individuals to work collectively for common organizational goals (Boateng, Mbarika, & Thomas, 2010). Organizations rely on work teams to conduct complex tasks that require a range of functional expertise and experiences (London, 2012).

Electronic communications have long provided convenient means for team members to function outside of face-to-face meetings (London, 2012) to complete complex tasks. However, easier complex task completion is due to the ability of organizational members to move beyond the bounds of time and space. New technologies create new opportunities to engage with non-traditional stakeholders, along with new ways for groups to interact.

### *Group Collaboration*

Another new opportunity for organizations is increased group collaboration. Increased group collaboration creates room for diverse participation. When using social media, users can foster effective collaboration and diverse involvement with each other despite the physical distance between them (Lim, Cha, Park, Lee, & Kim, 2012). Group members are not bounded, by space and time. Group members are bounded, by attachment to the mission and vision of the organization. Group members operate in conjunction with consumers who benefit from the fulfillment of the mission and vision of the organization. Through this connection, participation and group decision making becomes a collaborative effort (Turban, Liang, & Wu, 2011).

Group collaboration is a process where two or more individuals, groups, or organizations work together to accomplish a task or attain a goal (Turban et al., 2011). Group collaboration involves a series of interactions, communication, deliberation, and other activities. These activities include such things as search for information, asking questions, collecting answers, generating ideas, and solving problems (Turban et al., 2011). This deeper level of access to collaboration offers new opportunities.

In the digital world, Web 2.0 technologies offer new opportunities for virtual teamwork and learning (London, 2012). The lack of boundedness within these new communication technologies allowed organizations to interact in different ways. Communication technology advancements allowed organizations to embrace a new set of tools to accomplish team goals. Utilizing communication with social media tools requires business professionals to adopt a new set of tools, such as blogs, wikis, and other collaborative tools, to accomplish team goals (Cardon & Marshall, 2015).

## Digital Leadership

Along with changes in the way individuals and organizations communicate, essential adjustments are happening in the business environment that demand radical transformation in leadership (Dimovski, Grah, Penger, & Peterlin, 2010). With the conversion of organizations to a digital context, organizations must adopt new tools to collaborate, and new ways to collaborate. To use the new set of collaborative tools that the evolution of communication technology produced requires stakeholders to adopt new skills as well as new attitudes (Cardon & Marshall, 2015).

For this adoption of new collaboration tools to take place, leaders must adopt new skills that are relevant and effective in a digital environment. Not only do leaders need to do this, but organizational stakeholders must adopt new policies as well. Leaders need to adapt their leadership styles to accommodate the revolution that is taking place on the digital frontier. As the way people communicate and learn changes, so too do the trends in leadership across the new digital frontier (Petrucci & Rivera, 2018).

The "digital revolution" is changing how individuals and organizations communicate, by increasing organizational responsibility. This shift involves implications for leadership as leaders face new challenges as a result of digital disruption (Kane et al., 2019). With the advances in technology, making information almost instantaneously available, these same advances serve as a double edge sword to organizations. On one side, consumers are demanding increased authenticity and transparency. On the flip side, organizational authenticity is enlarging at a rate that some organizations are not comfortable with as stakeholders compel organizations to take more responsibility, by being transparent.

Individuals and organizations require significant changes in leadership style to adapt to technological innovations, by becoming more authentic and transparent in business operations and in how they communicate. At the same time, while making changes to leadership and using digital tools, leaders need to bridge generational gaps. Digital tools must be innovative enough for millennials but accessible for Gen Xers and baby boomers who were not born into the digital age (Hicks, 2018). The digital leader must bridge the divide between skill sets, communication styles and cultural viewpoints (Hicks, 2018).

The adaptation of new skills and attitudes of authenticity and transparency in a collaborative effort helps leaders gain an advantage in influencing others. When leaders adapt to new technologies, leaders acquire the potential to influence others in a higher capacity. Being leaders who can master social media will allow leaders for proper positioning to lead in this new area and allow leaders the ability to influence the new generation (Tredgold, 2014). The process of leaders adapting to new technologies amplifies the need for the strength of leaders to exemplify authentic leadership. In today's organizations, authentic leadership is critical, with authentic leadership reflecting open and transparent communication (Men, 2014).

## Demand for Authenticity and Transparency

The organization possesses access to information at all times and at all levels. At every level, the organization's leadership will know what is going on at all times to leave no fact behind (Bennis, 2013). Organizational knowledge can include any comment posted on social media, by any customer from any place, to become a source of action for the organization (Agostino & Sidorova, 2017). Due to the shift in information access, more people are demanding that leaders demonstrate authentic leadership, because of Social Media and advanced communication technologies (Tredgold, 2014).

As communication with stakeholders changes, there is a growing need for more casual leadership to match follower expectations of interactions that appear unscripted and genuine (Watson, 2017). Stakeholders expect that there are higher levels of open access to decision-makers. Concurrently, with open access, stakeholders want leaders to be authentic and transparent. Stakeholders want leaders to exhibit real and genuine interactions. Followers expect leaders to "Talk the Talk," but also to "Walk the Walk" (Tredgold, 2014).

### *Demand for Authenticity*

Stakeholders desire leaders to be authentic and transparent, as well as being consistent. As people demand more authentic, real-time interaction with those they admire, social media sites will become leadership platforms to increase visibility (Watson, 2017). Having a social media account provides an organization with real-time access to customers in their daily life, without the customers being directly involved (Agostino & Sidorova, 2017).

### *Open Access*

The phenomenon of the "digital revolution" shifted the perception of distance between leaders and followers in addition to the distance between leaders and consumers, by building informal relationships. Whereas the barriers of access to leaders are decreasing due to rapid modes of communication and advanced communication technologies such as Social Media. As boundaries are declining, many young people are looking to connect with leadership on a social level on a social media platform (Tredgold, 2014).

The shift in the perception of distance between the leader and the follower starts with building dialogue between leader and follower. The emergence of digital media fuels equal dialogues and strengthens the relationship between leaders and followers (Men, 2015). As a result of this, the discussions between leader and follower are expected to be equal and open. Stakeholders expect leaders to demonstrate their values and beliefs, which represent the vision and mission of who they lead (Steffens, Mols, Haslam, & Okimoto, 2016). With access to equal dialogue with leaders, stakeholders, and followers desire greater open access to the insights and vision of leaders (Men & Tsai, 2016). In the current business environment, younger generations have a higher expectation for leaders to connect to followers via social media (Tredgold, 2014).

### *Reduced Power Distance*

With this sense of dialogue between leader and followers, power distance is reduced, allowing leaders and followers to communicate friendly, authentically, and informally (Men, 2015). The desire to access leaders with higher levels of open access spread to stakeholders. The desire for a higher level of access is a significant change from past generations as young people have come to expect more significant levels of access. Young people want an informal communication channel to their leader that they can use whenever they feel the need, and there is a strong expectation on the leader to respond and support this (Tredgold, 2014).

As more and more people want access to leaders, the demand for access allows a more significant opportunity for interaction. With a higher level of interaction, there is a greater level of potential authenticity. If a leader has more opportunities to interact with followers, he or she may be able to give information about his or her relational style and build authentic relationships (Azanza, Gorgievski, Moriano, & Molero, 2018).

### *Demand for Transparency*

Along with the desire for authenticity in organizations, there is a demand for transparency. There is a sense that authenticity and transparency within organizations will become inevitable due to the instant access to information. The ubiquity of information and the accessibility of leaders will continue to grow in surprising ways, where transparency becomes inevitable (Bennis, 2013).

#### *Decision-Making*

Individuals are demanding transparency to aid in the decision-making process. As transparency aids in stakeholder involvement in identifying the information needed for decision making (Men, 2014). Once information is disseminated, organizations are responsible for the information accumulation, and thus have responsibility for transparency. Being transparent involves three components. Transparency includes substantial information, participation, and accountability (Men, 2014).

In attempting to be transparent, organizations strive to make actions and decisions understandable to all interested stakeholders (Men, 2014). Organizations want to increase the flow of information to the stakeholders who participate in the operation of the organization. Leaders want to make it easier for the flow of information to key stakeholders with the flow of communication, starting with leaders. Leaders who emphasize transparency make it possible for followers to share information with others (Hahm, 2017).

At the same time, the purpose of transparency is to improve understanding. In the process of helping stakeholders understand information, organizations are responsible for that information and their actions. An organization needs to be accountable for its words, activities, and decisions to be transparent (Men, 2014). Organizations are responsible for anything they have done, including weaknesses and limitations.

## The Need for Authentic Leadership in a Digital World

In the digital world, leaders need to be authentic and transparent. Leaders need to represent the values that they espouse. Stakeholders are demanding that organizations manifest authenticity and transparency. Through the demand for more open and transparent communication, authentic leadership practices fill in the gap.

### *Authentic Leadership*

Although definitions of authentic leadership may vary, each draws upon a central theme. In essence, authentic leaders are true to themselves, behave consistently with who they are, and have a strong influence on followers (Liu, Fuller, Hester, Bennett, & Dickerson, 2018). Authentic leaders are open and transparent. Authentic leaders act in ways that match their words with their fundamental and deeply rooted shared values and high moral standards of the organization (Men, 2014).

Albeit, openness, and transparency are components of authentic leadership; they are not all that comprises the construct of authentic leadership. Authentic leadership is a multi-dimensional leadership theory. Authentic leadership is similar to transformational theory and as well as ethical, charismatic, spiritual, and servant leadership (Covelli & Mason, 2017). Authentic leaders may be directive, participative, or autocratic as long as they behave in compliance with personal values and beliefs (Dimovski et al., 2010).

Albeit similar to other leadership constructs, authentic leadership encompasses several characteristics that make it unique from different leadership styles. Walumbwa, Avolio, Gardner, Wernsing, and Peterson (2008) defined authentic leadership as leader behavior that promotes positive psychological capacities. Positive psychological capacities, with positive ethical climates, foster higher levels of self-awareness, as well as an internalized moral perspective (Walumbwa et al., 2008). Positive psychological capacities, with positive ethical climates, provide balanced processing of information, along with relational transparency of leaders to followers, to foster positive self-development (Walumbwa et al., 2008).

*Self-Awareness*

Self-awareness refers to demonstrating an understanding of how one makes meaning of the world (Walumbwa et al., 2008), along with how over time, that process of making meaning impacts the way one views of themselves (Walumbwa et al., 2008). Within the process of self-awareness, leaders need to be mindful of the world in which they live. Mindfulness involves the capacity to live in full awareness of what one experiences, of full awareness of other people, and full awareness of the world in which they live (McKee & Massimilian, 2006).

Being mindful means being aware of and attending to oneself, the people in one's life, and one's environment (McKee & Massimilian, 2006). Mindfulness is critical to self-awareness, where it causes individuals to examine the world in which they live. For authentic leaders, self-awareness involves how leaders look at themselves and the extent to which leaders are aware of their strengths, weakness, and motivation (Liu, Liao, & Wei, 2015). Self-awareness also extends to leaders discerning how employees recognize their leadership (Liu et al., 2015).

*Internalized Moral Perspective*

Simultaneously, authentic leaders foster an internalized moral perspective with self-awareness. An internalized moral perspective represents the values and standards of an authentic leader. Authentic leaders generally do not conform to role expectations that are not consistent with their values and beliefs (i.e., what they believe is right, proper, or necessary) (Men, 2014). The values and beliefs of the leader act as a moral compass. An internalized moral perspective symbolizes self-regulation where one's behaviors and actions are guided by one's values and moral standards (Chaudhary & Panda, 2018).

An internalized moral perspective often indicates a positivist perspective. The positivist perspective of an internalized moral perspective guides decision making and behaviors, such as honesty, altruism, kindness, fairness, accountability, and optimism (Jiang & Men, 2017). However, not all internalized moral perspectives reflect a positivist view, as not all individuals share the same values and beliefs. What one may consider immoral another may consider moral.

*Balanced Processing*

Another aspect of authentic leadership is balanced processing. Balanced processing refers to leaders who show that they objectively analyze all relevant data before coming to a decision (Walumbwa et al., 2008). Mindful and self-awareness go along with balanced processing. With the concept of balanced processing related to the idea of self-awareness unbiased processing (Mazutis & Slawinski, 2008). Leaders need to be aware of data that applies to leadership decisions so that they can make informed decisions.

Balanced processing is vital when interacting with others. Balanced processing is critical in accurately self-assessing one's abilities and using this knowledge in communications with others (Mazutis & Slawinski, 2008). Accurately assessing one's self and one's abilities allow others to make informed decisions as well.

*Relational Transparency*

The final aspect of authentic leadership is relational transparency. A core characteristic of authentic leaders is that they build transparent relationships with their followers (i.e., relational transparency) (Azanza et al., 2018). Relational transparency relates to how one presents one's self and their thoughts and emotions. Relational transparency refers to presenting one's authentic self rather than a distorted self to others (Walumbwa et al., 2008). Chaudhary and Panda (2018) extended the definition of relational transparency, saying relational transparency related to the extent of the openness of sharing and the extent that one displays their real thoughts and emotions (Chaudhary & Panda, 2018).

## Authentic Leadership in a Digital World

Open and transparent communication is a necessary part of authentic leadership in the digital world. Authentic digital leadership is very similar to authentic leadership. However, there are some key differences. The differences between authentic digital leadership and authentic leadership are exhibited, by the enaction of the leader identity, as well as the application of components of authentic leadership digitally.

### *Digital Leader Identity*

Today, information and communication technologies infuse a variety of organizations and unify the digital and physical world more closely than ever before (Schwarzmüller et al., 2018). With advanced technology embedded in society, disruptive technologies such as mobile computing and virtual reality corrupt previously existing boundaries between online and offline settings, creating large-scale networks of people, computers, and objects (Schwarzmüller et al., 2018). This diffusion of advanced technology into organizations created dual leader identities between the physical world and the virtual world.

Due to the blurring of lines, digital leaders operate in dual dimensions. Advanced technology allows leaders to operate on a physical face-to-face plane as well as on a virtual plane. As a digital leader, leaders need to operate authentically in the physical and virtual dimension. To be authentic on a physical level, the leader must be as close as possible to his virtual identity (Dimitrov, 2018). That authentic image connects the virtual to the real identity and the virtual to the real affiliation of its followers (Dimitrov, 2018).

The physical level is different from the virtual dimension. On a virtual level, a leader only has access to digital tools to communicate, connect, and mobilize followers (Dimitrov, 2018). Authenticity on a virtual level requires that a leader become an online generator of influence, as well as an integrator of virtual identities, united around his/her ideas and goals (Dimitrov, 2018).

## *Digital Authentic Leadership Application*

As a leader in the digital world, leaders need to adjust their application of authentic leadership to the digital frontier. An authentic digital leader is responsible for delivering authenticity on a physical plane as well as a virtual plane. Digital authentic leaders operate in dual dimensions., with leadership efficiency of physical and virtual levels measured differently. To be efficient at both levels, leaders will apply authenticity differently.

On a physical level, leadership efficiency will be measured by virtual presence and support being replicated in real life and leading to real-life actions when needed (Dimitrov, 2018). Vice versa, with actual-life activities transformed into virtual influence (Dimitrov, 2018). While on a virtual level, the ability to participate and be present on the most social platforms and new media in the fastest and highest quality measures leadership efficiency (Dimitrov, 2018). The different requirements to be efficient in a digital setting require the authentic digital leader to apply the principles of authentic leadership in a separate manner.

### *Digital Self-Awareness*

Self-Awareness is even more critical in the digital era, where information that is shared online has the potential to go viral. Leaders are bounded in their communication to followers as followers can only perceive leaders through online interactions. Leaders need to be mindful of the digital world in which they live. Leaders interact in a separate manner with followers in a digital context.

### *Digital Internalized Moral Perspective*

In a digital world, stakeholders perceive a moral perspective through the online presence of the individual or the organization. Individuals and organizations need to take into account what they participate in and that what they participate in should represent their values. The internalized moral perspective of individuals and organizations is reduced down to how they engage online. Every comment, like, and share reflects what that person or organization believes.

### *Digital Balanced Processing*

The digital world is very unforgiving. Organizations and leaders must practice balanced processing. Organizations and leaders need to take into account relevant information. Lack of understanding of pertinent information created chaos within several organizations lately. In a digital world, with greater access to information, there is more significant potential for backlash and potential loss of profits due to organizational missteps. For instance, lack of awareness and balanced processing recently led to calls for boycotts of H&M, Gucci, and Prada.

*Digital Relational Transparency*

Relational transparency is critical in the digital world. In a digital environment, all the stakeholders see is how the individual and organization participates online. One needs to be aware of how one presents one's self and one's thoughts and emotions. The individual's presence online should match their physical presence and how they act offline.

## Challenges to Digital Transparency and Authenticity

While leaders attempt to be authentic and transparent in today's world, those efforts are not always successful. Social media and advanced communication technologies have created opportunities for increased information flows. Albeit, advanced communication technologies allow for more transparency in communication, organizations find that open communication is problematic when used in specific ways.

## Challenges to Digital Transparency

### *Expectation of Transparency*

New technology tools, such as social media, provide an organization with innovative ways to share information and remain open with the public (Men, 2014). New technology tools also escalate the publics' expectation of organizational transparency (Men, 2014). Organizational transparency may expose organizations to unintentional risk. Social media engagement may expose companies to internal and external threats, from intellectual property leaks and management critique internally to blatant attacks externally (Porter, Anderson, & Nhotsavang, 2015).

*Control of Information Flows*
Other issues arise when organizations lose control of information flows. Social media may present common challenges for practitioners and executives related to accepting the lack of control associated with social media (Porter et al., 2015). Some organizations do not trust employees with organizational information and feel that Web 2.0 and social networking are problematic when used by employees (Burrus, 2010). The lack of trust affects the relational transparency of leaders. When an organization feels a threat to its control of information flows, some leaders are reluctant to affirm programs that allow higher levels of openness (Burrus, 2010).

## Challenges to Digital Authentic Leadership

### *Challenges to Digital Self-Awareness*

There is potential for negative backlash from consumers, and leaders need to be aware of their actions. Leaders need to be mindful of past online behaviors as well. There have been several instances of celebrities, leaders, and organizations apologizing over comments that were made on Social Media years ago. Perceived negative comments that have received backlash have cost people their careers. Leaders need to be mindful and aware of what they believe, and their comments and digital expressions should reflect those beliefs.

### *Challenges to Digital Internalized Moral Perspective*

The values and beliefs of the leader act as a moral compass. However, at times the internalized moral compass of an organization is forgotten. There is a sense of anonymity on the Internet that allows people to espouse values online that they would never utter person-to-person.

### *Challenges to Balanced Digital Processing*

Organizations and leaders must practice balanced processing. Organizations and leaders need to take into account relevant information. Organizations have a more significant potential for backlash and potential loss of profits due to organizational missteps. For instance, lack of awareness and balanced processing recently in several organizations led to backlash and calls for boycotts in several industries.

Several instances of lack of awareness and balanced processing have sparked outrage and backlash from minorities against organizations, including Gucci, Burberry, and several others. For example, Gucci sold sweaters with a symbol that looked like the buffoonish character Sambo (which represented a derogatory depiction of blackface). Whereas Burberry models walked the runway with nooses hanging around their neck. If these organizations would have been aware of the derogatory history of these items, then a better-informed decision would have been made.

#### *Challenges to Digital Relational Transparency*

Currently, the world is very divisive, and that divisiveness reflects in the digital domain also. The digital realm has given people a voice to express feelings of dissent and divisiveness. Digital leaders need to take into consideration how their personal opinions and emotions reflect on their organization. Individuals have gotten fired for making inappropriate comments online. Pitfalls to expressing oneself are that others may not agree with how one expressed themself. If one is open and transparent about one's opinion, anyone has a right to disagree with one's opinion, especially with a perceived unpopular position.

## Conclusion

Advanced technologies and rapid modes of communication have acted as catalysts for change. Communication technologies that include Web 2.0 technologies shifted how individuals communicate. The lack of boundedness within these new communication technologies allowed organizations to embrace a new set of tools to accomplish team goals. To adapt to these changes, leaders must adopt new skills that are relevant and effective in a digital environment. Leaders must adjust their leadership styles to accommodate the new business frontier to adapt to the shift to a digital context that is taking place. Leaders must adapt to their leadership styles to help their organizations survive in turbulent times, but to also demonstrate a higher level of authenticity and transparency.

## References

Agostino, D., & Sidorova, Y. (2017). How social media reshapes action on distant customers: Some empirical evidence. *Accounting, Auditing & Accountability Journal, 30*(4), 777–794.

Ahlquist, J. (2014). Trending now: Digital leadership education using social media and the social change model. *Journal of Leadership Studies, 8*(2), 57–60.

Andriole, S. J. (2012). Managing technology in a 2.0 world. *IT Professional Magazine, 14*(1), 50–57.

Azanza, G., Gorgievski, M. J., Moriano, J. A., & Molero, F. (2018). Influencing salespeople's work outcomes through authentic leadership. *Leadership & Organization Development Journal, 39*(7), 926–944.

Bennis, W. (2013). Leadership in a digital world: Embracing transparency and adaptive capacity. *MIS Quarterly, 37*(2), 635–636.

Boateng, R., Mbarika, V., & Thomas, C. (2010). When web 2.0 becomes an organizational learning tool: Evaluating web 2.0 tools. *Development and Learning in Organizations: An International Journal, 24*(3), 17–20.

Burrus, D. (2010). Social networks in the workplace: The risk and opportunity of business 2.0. *Strategy & Leadership, 38*(4), 50–53.

Cardon, P. W., & Marshall, B. (2015). The hype and reality of social media use for work collaboration and team communication. *International Journal of Business Communication, 52*(3), 273–293.

Chaudhary, R., & Panda, C. (2018). Authentic leadership and creativity. *International Journal of Productivity and Performance Management, 67*(9), 2071–2088.

Christidis, K., Mentzas, G., & Apostolou, D. (2011). Supercharging enterprise 2.0. *IT Professional Magazine, 13*(4), 29–35.

Covelli, B. J., & Mason, I. (2017). Linking theory to practice: Authentic leadership. *Academy of Strategic Management Journal, 16*(3), 1–10.

Darwis, Y. (2013). The urgency of communication media (e-commerce) in indonesia's creative industry as an effort to increase international business competition: A case study of the fashion industry. *International Journal of Organizational Innovation (Online), 5*(3), 206–220.

Denstadli, J. M., Julsrud, T. E., & Hjorthol, R. J. (2012). Videoconferencing as a mode of communication: A comparative study of the use of videoconferencing and face-to-face meetings. *Journal of Business and Technical Communication, 26*(1), 65–91.

Dimitrov, A. (2018). The digital age leadership: A transhumanistic perspective. *Journal of Leadership Studies, 12*(3), 79–81.

Dimovski, V., Grah, B., Penger, S., & Peterlin, J. (2010). Authentic leadership in contemporary slovenian business environment: Explanatory case study of hermes softLab. *Organizacija, 43*(5), 214–223.

Gardner, B. (2013). Making sense of enterprise 2.0. *Vine, 43*(2), 149–160.

Hahm, S. (2017). Information sharing and creativity in a virtual team: Roles of authentic leadership, sharing team climate and psychological empowerment. *KSII Transactions on Internet & Information Systems, 11*(8), 4105–4119.

Hicks, M. (2018). How hr execs can use technology to connect a divided workforce. *Strategic HR Review, 17*(1), 23–28.

Jiang, H., & Men, R. L. (2017). Creating an engaged workforce: The impact of authentic leadership, transparent organizational communication, and work-life enrichment. *Communication Research, 44*(2), 225–243.

Kane, G. C., Phillips, A. N., Copulsky, J., & Andrus, G. (2019). How digital leadership is(n't) different. *MIT Sloan Management Review, 60*(3), 34–39.

Khrais, L. T. (2017). Framework for measuring the convenience of advanced technology on user perceptions of internet banking. *Journal of Internet Banking and Commerce, 22*(3), 1–18.

Lim, S., Cha, S. Y., Park, C., Lee, I., & Kim, J. (2012). Getting closer and experiencing together: Antecedents and consequences of psychological distance in social media-enhanced real-time streaming video. *Computers in Human Behavior, 28*(4), 1365–1378.

Liu, S., Liao, J., & Wei, H. (2015). Authentic leadership and whistleblowing: Mediating roles of psychological safety and personal identification. *Journal of Business Ethics, 131*(1), 107–119.

Liu, Y., Fuller, B., Hester, K., Bennett, R. J., & Dickerson, M. S. (2018). Linking authentic leadership to subordinate behaviors. *Leadership & Organization Development Journal, 39*(2), 218–233.

London, M. (2012). Generative team learning in web 2.0 environments. *Journal of Management Development, 32*(1), 73–95.

Mazutis, D., & Slawinski, N. (2008). Leading organizational learning through authentic dialogue. *Management Learning, 39*(4), 437–456.

McAfee, A. P. (2006). Enterprise 2.0: The dawn of emergent collaboration. *MIT Sloan Management Review, 47*(3), 21–28.

McKee, A., & Massimilian, D. (2006). Resonant leadership: A new kind of leadership for the digital age. *Journal of Business Strategy, 27*(5), 45–49.

Men, L. R. (2014). Internal reputation management: The impact of authentic leadership and transparent communication. *Corporate Reputation Review, 17*(4), 254–272.

Men, L. R. (2015). The internal communication role of the chief executive officer: Communication channels, style, and effectiveness. *Public Relations Review, 41*(4), 461–471.

Men, L. R., & Tsai, W. H. S. (2016). Public engagement with ceos on social media: Motivations and relational outcomes. *Public Relations Review, 42*(5), 932–942.

Michelman, P. (2019). Key words for digital transformation. *MIT Sloan Management Review, 60*(2), 1–7.

Montague, I., Gazal, K. A., Wiedenbeck, J., & Shepherd, J. (2016). Forest products industry in a digital age: A look at e-commerce and social media. *Forest Products Journal, 66*(1–2), 49–57.

Petrucci, T., & Rivera, M. (2018). Leading growth through the digital leader. *Journal of Leadership Studies, 12*(3), 53–56.

Porter, M. C., Anderson, B., & Nhotsavang, M. (2015). Anti-social media: Executive twitter "engagement" and attitudes about media credibility. *Journal of Communication Management, 19*(3), 270–287.

Rice, R. E., Evans, S. K., Pearce, K. E., Sivunen, A., Vitak, J., & Treem, J. W. (2017). Organizational media affordances: Operationalization and associations with media use. *Journal of Communication, 67*(1), 106–130.

Schwarzmüller, T., Brosi, P., Duman, D., & Welpe, I. M. (2018). How does the digital transformation affect organizations? Key themes of change in work design and leadership. *Management Revue, 29*(2), 114–138.

Steffens, N. K., Mols, F., Haslam, S. A., & Okimoto, T. G. (2016). True to what we stand for: Championing collective interests as a path to authentic leadership. *The Leadership Quarterly, 27*(5), 726–744.

Tredgold, G. P. (2014). Are you connected? Leadership in the era of social media. *Development and Learning in Organizations: an International Journal, 28*(6), 9–11.

Trimi, S., & Galanxhi, H. (2014). The impact of enterprise 2.0 in organizations. *Service Business, 8*(3), 405–424.

Turban, E., Liang, T., & Wu, S. P. J. (2011). A framework for adopting collaboration 2.0 tools for virtual group decision making. *Group Decision and Negotiation, 20*(2), 137–154.

Wagner, T. F., Baccarella, C. V., & Voigt, K. I. (2017). Framing social media communication: Investigating the effects of brand post appeals on user interaction. *European Management Journal, 35*(5), 606–616.

Walumbwa, F. O., Avolio, B. J., Gardner, W. L., Wernsing, T. S., & Peterson, S. J. (2008). Authentic leadership: Development and validation of a theory-based measure. *Journal of Management, 34*(1), 89–126.

Watson, O. (2017). The future of leadership: Robots, remote working and real-time reactions. *Strategic HR Review, 16*(2), 89–90.

CHAPTER 3

# Authentic Leadership for the Christian Woman

*E. Ashley Newcomb*

## Introduction

For a Christian woman, the idea of a leadership role can be contradictory or even ambiguous in the context of our faith. In contemporary Christianity, the availability of roles in church leadership for women varies by denomination. Denominations such as the Pentecostal Church of God allow female pastors, while some denominations such as Assemblies of God only allow women to serve as pastors alongside their husbands. However, many more denominations such as Southern Baptists do not allow women to serve as the pastor for the congregation at all. Although denominations such as Southern Baptists do not allow women to pastor the congregation, women are often allowed to hold positions of leadership within children's and women's ministries. In addition to bylaws of denominations that provide guidance regarding the roles that women are allowed to hold within that specific domination, Scripture can also feel

E. Ashley Newcomb (✉)
School of Business and Leadership, Regent University, Virginia Beach, VA, USA
e-mail: eliznew@mail.regent.edu

Millbrook, AL, USA



B. E. Winston (eds.), *Transparent and Authentic Leadership*, Christian Faith Perspectives in Leadership and Business,
https://doi.org/10.1007/978-3-030-61996-1_3

contradictory regarding where and when women are allowed to occupy leadership positions. For example, Scripture such as 1 Timothy 2:11–13 (NKJV) states, "Let a company learn in silence with all submission. And I do not permit a woman to teach or to have authority over a man, but to be in silence" while other Scripture such Judges 4:4–5 (NKJV) contains an example noting that "Now Deborah, a prophetess, the wife of Lapidoth, was judging Israel at that time… And the children of Israel came up to her for judgment."

Still, the role of leadership for a Christian woman can spread outside the walls of a church and into the secular arena. The Christian church can provide guidance regarding exercising ethical behavior in the workplace (Miller, 2007). However, many Christians in the secular working environment experience hesitation or even fear in expressing their spiritual or religious identities as to avoid offending coworkers or clients (Lips-Wiersma & Mills, 2002). The environments present within contemporary workplaces and other organizations are not always conducive to the outward expression of faith and religious values, but our faith is a part of our very essences that cannot be left behind based on our physical location (Williams, 2010). These same environments are often not supportive of females assuming leadership positions within an organization. Growe and Montgomery (1999) noted that women who work toward the achievement of leadership roles in pursuit of productive professional careers often meet with resistance planted by social beliefs that men are best suited for leadership positions. Leadership behaviors engaged by women, such as the increased personal interaction with subordinates, contradict the social norms associated with organizational leaders (Growe & Montgomery, 1999). Thus, women who desire a career path that includes becoming a leader face a choice about when and how to adjust their personal and professional behavior to align with expectations of society, or whether to embrace a leadership approach true to who they are and whom they were shaped and are still being shaped to become. Christian women face this challenge on two fronts: one of professional career and one of faith in a secular world.

## Authentic Leadership

Even before the formalized field of organizational research, people have studied and examined leaders and leadership approaches. For countless years both formal and informal examinations have attempted to determine precisely what leadership is, what makes leaders so appealing to others, and why individuals follow a select few designated as leaders. An important note is that the identification of "leader" is not a formal position in an organization, government, or any other group. Instead, a leader is a specific person, and this person exists alongside another person or among other people. Yukl (2013) explained that it is quite possible for a leader not to be a manager in an organization and for a manager in an organization not to be a leader. Leaders are those who engage in the art of influence to accomplish a goal. Yukl (2013) defined leadership as:

> A process of influencing others to understand and agree about what needs to be done and how to do it, and the process of facilitating individual and collective efforts to accomplish shared objectives. (p. 7)

In addition to this conversation, Northouse (2016) defined leadership as "a process whereby an individual influences a group of individuals to achieve a common goal." In understanding that leadership is a process between one leader exerting influence over one or more individuals, it is understood that leadership is a relationship between people.

The approach to leadership and the study of leadership theory has evolved, seemingly with the current events and sociological climate of the times. The origin of authentic leadership theory lies in the transformational leadership theory. Transformational leadership theory as a process serves to provide personal growth for both the follower and, as a result, the leader as well (Arnold, Turner, Barling, Kelloway, & McKee, 2007). Authenticity was observed as an essential element of transformational leadership but was under-developed as an actual leadership approach (Northouse, 2016). However, a growing number of scholars and practitioners have expressed interest in the importance of authenticity in leaders. Hackman and Johnson (2013) noted that many people believe that "authenticity is the most important virtue for leaders" (p. 355). Luthans and Avolio (2003) described authentic leadership as the optimal result from the merging of positive organizational behavior.

Yukl (2013) noted that authentic leadership is "based on positive psychology and psychological theories of self-regulation" (p. 351). Wong and Cummings (2009) noted that authentic leaders behave in a manner consistent with their espoused values. Thus, the values that the authentic leader publicize to others are reinforced by his or her behavior, thereby increasing the leader's credibility (Wong & Cummings, 2009). The ability of an authentic leader to effectively role model his or her values of honesty, integrity, and highly ethical behavior influence the follower's perception of the leader's authenticity (Wong & Cummings, 2009). Walumbwa, Avolio, Gardner, Wernsing, and Peterson (2008) defined authentic leadership theory as:

> A pattern of leader behavior that draws upon and promotes both positive psychological capacities and a positive ethical climate, to foster greater self-awareness, an internalized moral perspective, balanced processing of information, and relational transparency on the part of leaders working with followers, fostering positive self-development. (p. 94)

This definition identified four central concepts for authentic leadership: positive psychological capacities, self-awareness and self-regulation, developing relationships between leaders and followers, and the continual growth and development of both leaders and followers (Walumbwa et al., 2008). Walumbwa et al. (2008) explained that authentic leadership theory is still in its infancy and may grow or change through further rigorous research.

### *Intrapersonal, Interpersonal, and Developmental Approach*

Authentic leaders are viewed by their followers as "people who are hopeful, optimistic, resilient, and transparent" (Wong & Cummings, 2009, p. 7). Northouse (2016) noted that there are three basic orientations regarding authentic leadership and two modes of approach. The first orientation focuses on the process of development that occurs internally within the leader himself or herself. Researchers emphasizing this intrapersonal orientation give elevated value to life experiences and how the leader adjusts according to the experience, how the leader processes development from self-reflection, and how the leader's uniqueness or individuality manifests (Northouse, 2016). Authenticity in a leader is linked to high levels of self-esteem, the ability to effectively self-regulate based on internalized values and beliefs, and relative immunity from external threats (Walumbwa et al., 2008). Authentic leaders possess a self-awareness and can more accurately conduct self-assessments without interference from a heightened need toward self-protection than non-authentic individuals (Wong & Cummings, 2009).

The second orientation examines the interpersonal interactions between the authentic leader and follower (Northouse, 2016). In addition to self-actualization and understanding their own personal values and beliefs, it is equally important that authentic leaders effectively communicate who they are and what they believe to their followers (Eriksen, 2009). Authenticity in the leadership relationship held between the leader and the follower is a reciprocal relationship as even through the process of the leader inspiring the follower toward higher aspirations, the follower is holding the leader to higher standards of expectations (Avolio & Gardner, 2005). Walumbwa et al. (2008) explained that authentic leaders are more comfortable embracing their strengths and weaknesses for the sake of personal growth and are "consequently more comfortable forming transparent, open, and close relationships with others" (p. 93). Leroy, Anseel, Gardner, and Sels (2015) discussed the relationship between leaders and followers in authentic leadership noting that authentic leadership not only strengthened the relationship between leader and follower but also increased the level of basic needs satisfaction as perceived by the follower.

The third orientation examines a developmental approach in which an individual grows into an authentic leader over a lifetime (Northouse, 2016). Authentic leaders grow, develop, and mature continuously throughout their lifetimes (Eriksen, 2009). Many of the events in a person's life affect that individual's personal and professional behavior. These life experiences shape an individual's world view and create a narrative process by which the individual learns about himself or herself and grows, adapts, or otherwise changes in the context of his or her personal and professional image (Avolio & Gardner, 2005). By definition and nature, authentic leaders are self-aware and seek opportunities to learn about themselves and their behavior while looking for opportunities to apply that information for personal growth (Avolio & Gardner, 2005). As events occur throughout life rather than a single season of activity, growth as a person and as an authentic leader occurs throughout life as well.

### *Practical and Theoretical Application*

In addition to the intrapersonal, interpersonal, and perpetual development orientations of authentic leadership, there are two approaches to understanding the application of authentic leadership: the practical approach and the theoretical approach (Northouse, 2016). Under the practical approach, authentic leaders are found to have five chief characteristics, including:

> (1) They understand their purpose, (2) they have strong values about the right thing to do, (3) they establish trusting relationships with others, (4) they demonstrate self-discipline and act on their values, and (5) they are passionate about their mission. (Northouse, 2016, p. 197)

The theoretical approach yielded four components of authentic leadership. These components are self-awareness, internalized moral perspective, balanced processing, and relational transparency (Luthans & Avolio, 2003).

Hackman and Johnson (2013) explained that authentic leaders possess heightened levels of self-awareness and that this heightened self-awareness contributes to increased levels of self-esteem, positive emotions, and confidence. There is a minimal amount of discrepancy between who the individual actually is and who the individual views as his or her ideal self for the authentic leader (Wong & Cummings, 2009). Authentic leaders also have an elevated ability to recognize their strengths and shortcomings and are less defensive regarding the discussion of personal weaknesses and the improvement of such (Hackman & Johnson, 2013). With elevated self-awareness and willingness to inventory and correct weaknesses, authentic leaders are intrinsically motivated and rewarded. These traits afford the authentic leader the ability to act in accordance with his or her internalized values without the desire to sacrifice his or her values to seek the approval of others (Hackman & Johnson, 2013). However, authentic leaders do value relationships with others and strive to maintain open and honest relationships with their followers (Oc, Daniels, Diefendorff, Bashshur, & Greguras, 2019).

In addition to the five characteristics of authentic leadership theory outlined, Northouse (2016) also noted that positive psychological attributes, moral reasoning, and events that were critical moments in the authentic leader's life influenced that person's leadership approach. Luthans and Avolio (2003) listed the positive psychological attributes of authentic leadership as confidence, hope, optimism, and resilience. Confidence is defined here as "the belief that one has the ability to successfully accomplish a specified task" (Northouse, 2016, p. 204). Luthans and Avolio (2003) argued that confidence, or self-efficacy, was a foundational attribute of authentic leadership. Self-efficacy is interrelated with self-regulation and self-motivation and has positively correlated through research to work-related performance (Luthans & Avolio, 2003).

The next attribute, hope is described as "a positive motivational state based on willpower and goal planning" (Northouse, 2016, p. 204). The hope that a leader has influences the developmental process of an authentic leader and his or her leadership approach (Luthans & Avolio, 2003). Northouse (2016) posited that the hope possessed by an authentic leader "inspires followers to trust them and believe in their goals" (p. 204). Rego, Sousa, Marques, and Pina e Cunha (2014) explained that as followers often view authentic leaders as trustworthy individuals, the follower will often adopt the level of hope demonstrated by the authentic leader.

Similar to hope, optimism "refers to the cognitive process of viewing situations from a positive light and having favorable expectations about the future" (Northouse, 2016, p. 204). Optimism is one of the constructs that contributes to an authentic leader's psychological capital, which leaders can use toward the accomplishment of goals (Stander, Beer, & Stander, 2015). The optimism experienced and displayed by the authentic leader is not only a defining characteristic of his or her leadership approach but can also translate into increased loyalty and job satisfaction of authentic leader's followers (Walumbwa et al., 2008). However, Luthans and Avolio (2003) noted that external events could influence optimism and, thus, optimism is relatively temporary in nature.

Luthans and Avolio (2003) noted a final positive psychological attribute to authentic leadership as resilience. Northouse (2016) defined resilience as "the capacity to recover from and adjust to adverse situations. It includes the ability to positively adapt to hardships and suffering" (p. 204). Luthans and Avolio (2003) expressed the importance of an authentic leader to be able to face the trials and tribulations present in the competitive corporate environment, to survive these challenges, and to still have the spirit by which to continue to progress through life.

Moral reasoning and critical life events are also crucial to the development and application of the authentic leader's approach to leadership. Moral reasoning focuses on the leader's ability to decipher right from wrong under higher moral obligation and to ignore personal interest to act out of the best interest for others (Avolio & Gardner, 2005). Northouse (2016) noted that this higher moral reasoning allows the "authentic leader to make decisions that transcend individual differences and align individuals toward a common goal" (p. 204). Critical life events influence the authentic leader's life, opinion, and even worldview. Luthans and Avolio (2003) noted that both positive and negative life events could serve to strengthen, educate, and equip authentic leaders. Thus, both positive and negative events can yield positive results for an individual's personal and professional development.

## Women in Authentic Leadership

As discussed earlier, authentic leaders possess an intimate self-awareness and understanding of their strengths and weaknesses. Women in organizational leadership positions often face challenges to their leadership identities specific for their gender. Growe and Montgomery (1999) noted that many barriers to women in leadership exist based on stereotypes, differences in physical appearance, and male perception of a woman's emotional state. Eagly and Johannesen-Schmidt (2001) explained that women in organizational leadership positions are often confined by both the constraints of the actual position and constraints placed on them because of expectations and perceptions assigned to their gender. In addition to creating confinements within leadership roles, these stereotypes and perceptions can even prevent a woman from receiving an opportunity to serve in a leadership position within an organization (Hoyt & Murphy, 2016).

In returning to the origin of woman, woman was not created to compete with man. Woman was designed to work alongside man. Genesis 2:15 (NKJV) states, "Then the Lord God took the man and put him in the garden of Eden to tend and keep it." Therefore, man was created specifically to tend to God's creation. Genesis 2:20–22 (NKJV) further states,

> 20So Adam gave names to all cattle, to all the birds of the air, and to every
> beast of the field. But for Adam there was not found a helper comparable
> to him. 21 And the Lord God caused a deep sleep to fall on Adam, and
> he slept; and He took one of his ribs, and closed up the flesh in its place.
> 22Then the rib which the Lord God had taken from man He made into
> woman, and He brought her to the man.

Thus, woman and man were made comparable to one another, and both were intended to work alongside each other to tend God's creation. Throughout the years, God used both males and females to lead His people and to provide a lineage for the deliverance of the Messiah. Many women served in positions of influence and leadership throughout the Bible. Two such women who demonstrated authentic leadership traits were Deborah and Naomi. Both of these women served in leadership positions while being true to themselves and God. While Deborah's leadership was a formal position among her people, Naomi's leadership was an informal position within her family.

### *Deborah*

As a Biblical leader, Deborah demonstrated traits associated with authentic leadership. Deborah was a prophetess appearing in Judges 4 and Judges 5. Although the society in which Deborah lived was patriarchal, Deborah held a position of power and authority over all of God's people (Webb, 2015). God appointed Deborah as judge over the Israelites, and she provided Israel with instructions from God for matters including military battles. Järlemyr (2016) explained that the period in which Deborah was prophetess was a desperate and dark time for Israel. Deborah was appointed to serve as the judge for Israel in a time that was characterized with internal brokenness and disunity among God's people (Webb, 2015). This brokenness and national disparity resulted from Israel's disobedience to God (Dalgish, 1970). Deborah easily could have followed the pattern of the Israelites in violating the laws set forth by God, but instead she followed God's will.

During this time, Deborah was publicly recognized as a person of wisdom and authority (Webb, 2015). She lived her life consistently in accordance with God's laws in a manner observable by the Israelites. The people of Israel trusted her judgment and sought her out when unable to resolve their issues privately (Webb, 2015). Assis (2005) explained that Deborah's actions and behaviors were consciously and intentionally not to bring glory to herself but to God. She acknowledged that she was raised up by God for His purposes, at that place, and during those times (Webb, 2015). As such, Deborah understood her position in the context of this disparity of the times, yet was still optimistic that Israel would overcome its hardships.

Deborah spoke with authority and confidence in relaying the word of God. She was confident that Israel could and would accomplish the goal established by God regarding the defeat of Sisera. However, Deborah recognized her own personal limitations and the limitations of what liberties her status in society would allow her (Webb, 2015). In recognition of these things, she called for Barak who was known for his military prowess, to commission him for God's work in accordance with God's will (Webb, 2015). This confidence in Israel and Israel's army was despite the fact that "Sisera's army is significantly stronger since it is fortified by his great defense" (Assis, 2005, p. 6). Barak had such confidence in and through Deborah that he refused to go into battle without Deborah to accompany his army, which she did (Judges 4:8–10). Assis (2005) noted that Barak did not request her presence at the battle to be subordinate to him, but instead requested her appearance due to the relationship and connectedness he felt to her. As an act of reassurance, Deborah accompanied him to the battlefield. Regardless of this personal reassurance, she prophesied that, as Barak did not submit fully to the will of God, his final victory would be taken from him and placed in the hands of someone else. Therefore, Deborah possessed a sense of purpose, personal values, relationship connectedness, consistency, and heart in alignment with authentic leadership.

### *Naomi*

Naomi appears in the Book of Ruth in the Old Testament. Naomi was the wife of Elimelech and the mother of two sons, Mahlon and Kilion. As famine struck the land, Elimelech took Naomi and their sons from the land of Judah to the country of Moab (Ruth 1:1–2, NKJV). This famine created a sense of desperation among the families and Elimelech's relocation of his family was a desperate attempt at preservation (Webb, 2015). In addition, Kennedy (1970) noted that the story of Ruth occurs during the period of Judges so it is quite possible that coupled with the desperation of the drought was the disparity the Israelites faced from turning their backs on God's law. Elimelech died after reaching Moab, leaving Naomi a widow in a foreign land (Kennedy, 1970). Her sons each married a woman from the Moabite people, then both of her sons died after a period of about ten years (Ruth 1:3–5, NKJV). The society in which Naomi lived was patriarchal and her entire existence was reliant on a male benefactor to establish her way (Webb, 2015). Thus, with the famine, the relocation to Moab, and after ten years of residence in Moab, Naomi experienced economic hardships and a loss of her home, her husband, and her sons.

Naomi was grief-stricken over the loss of her husband and sons but experienced a sense of hope when she heard of a period of prosperity occurring in her homeland of Bethlehem (Webb, 2015). This sense of hope gave Naomi the strength and encouragement she would need to make the long migration back to Bethlehem (Webb, 2015). Naomi was transparent with her grief and bitterness after her life experiences. However, regardless of Naomi's personal situation she continued to attempt to put the best interests of her daughters-in-law above her own. In Ruth 1:11–13 (NIV), Naomi urged the widows of her deceased sons to return to their own families in what she believed was their best interest.

Masenya (2016) explained that the religious beliefs of their time would have continued to bind the living together with the dead. Thus, Naomi's husband and sons would have continued to connect Naomi and her daughters-in-law and, in a sense, guide their behavior. However, Naomi realistically recognized that she had nothing further to offer her daughters-in-law by means of the care and protection marriage would have provided. In this belief, Naomi released her daughters-in-law to return to their families as this would have afforded the women opportunities to find new husbands in accordance with the law (Kennedy, 1970). By that time, she had built such a strong interpersonal connection with them and earned such esteem from them that they both initially refused to leave her side (Webb, 2015). Although Orpah eventually accepted this dismissal and returned to her family, Ruth remained with Naomi. After this narrative in which Naomi encouraged her daughters-in-law to return to their family, she returned to her native Bethlehem with her daughter-in-law Ruth who refused to leave her side. Upon her return to Bethlehem, Naomi instructed the town to refer to her as Mara "because the Almighty has made my life very bitter" (Ruth 1:20, NIV). The transparency demonstrated by Naomi and the solid bond she formed with Ruth so much so that Ruth refused to leave her are both characteristics of authentic leaders(Avolio & Gardner, 2005).

Although Naomi had many adverse events influencing the direction of her life, she continued to persevere. In Bethlehem, Naomi continued to put Ruth's interests as paramount, attempting to better her circumstances. Naomi sent Ruth to glean wheat from the fields and upon learning that Ruth was well received in Boaz's fields, expressed optimism over their future (Kennedy, 1970). Naomi used her influence with Ruth to encourage Ruth to seek out Boaz while he was on the threshing floor, to receive the provisions and security that he could offer her as a close male relative (Ruth 3:1–18). As with the custom of the day, Naomi knew that once Boaz redeemed Ruth, the bloodline of Naomi's husband and son would continue through Ruth's first child with Boaz (Van Wolde, 1997). Thus, with Ruth's first child Naomi expanded her role to include grandmother. Naomi experienced personal growth from a period of sorrow to a period of joy. Naomi was resilient through tribulations, was passionate about ensuring Ruth would receive provisions and security and her family's bloodline would continue, and maintained her hope and optimism when she believed she and Ruth had an opportunity to rectify their hardships. With these traits, Naomi behaved as an authentic leader for her family.

## Applying Authentic Leadership

The journey toward a true authentic leadership approach is just that—a journey. Authentic leaders possess a self-awareness that is deeply personal and often creates a more intimate vulnerability than other leadership approaches. Authentic leaders nurture transparent relationships with others in which they show the good, the bad, and the ugly of their humanity. Both men and women alike often experience situations in which they can feel like they must balance personal identity with professional identity. Women often balance familial roles such as mother, daughter, or wife with organizational functions such as a supporting subordinate or an organizational leader. Women in the workplace often face roles that may seem contradictory. These contradictions, in addition to other imposed personal constraints, can cause women to feel frustrated with their organizational performance and their perception of personal acceptance within the workplace (Hoyt & Murphy, 2016). Authentic leaders assess these points of frustration to identify any weaknesses and to examine these life events to further their personal and professional growth. As with Deborah and Naomi, authentic leaders understand who they are and where they are in their life journey. Deborah shows that authentic leadership traits can result in wins for seemingly impossible battles, while Naomi shows that authentic leadership traits can overcome hardships and restore one's joy, however that joy may manifest to each person. Deborah and Naomi were true to their beliefs and held firm in difficult times. They believed in the greater good and believed that God's will should be glorified above all else. More importantly, their behavior reflected their espoused beliefs.

Deborah and Naomi experienced life events that tested their character, values, and beliefs. Shamir and Eilam-Shamir (2018) explained that leaders acquire authentic leadership traits as life events prove the individual's identity and associated value system. Through life events, individuals experience catalysts for defining, redefining, strengthening, and clarifying their character, values, and beliefs. Avolio and Reichard (2008) noted that the processes associated with authentic leadership are not exclusive to leadership positions but can also pertain to the theory of authentic followership. Authentic followership possesses the same traits as the leadership component. Authentic followers develop a strong sense of self with personal characteristics, values, and beliefs, develop confidence and comfort with their identity, and develop psychological ownership of their lives on a personal and professional level (Avolio & Reichard, 2008). In addition, authentic followers operate under transparency and build environments of trust and intentional vulnerability in relationships with others (Avolio & Reichard, 2008). Thus, authentic leaders and authentic followers are two sides of the same coin.

When applying authentic leadership or followership, an essential understanding involves the authenticity of purpose. Authentic leaders, and by proxy authentic followers, do not seek out roles; instead, these individuals act out according to their true selves and, therefore, enter positions that align with their personal goals, values, beliefs, and character (Shamir & Eilam-Shamir, 2018). An individual who is an authentic leader did not seek out the leadership role. This person became a leader because the leadership position aligned with his or her naturally occurring gifts, personality, and life-long development. Likewise, the authentic follower became a follower for the same reasons and through the same type of circumstances. Authentic people do not assume false personas for different "roles" internal and external to organizations but are consistent in behavior (Shamir & Eilam-Shamir, 2018). Finally, authentic people do not adhere to popularized beliefs, values, or actions, or value-based fads. Authentic people behave in a manner consistent with what they honestly believe and value and what they have personally found to be right in the grand scheme of life (Shamir & Eilam-Shamir, 2018). An authentic person is not concerned with the external opinion or societal pressures when developing and behaving in accordance with what he or she knows internally to be the difference between right and wrong. Even in the face of adversity, the authentic person will stand firm in his or her personal beliefs.

## Conclusion

An essential component of the authentic leadership approach is the authenticity of self. Authentic leaders and followers are aware of their personal identities, their strengths and weaknesses, and their honest connection to others. Authentic leaders possess the ability to self-regulate, to make decisions based on an awareness of their own limitations, and to form transparent relationships with others without feeling threatened. Authentic leaders are optimistic, hopeful, confident, and resilient, drawing from internalized beliefs and values while being able to resist any temptation to behave in a manner by which to receive the praise and approval of others. Women in the workplace often experience challenges resulting from their gender and external stereotypes and prejudices related to their gender. However, through life events, women can develop in their authentic leadership approach and use negativity toward positive results. Christian women can draw from the examples provided by women of faith in the Bible for guidance and affirmation. Women such as Deborah and Naomi faced challenges during difficult times, but still accomplished the goals set before them through their faith and authentic leadership traits.

## References


Arnold, K. A., Turner, N., Barling, J., Kelloway, E. K., & McKee, M. C. (2007). Transformational leadership and psychological well-being: The mediating role of meaningful work. *Journal of Occupational Health Psychology, 12*(3), 193–203. https://doi.org/10.1037/1076-8998.12.3.193.

Assis, E. (2005). "The hand of a woman": Deborah and Yael (Judges 4). *Journal of Hebrew Scriptures, 5.* https://doi.org/10.5508/jhs.2005.v5.a19.

Avolio, B. J., & Gardner, W. L. (2005). Authentic leadership development: Getting to the root of positive forms of leadership. *Leadership Quarterly, 16,* 315–338.

Avolio, B. J., & Reichard, R. J. (2008). The rise of authentic followership. In R. E. Riggio, I. Chaleff, & J. Lipman-Blumen (Eds.), *The art of followership: How great followers create great leaders and organizations* (pp. 325–337). San Francisco: Jossey-Bass.

Dalgish, E. R. (1970). Judges. In C. J. Allen, J. I. Durham, R. L. Honeycutt, W. J. Fallis, & J. F. Green (Eds.), *The Broadman Bible commentary* (Vol. 2). Nashville: Broadman.

Eagly, A. H., & Johannesen-Schmidt, M. C. (2001). The leadership styles of women and men. *Journal of Social Issues, 57*(4), 781–797.

Eriksen, M. (2009). Authentic leadership: Practical reflexivity, self-awareness, and self-authorship. *Journal of Management Education, 33*(6), 747–771.

Growe, R., & Montgomery, P. (1999). *Women and the leadership paradigm: Bridging the gender gap*. Retrieved from: https://www.researchgate.net/profile/Roslin_Growe/publication/242783132_Women_and_the_leadership_paradigm_bridging_the_gender_gap/links/575f609508ae414b8e5497d7.pdf.

Hackman, M. Z., & Johnson, C. E. (2013). *Leadership. A communication perspective*. (6th ed.). Long Grove: Waveland.

Hoyt, C. L., & Murphy, S. E. (2016). Managing to clear the air: Stereotype threat, women, and leadership. *The Leadership Quarterly, 27*(3), 387–399.

Järlemyr, S. (2016). A tale of cross-dressers, mothers, and murderers: Gender and power in Judges 4 and 5. *Svensk Exegetisk Årsbok, 81*, 49–62.

Kennedy, J. H. (1970). Ruth. In C. J. Allen (Ed.), *Broadman Bible Commentary* (Vol. 2). Nashville: Broadman.

Leroy, H., Anseel, F., Gardner, W., & Sels, L. (2015). Authentic leadership, authentic followership, basic need satisfaction, and work role performance: A cross-level study. *Journal of Management, 41*(6), 1677. https://doi.org/10.1177/0149206312457822.

Lips-Wiersma, M., & Mills, C. (2002). Coming out of the closet: Negotiating spiritual expression in the workplace. *Journal of Managerial Psychology, 17*(3), 183–202.

Luthans, F., & Avolio, B. J. (2003). Authentic leadership development. In K. S. Cameron, J. E. Dutton, & R. E. Quinn. (Eds.), *Positive organizational scholarship* (p. 241–258). San Francisco: Berrett-Koehler.

Masenya, M. (2016). Who calls the shots in Naomi's life? reading the Naomi-Ruth story within the African religio-cultural context. *Acta Theologica, 36*, 84. https://doi.org/10.4314/actat.v36i1.6s.

Miller, D. W. (2007). *God at work: The history and promise of the Faith at Work movement* (Kindle). New York: Oxford University Press.

Northouse, P. G. (2016). *Leadership. Theory and practice*. (7th ed.). Thousand Oaks: Sage.

Oc, B., Daniels, M. A., Diefendorff, J. M., Bashshur, M. R., & Greguras, G. J. (2019). Humility breeds authenticity: How authentic leader humility shapes follower vulnerability and felt authenticity. *Organizational Behavior and Human Decision Process*, 1–14.

Rego, A., Sousa, F., Marques, C., & Pina e Cunha, M. (2014). Hope and positive affect mediating the authentic leadership and creativity relationship. *Journal of Business Research, 67*(2), 200–210. https://doi.org/10.1016/j.jbusres.2012.10.003.

Shamir, B., & Eilam-Shamir, G. (2018). "What's your story?" A life-stories approach to authentic leadership development. In *Leadership Now: Reflections on the Legacy of Boas Shamir* (pp. 51–76). London: Emerald Publishing Limited.

Stander, F. W., De Beer, L. T., & Stander, M. W. (2015). Authentic leadership as a source of optimism, trust in the organisation and work engagement in the public health care sector. *SA Journal of Human Resource Management, 13*(1), 1–12.

Van Wolde, E. (1997). Texts in dialogue with texts: Intertextuality in the Ruth and Tamar narratives. *Biblical Interpretation, 5*(1), 1–28. https://doi.org/10.1163/156851597X00012.

Walumbwa, F. O., Avolio, B. J., Gardner, W. L., Wernsing, T. S., & Peterson, S. J. (2008). Authentic leadership: Development and validation of a theory-based measure. *Journal of Management, 34*(1), 89–126.

Webb, B. G. (2015). *Judges and Ruth. God in chaos.* Wheaton: Crossway.

Williams, R. R. (2010). Space for God: Lived religion at work, home, and play. *Sociology of Religion, 71*(3), 257–279.

Wong, C. A., & Cummings, C. G. (2009). The influence of authentic leadership behaviors on trust and work outcomes of health care staff. *Journal of Leadership Studies, 3*(2), 6–23.

Yukl, G. (2013). *Leadership in organizations* (8th ed.). Boston: Pearson.

CHAPTER 4

# The Leadership of an Authentic King

*Tim Gregory*

## Christians as Authentic Leaders: A Biblical Perspective with Practical Application

Organizational leaders who uphold high standards of ethical conduct are often identified by their followers as being authentic and genuine in their behavior towards other (Zhu, He, Treviño, Chao, & Wang, 2015). Authentic leaders can be recognized by their followers as upholding the highest standards of ethical conduct and morality, as their words and actions align, allowing them to be a positive and productive influence on their followers and their organization (Leroy, Palanski, & Simons, 2011). They are aware of their behavior and the influence that behavior has on others, they understand the perception others hold of them and how their values and morals influence those they lead (Avolio & Gardner, 2005). Authentic leaders are optimistic and hopeful, they have the unique ability to project a positive belief in future events to those they lead (Avolio & Gardner, 2005). Peus et al. (2012) found that a leader's self-knowledge

T. Gregory (✉)
Family Worship Center, Santa Fe, TX, USA
e-mail: pastortimgregory@gmail.com



B. E. Winston (eds.), *Transparent and Authentic Leadership*, Christian Faith Perspectives in Leadership and Business, https://doi.org/10.1007/978-3-030-61996-1_4

and self-confidence were both antecedents of the perceived authenticity of a leader by their followers. Peus et al. (2012) also found empirical evidence of the power of perceived authentic leadership to create organizational commitment and job satisfaction in subordinates, prompting them to exert extra effort in their daily task and creating a willingness in them to go above and beyond the call of duty for their perceived authentic leader.

Sidani and Rowe (2018) rightly point out that a person who is authentic in their behavior cannot be considered a leader unless their behavior is embraced by followers who grant a moral legitimacy to the individual and their behavior, which makes them an authentic leader. Darvish and Rezaei (2011) in a quantitative study found that team members will willingly follow leaders they perceive as authentic in character and nature, and those same team members were likely to remain committed and satisfied employees. Leaders who are perceived as authentic are also perceived as effective leaders by their followers, inspiring followers to engage in ventures they may never had considered before (Puls, Ludden, & Freemyer, 2014). Unfortunately, with the growing moral failures of many of our political leaders, and corporate scandals such as Enron, the confidence that subordinates are willing to place in their leaders is limited and their perception of those leaders is often tainted by the behavior of other leaders who have failed morally and ethically (Sidani & Rowe, 2018). Authentic Christian leaders are needed to establish the confidence and commitment of organizational members, which is needed to help companies successfully move forward in their mission and goals. The biblical character of King Josiah serves as a strong exemplar for Christians and secular leaders alike, who desire to be perceived as authentic, to model their behavior after.

Josiah was the sixteenth king of the Southern Kingdom of Judah and he was the last of its kings to have a successful and prosperous reign (Fried, 2002). Josiah brought great reform to the kingdom, as he whole heartedly embraced God's law and won the hearts of the people. The Scriptures note is greatness by saying, "Before him there was no king like him, who turned to the Lord with all his heart, with all his soul, and with all his might, according to all the law of Moses; nor did any like him arise after him" (2 Kgs 23:25, NRSV). Clark (1977) points out that Josiah's conduct was so exemplary and his labors for God so zealous, that David may have been greater, but he was not a better man then Josiah. Josiah represents an example of authentic leadership from the pages of Scriptural history that provides a model whom today's leader can learn from, and if the principles that Josiah led by are applied by organizational leaders of today, they will certainly find themselves leading in the exemplary manner that he did. As we study the life and works of King Josiah, we can identify at least eight themes that helped him to excel as an authentic leader.

### *Authentic Leaders Value Moral Integrity*

The writer of 2 Chronicles points out the integrity of King Josiah and how he did the right things in the sight of God, following after the example of King David (2 Chr 34:2). Josephus, the Jewish historian, states that the integrity of Josiah's nature was demonstrated in his virtuous actions and his impeccable character (Josephus, Antiquities10 (49)). Josiah's inner integrity was testified to by his outward actions, he demonstrated the way he expected others to live, his life served as an example for those he led to model their own lives after (Josephus, Antiquiteies10 (50)). Keil and Delitzsch (1969) believes Josiah learned the value of integrity early on from his mother, and then after the death of his father, from the righteous leaders and teachers who were responsible for guiding and educating him. King Josiah, as an authentic leader, leaned the value of integrity and led in a manner that demonstrated the strength of his character for all to see.

The integrity of a leader speaks to the cohesiveness of their actions and words, which is determined by follower perception (Leroy et al., 2011). When the moral and ethical behavior of a leader's character is demonstrated in a way that brings their words and actions into alignment, they create a positive perception of their integrity for follower to identify with (Zhu et al., 2015). In conducting a study of 49 teams in the service industry, Leroy et al. (2011) found that authentic leadership was directly related to the affective commitment level of organizational members, which was fully mediated through the perception that subordinates had of the leader's behavioral integrity. Authentic leaders are often perceived by their followers as having moral standards and being aware of how they behave in regard to those standards (Avolio & Luthans, 2006). Their followers see them as being fair and balanced in their decision-making, as well as being transparent in their behavior and decisions (Avolio & Luthans, 2006). Authentic leaders, who value moral integrity, are seen by their followers as doing the right things for the right reasons.

Leaders who are perceived as authentic have the ability to set the standard of behavior within their organizations, becoming role-models for subordinates to model their own behavior after (Avolio, Gardner, Walumbwa, Luthans, & May, 2004). Authentic leaders who model strong moral integrity can create a culture that promotes and expects strong moral and ethical practices from its members (Hannah, Avolio, & Walumbwa, 2011). The courage authentic leaders demonstrate in making moral and ethical decisions has a direct influence on the way their followers behave and understand acceptable moral and social practices (Hannah et al., 2011). Authentic leaders who are perceived as having moral integrity have the ability to positively influence the behavior of their subordinates, increasing the loyalty and commitment levels of members in a way that promotes their willingness to go the extra mile in fulfilling the goals and mission of the organization (Hannah et al., 2011; Leroy et al., 2011; Zhu et al., 2015).

> Principle 1: Christians, as authentic leaders, value their own moral integrity and are diligent to lead their organizations in a manner where others can behold the strength of that integrity and use it as a benchmark for their own behavior.

### *Authentic Leaders Value and Inspire Teamwork*

As Josiah set his heart to repair the Temple, he delegates responsibility for the task to others who have both ability and integrity. Josiah entrusted the high priest Hilkiah with the responsibility of accounting for the finances that were given for the repair of the temple (2 Kgs 22:4). From there, others were also involved in distributing the money to the craftsman who were employed to complete the repairs (2 kgs 22:5–6). The project of repairing the Temple was a well-organized endeavor, where individuals with varying talents and skill were called upon by the king to ensure the task was a successful one (Myers, 1965). The organization and incorporation of multiple participants shows the project was well planned before any work began (Myers, 1965). King Josiah, as an authentic leader, values teamwork and inspires those around him who have demonstrated both ability and integrity, to help carry out the plans for the renovating of the Temple of God.

Authentic leaders recognize the potential of accomplishing great things with the help of others and are able to motivate teams in a manner that keeps them focused on the task at hand, which increases the collective effectiveness of the team (Xiong & Fang, 2014). Leaders are able to influence the behavior and performance of a team by the way they behave themselves, for they create a standard for others to follow (Gillette & McCollom, 1990). The behavior of a leader dictates what is and what is not acceptable as a member of the team (Gillette & McCollom, 1990). As leaders demonstrate an authentic willingness to make sacrifices for the sake of the organization and the mission and goals of the team, they have the potential to create a perception of a strong and dedicated leader in the eyes of those they lead (Sivasubramaniam, Murry, Avolio, & Jung, 2002). This in-turn has the potential to motivate team members to willingly and enthusiastically make sacrifices of their own for the good of the team and the organization (Sivasubramaniam et al., 2002).

Leaders who are able to establish goals that team members perceive as noble and worthy are able to inspire them in a manner that motivates them to make sacrifices to achieve those goals; exerting the effort and commitment needed to do so (LaFasto & Larson, 2001). As leaders create a positive image of themselves in the eyes of their followers, they often demonstrate the ability to motivate them to envision an optimistic future, which can inspire them to go the extra-mile to achieve that future (Arrow, McGrath, & Berdahl, 2000). The ability of a leader to create a vison of accomplishing a worthy cause can help to strengthen and sustain teams in pushing forward with their mission when the team encounters hard and challenging times (LaFasto & Larson, 2001). Authentic leaders are able to both inspire and motivate team members, they see the value of working as a team, and as such, incorporate those organizational members who have the skills and integrity needed to be a productive part of the team's efforts to achieve the set goals of the organization (Sivasubramaniam et al., 2002; Xiong & Fang, 2014).

> Principle 2: Christians, as authentic leaders, understand the necessity of team work to accomplish great ventures and they inspire those they lead, who have both ability and integrity, to diligently engage in the varying organizational task and projects they set-out to accomplish.

### *Authentic Leaders Communicate Honest Expressions*

As the repairs to the Temple went forth a copy of the Law was found and given to Hilkiah the high priest (2 Kgs 22:8). This was a significant event for the Law had not been followed for many generations, and the people and the king were unaware of its existence (2 Kgs 22:13). Once found, the lost book of the Law is brought to the king and read to him by Shaphan (2 Kgs 22:10). When the king hears the words of the book and realizes the disobedience of himself and his people, he is grieved to his core and tears his clothes (2 Kgs 22:11). In tearing his garments before the royal court, Josiah openly expresses the deep morning he feels for the sins of the nation he leads and hopes that it is not too late to change (House, 1995). Josiah, as an authentic leader, communicates an honest expression of the grief he feels inside with those he leads.

Leaders who are effective within their organizations have learned how to skillfully communicate their emotions to others in a healthy and productive manner that is able to bring the best out of their subordinates (Hackman & Johnson, 2009). The transparency that is associated with authentic leaders is displayed in the honest and healthy way they express their emotions for their subordinates to see, which can play a role in the amount of influence they exert of others (Miao, Humphrey, & Qian, 2018). Effective organizational leaders are able to use emotional expression as a conduit to communicate their thought, helping their subordinate to better understand where they stand on certain issues and what their expectations are (Mayer, Caruso, & Salovey, 2016). The ability of leaders to communicate an honest expression of their emotions in a healthy manner creates a positive environment where creativity is fostered, optimism about reaching goals is cultivated, and greater cooperation amongst employees is encouraged (Hackman & Johnson, 2009).

Leaders who learn to communicate an honest expression of their emotions have the ability to create an emotional bond between themselves and their subordinates, as well as promoting a workplace environment where strong bonds are formed between organizational members (Eisenberg & Goodall, 2004). Often times these leaders are also able to read and understand the emotional stance of others, which serves as a means to create empathic bonds that allow them to manage the anxieties of their subordinates (Gardner, Fischer, & Hunt, 2009). Based on their research, Miao et al. (2018) suggest that organizations should recruit and promote individuals for leadership who are able to effectively communicate an honest expression of their emotions, for these individuals are able to employ effective leadership styles, such as authentic leadership practices, to influence their followers and achieve desirable outcomes throughout the organization. Authentic leaders are able to communicate and honest expression of their emotions in a healthy manner that promotes trust and unity towards the achievement of organizational goals.

> Principle 3: Christians, as authentic leaders, communicate honest expressions of their joy and sorrow with those they lead, which promotes a culture of trust within their organizations that positively influences the performance of their followers.

### *Authentic Leaders Are Unassuming*

After the book of the law is read to Josiah, he seeks council on the direction he should take and sends members of his court to the prophetess Huldah for advice on what he should do (2 Kgs 22:13–14). Josiah doesn't jump to conclusions and act presumptuously, but instead seeks wise council before making any decisions about what he should do as the leader of the nation. Na'aman (2011) points out that when kings in the Near East sought to bring about some form of cult reform, they required justification before the priests and elite. The prophetess Huldah provides the justification Josiah will need, as he sets out to bring reform to the nation, by verifying the book of the Law as authentic and sending back her support for the reform Josiah looks to initiate (Na'aman, 2011). King Josiah, as an authentic leader, is unassuming in his actions and desire to bring reform, seeking council before he makes any movement.

Beshears and Gino (2015) report that one of the reasons for poor decision making is cognitive biases, which is our system of thinking that creates our personal understating and perception of things. One-way leaders can effectively overcome their own cognitive bias is to seek out the advice of solid council before making big decision. Yaniv (2004) in an empirical study found that organizational leaders who seek out and use the advice of solid council, significantly improved their decision making over those leaders who do not. Organizational leaders are able to seek out solid advice that will keep them from acting presumptuously on bad information or cognitive biases in a variety of ways, those ways could include: discrete advice, counsel, coaching, and mentoring (Garvin & Margolis, 2015).

Discrete advice from an independent advisor can help to give leaders options concerning individual matters from the perspective of a none bias person, which can considerably improve their ability to make accurate decisions (Yaniv, 2004). When leaders obtain counsel, they seek out those individuals who are able to provide guidance on how to approach a variety of unfamiliar and complex situations (Garvin & Margolis, 2015). Coaching provides leaders with the help of an experienced professional to guide them in the choices they are making and to help them understand the impact of those choices, coaches help leaders to manage their personal behavior (McKenna & Maister, 2005). Mentoring gives organizational leaders access to the perception of a more experienced leader who has traveled the same road they are on to help them in their judgement choices and management decisions (Janasz & Peiperl, 2015). Authentic leaders can find a genuine advantage in seeking the help and guidance of others to ensure they are unassuming in the direction they are leading their organizations.

> Principle 4: Christians, as authentic leaders, are unassuming in the direction they lead their organizations, seeking wise council and researching the matter before committing to any action.

### *Authentic Leaders Keep Followers Informed*

After Josiah receives council from the prophetess Huldah, the Scriptures record that he went up to the house of the Lord and all of Judah went with him, both the ordinary people of his kingdom and the political and religious elite (2 Kgs 23:2). When the people were all gathered, the king read the words of the book of the Law to them (2 Kgs 23:2). Josiah does not conceal the truth from the people, but rather relays it to them so that they will understand the situation and the measures that must be taken to set things right. Through this act of relaying the truth according to the discovered book, which had been authorized by the prophetess Huldah, Josiah prepares the way for the reform he seeks to enact (Na'aman, 2011). In reading the discovered book to his followers, Josiah is informing the assembly of both the privileges and obligations that are inherent in their relationship with the Lord their God (House, 1995). King Josiah, as an authentic leader, keeps his followers informed of the events that have transpired and how those events were going to affect his leadership decisions.

Every leader has a unique style of communication, that is a set of interpersonal behaviors, which are used to relay ideas in the most efficient manner possible to their subordinates in order to reach the given goals of their organization (de Vries, Bakker-Pieper, & Oostenveld, 2010). Effective leaders communicate in a style that creates a shared understanding between themselves and those they lead, so that their course of action may be understood and embraced by both their subordinates and peers (Konopaske, Ivencevich, & Matteson, 2018). When leaders fail to clearly communicate the purpose for their actions and decisions, subordinates can feel left out of the loop and anxiety can set-in (Carlson & Zmud, 1999). Organizational leaders who fail to clearly communicate their decisions making process and job-related information to their subordinates, will have difficulty motivating them to embrace the goals of the company and laboring to see those goals accomplished (Mayfield, Mayfield, & Sharbrough, 2015).

Leaders who clearly communicate the goals of the organization and the reasons for those goals can help to foster an environment where followers are motivated to labor towards the realization of those goals (Hatch & Cunliffe, 2013). As leaders are diligent in their efforts to keep organizational members informed, they are able to communicate a vibrant picture of the company's future that members can embrace as their own, motivating them to go the extra mile to reach that future (Collins & Porras, 1996). These leaders assure that there is a richness of communication, where the quality of information and the amount that is being relayed is given in a manner that subordinates can actually absorb and readily understand (Konopaske et al., 2018). Authentic leaders who remain transparent will be diligent in keeping organizational members clearly informed of the various happenings, events, and goals that are emerging within the organization.

Principle 5: Christians, as authentic leaders, keep organizational members informed of the events and data that are affecting their leadership decision making.

### *Authentic Leaders Are Humble*

The Scriptures note the humility expressed by Josiah when he first hears the book of the law read. The prophetess Huldah declares this humility, which Josiah demonstrated before the Lord, and how this demonstration of humility got the attention of God (2 Chr 34:27). The king's humility was openly expressed in the grief he felt and the guidance he sought, as his heart became soft before God, which in—turn allowed him to receive the wisdom of the book and the prophetess Huldah (Keil & Delitzsch, 1969). King Josiah, as an authentic leader, has an attitude of humility, which allows him to find the guidance he needs to make it out of a difficult situation.

Humility must be expressed to be perceived as humility, which means it is much more than an inner emotional sensation. Expressed humility can be defines as "an interpersonal characteristic that emerges in social context that connotes a manifested willingness to view oneself accurately, a displayed appreciation of others' strengths and contributions, and teachability" (Owens, Johnson, & Mitchell, 2013, p. 1518). Collins (2001), in *Good to Great*, points out that one of the distinguishing qualities of a level 5 Leader (the highest level of executive capability) is their humility. This humility should never be mistaken for weakness, for these leaders are indeed ambitious, but they are not self-serving, they seek a larger goal in moving their companies to greatness (Collins, 2001). The humility of an organizational leader has the capacity to build high levels of trust in their followers and commitment to the mission of the company (Caldwell, 2017).

Organizational leaders can be strategic in their expression of humility by staying aware of their own ignorance, which could help to create in them an appetite for continuous learning (Murphy, 1996). Murphy (1996), in examining high-performing leaders, found that a commonality shared by them all was that of humility and the absence of pride and self-indulgence. Leaders who express high levels of perceived humility are able to create buy-in amongst their followers, as they empower them to help reach the goals of the organization (Morris, Brotheridge, & Urbanski, 2005). Authentic leaders who express humility in a manner that is perceivable by their followers, have the potential to move them to accomplish great undertakings, which helps their organizations in the fulfillment of their mission.

Principle 6: Christians, as authentic leaders, maintain an attitude of humility, which allows them to receive guidance and input from other members of their organization and raises the commitment level of their followers.

### *Authentic Leaders Are just*

As Josiah moves through the land bringing about dramatic reform, he comes across the grave of an old prophet of God (2 Kgs 23:16). The grave catches the attention of the king and he enquires about it (2 Kgs 23:17). The king is told the grave belongs to the prophet whom had foretold of the things he was currently doing (2 Kgs 23:17). Three hundred and twenty-six years before Josiah was born a prophet of God had come to Bethel to prophecy against the pagan worship that had been instituted, and through a string of events ends up dying there (Jamieson, Fausset, & Brown, 1945). Josiah had the unique privilege of being one of only two people called by name in the Old Testament before he was borne (1 Kgs 13:2). In an act of justice, the king commands that the grave of the prophet of God be left alone, for the graves around him held the bones of pagan prophets, whom he had dug up and burnt on the altar that Jeroboam had set up (2 Kgs 23:15). Josiah was known as a king who sought to rule and lead justly. Josephus, in speaking of Josiah and the way he ruled, said, "He ordained certain judges and overseers, that they might order the matters to them severally belonging, and have regard to justice above all things, and distribute it with the same concern they would have about their own soul" (Josephus, Antiquities10 (53)). King Josiah, as an authentic leader, seeks to rule and lead in manner that assures justice for all, without showing respect of person.

Followers desire fairness and justice in their leaders, they want to know the individual they are committing to follow after is one who upholds just standards towards all in their leadership practices (Gottfried & Trager, 2016). In fact, research has shown that subordinates are more likely to find meaning in the work they do, which will inspire them to diligently labor at the task they are given, when they believe their leader is one who seeks to lead with justice and fairness towards all (Lips-Wiersma, Haar, & Wright, 2018). Graen, Hui, and Tylor (2006) found that when the relationship between a leader and their followers was supported by fairness and trust, followers performed their task better and had a strong understanding of why they were doing the task at hand. The perceived relationship of fairness that followers have of themselves and their leaders has been shown to be a predictor of project success (Graen et al., 2006). Leaders would be wise to develop relationship with their followers that both demonstrate and create a perspective of fairness and justice in their behavior patterns.

Leaders who enact decision making procedures based on perceived just and fair practices have the capability of increasing desired organizational citizenship behavior (van Dijke, Creamer, Mayer, & Quaquebeke, 2012). This behavior can in-turn contribute to the organization functioning more proficiently in a manner that could help to reach the goals of the company (van Dijke et al., 2012). When leaders apply the same standards to everyone it creates a perception in the eyes of their followers that they are just and fair, which can serve to motivate them to go the extra-mile to help reach the goals of their organization (Bacha & Walker, 2013; Lips-Wiersma et al., 2018). Authentic leaders project an image of fairness and justice in their leadership behavior, which creates a relationship between them and their followers that motivates their followers to willingly go the extra-mile to help the organization reach its goals and fulfill its mission.

> Principle 7: Christians, as authentic leaders, seek to lead in a manner that assures just treatment for all, regardless of a person's organizational position or status.

### *Authentic Leaders Commit to the Right Path*

After King Josiah reads the book of the Law to the people, he commits to follow the laws and decrees declared throughout it (2 Chr 34:31). Josiah's father and grandfather had led the people in forsaking the teachings of the law, but Josiah was a different kind of leader and would guide the people along the right path, one that would help the nation to prosper and experience peace (2 Kgs 23:25). Josiah's commitment to follow the law of God was one in which the people would also be pledged too, making a vow to God to loyally follow His law and precepts (Cogan & Tadmor, 1988). King Josiah led the people in the path they should take, and the nation took notice and followed in his way (Cogan & Tadmor, 1988). King Josiah, as an authentic leader, committed himself to taking the right path, both ethically and strategically, and led his nation along that same path.

Leaders who commit to taking the right path for the future benefit of their organization will almost certainly experience a variety of challenges, but if they have clearly communicated their values and purpose to their followers, they will find the path a little less challenging

(Kouzes & Posner, 2007). When followers perceive their leaders are committed to seeing the right thing done, and that they understands the path they are on and how to successfully deal with the trials they will face, they are more likely to commit themselves to the same path (Chen & Wang, 2007). Abrell-Vogel and Rowold (2014) in an empirical study that examined the effects of leader behavior on follower behavior, found there was a direct link between the commitment of followers towards change and reaching an organizational goal to the perceived commitment demonstrated by their leader; the stronger the leader's commitment was the stronger the follower's commitment was. Leaders desiring to reach the goals their organization has set or to take their organization in a new direction will need to be committed to following through on the path they take if they want their followers to commit to it as well.

Leaders should share the values that direct their behavior, so that their followers have a clear understanding of the direction they are leading the company and what their purpose is in doing so (Kouzes & Posner, 2007). The strength of a leaders resolve to commit themselves to a certain course of action will be determined by the values that have been instilled in them, which in-turn will affect the way their followers perceive them and the commitment they are willing to exert to the leaders course of action (Kalberg, 1975; Montani, Courcy, & Vandenberghe, 2017). Authentic leaders are often noted for sharing their values and being guided by them; the identity they project is a true statement of who they are (Avolio & Gardner, 2005; Hannah et al., 2011). Authentic leaders commit to doing what they believe is right for their organizations, which is dictated by their inner values; values they have purposely communicated to those they lead.

Principle 8: Christians, as authentic leaders, commit to taking to right path ethically and strategically, so that they may lead their organizations in a way that ensures their profitability and moral veracity.

## Summary

Authentic leaders have the ability to lead their followers in a manner that produces commitment, loyalty, and even productivity in their observable behavior, creating an environment within their organizations where great things are both expected and accomplished. Josiah was authentic in his leadership practices, displaying the highest level of ethical behaviors for all to witness, which enabled him to effectively lead his nation to a great

**Table 4.1** Leadership Principles for Authentic Leaders

| *Principle* | *Christians, as authentic leaders* |
|---|---|
| 1 | Value their own moral integrity and are diligent to lead their organizations in a manner where others can behold the strength of that integrity and use it as a benchmark for their own behavior |
| 2 | Understand the necessity of team work to accomplish great ventures and they inspire those they lead, who have both ability and integrity, to diligently engage in the varying organizational task and projects they set-out to accomplish |
| 3 | Communicate honest expressions of their joy and sorrow with those they lead, which promotes a culture of trust within their organizations that positively influences the performance of their followers |
| 4 | Are unassuming in the direction they lead their organizations, seeking wise council and researching the matter before committing to any action |
| 5 | Keep organizational members informed of the events and data that are affecting their leadership decision making |
| 6 | Maintain an attitude of humility, which allows them to receive guidance and input from other members of their organization and raises the commitment level of their followers |
| 7 | Seek to lead in a manner that assures just treatment for all, regardless of a person's organizational position or status |
| 8 | Commit to taking to right path ethically and strategically, so that they may lead their organizations in a way that ensures their profitability and moral veracity |

revitalization. Organizational leaders who adopt the leadership principles displayed by King Josiah will find themselves well positioned to lead their companies and followers in a productive and positive manner. The leadership principles that have been identified in the life and behavior of Josiah have the potential to enable leaders, who implement them into their daily leadership practices, to usher in great revitalization movements within their organizations (Table 4.1).

## References

Abrell-Vogel, C., & Rowold, J. (2014). Leaders' commitment to change and their effectiveness in change—A multilevel investigation. *Journal of Organizational Change Management, 27*(6), 900–921.

Arrow, H., McGrath, J. E., & Berdahl, J. L. (2000). *Small groups as complex systems: Formation, coordination, development and adaptation.* Thousand Oaks, CA: Sage.

Avolio, B., & Luthans, F. (2006). *The high impact leader: Moments matter for accelerating authentic leadership development*. New York: McGraw-Hill.

Avolio, B. J., & Gardner, W. L. (2005). Authentic leadership development: Getting to the root of positive forms of leadership. *The Leadership Quarterly, 16*(3), 315–338.

Avolio, B. J., Gardner, W. L., Walumbwa, F. O., Luthans, F., & May, D. R. (2004). Unlocking the mask: A look at the process by which authentic leaders impact follower attitudes and behaviors. *The Leadership Quarterly, 15*(6), 801–823.

Bacha, E., & Walker, S. (2013). The relationship between transformational leadership and followers' perceptions of fairness. *Journal of Business Ethics, 116*(3), 667–680.

Beshears, J., & Gino, F. (2015, May). Leaders as decision architects. *Harvard Business Review, 93,* 52–61.

Caldwell, C. (2017). Understanding level 5 leaders: The ethical perspectives of leadership humility. *Journal of Management Development, 36*(5), 724–732.

Carlson, J. R., & Zmud, R. W. (1999). Channel expansion theory and the experimental nature of media richness perceptions. *Academy of Management Journal, 42*(2), 153–170.

Chen, J., & Wang, L. (2007). Locus of control and the three components of commitment to change. *Personality and Individual Differences, 42*(3), 503–512.

Clark, A. (1977). *Clark's Commentary: The Holy Bible, containing the Old and New Testaments*. Nashville: Abingdon.

Cogan, M., & Tadmor, H. (1988). *II Kings: A new translation* (1st ed., Vol. 11.). Garden City, NY: Doubleday.

Collins, J. C. (2001). *Good to great: Why some companies make the leap–and others don't* (1st ed.). New York, NY: HarperBusiness.

Collins, J. C., & Porras, J. I. (1996, September–October). Building your company's vision. *Harvard Business Review, 74,* 65–78.

Darvish, H., & Rezaei, F. (2011). The impact of authentic leadership on job satisfaction and team commitment. *Management & Marketing (Bucharest, Romania), 6*(3), 421.

de Vries, R. E., Bakker-Pieper, A., & Oostenveld, W. (2010). Leadership = communication? The relations of leaders' communication styles with leadership styles, knowledge sharing and leadership outcomes. *Journal of Business and Psychology, 25*(3), 367–380.

Eisenberg, E. M., & Goodall, H. L. (2004). *Organizational communication: Balancing creativity and constraint* (4th ed.). Boston: Bedford/St. Martin's.

Fried, L. S. (2002). The high places (Bāmôt) and the reforms of Hezekiah and Josiah: An archaeological investigation. *Journal of the American Oriental Society, 122*(3), 437–465.

Gardner, W. L., Fischer, D., & Hunt, J. G. (2009). Emotional labor and leadership: A threat to authenticity? *The Leadership Quarterly, 20*(3), 466–482.

Garvin, D. A., & Margolis, J. D. (2015, January/February). The art of giving and receiving advice. *Harvard Business Review, 93,* 60–71.

Gillette, J., & McCollom, M. (1990). *Groups in context: A new perspective on group dynamics.* Reading, MA: Addison-Wesle.

Gottfried, M., & Trager, R. (2016). A preference for war: How fairness and rhetoric influence leadership incentives in crises. *International Studies Quarterly, 60*(2), 243–257.

Graen, G. B., Hui, C., & Taylor, E. A. (2006). Experience-based learning about LMX leadership and fairness in project teams: A dyadic directional approach. *Academy of Management Learning & Education, 5*(4), 448–460.

Hackman, M. Z., & Johnson, C. E. (2009). *Leadership a communication perspective* (5th ed.). Long Grove: Waveland Press.

Hannah, S. T., Avolio, B. J., & Walumbwa, F. O. (2011). Relationships between authentic leadership, moral courage, and ethical and pro-social behaviors. *Business Ethics Quarterly, 21*(4), 555–578.

Hatch, M. J., & Cunliffe, A. L. (2013). *Organization theory: Modern, symbolic, and postmodern perspectives* (3rd ed.). Oxford and New York;: Oxford University Press.

House, P. R. (1995). *1, 2 Kings* (Vol. 8). Nashville, TN: Broadman & Holman.

Jamieson, R., Fausset, A. R., & Brown, D. (1945). *A commentary, critical, experimental and practical, on the Old and New Testaments.* Grand Rapids, MI: W. B. Eerdmans.

Janasz, S. d., & Peiperl, M. (2015, April). Managing yourself: CEOs need mentors too. *Harvard Business Review, 93,* 100–103.

Josephus, F. (1987). *The works of Josephus: Complete and unabridged* (W. Whiston, Tran. Vol. New updated Edition). Peabody, MA: Hendrickson Publishers.

Kalberg, S. (1975). The commitment to career reform: The settlement movement leaders. *Social Service Review, 49*(4), 608–628.

Keil, C. F., & Delitzsch, F. (1969). *Commentary on the Old Testament: 1 & 2 Kings, 1 & 2 Chronicles, Ezra, Nehemiah, Esther* (Vol. 3). Grand Rapids: W. B. Eerdmans.

Konopaske, R., Ivancevich, J., & Matteson, M. (2018). *Organizational behavior & management* (11th ed.). New York: McGraw Hill.

Kouzes, J. M., & Posner, B. Z. (2007). *The leadership challange* (4th ed.). San Francisco: Jossey-Bass.

LaFasto, F. M. J., & Larson, C. E. (2001). *When teams work best: 6,000 team members and leaders tell what it takes to succeed.* Thousand Oaks, CA: Sage.

Leroy, H., Palanski, M., & Simons, T. (2011). Authentic leadership and behavioral integrity as drivers of follower commitment and performance. *Journal of Business Ethics, 107*(3), 255–264.

Lips-Wiersma, M., Haar, J., & Wright, S. (2018). The effect of fairness, responsible leadership and worthy work on multiple dimensions of meaningful work. *Journal of Business Ethics, 161,* 1–18.

Mayer, J. D., Caruso, D. R., & Salovey, P. (2016). The ability model of emotional intelligence: Principles and updates. *Emotion Review, 8*(4), 290–300.

Mayfield, J., Mayfield, M., & Sharbrough, W. C. (2015). Strategic vision and values in top leaders' communications: Motivating language at a higher level. *International Journal of Business Communication, 52*(1), 97–121.

McKenna, P. J., & Maister, D. H. (2005). *FIrst among equals: How to manage a group of professionals* (First Free Press pbk ed.). New York: Free Press.

Miao, C., Humphrey, R. H., & Qian, S. (2018). Emotional intelligence and authentic leadership: A meta-analysis. *Leadership & Organization Development Journal, 39*(5), 679–690.

Montani, F., Courcy, F., & Vandenberghe, C. (2017). Innovating under stress: The role of commitment and leader-member exchange. *Journal of Business Research, 77,* 1–13. https://doi.org/10.1016/j.jbusres.2017.03.024.

Morris, J. A., Brotheridge, C. M., & Urbanski, J. C. (2005). Bringing humility to leadership: Antecedents and consequences of leader humility. *Human Relations, 58*(10), 1323–1350.

Murphy, E. C. (1996). *Leadership IQ: a personal development process based on a scientific study of a new generation of leaders.* New York: Wiley.

Myers, J. M. (1965). *I Chronicles* (2nd ed., Vol. 12.). Garden City, NY: Doubleday.

Na'aman, N. (2011). The 'discovered book' and the legitimation of Josiah's reform. *Journal of Biblical Literature, 130*(1), 47–62.

Owens, B. P., Johnson, M. D., & Mitchell, T. R. (2013). Expressed humility in organizations: Implications for performance, teams, and leadership. *Organization Science, 24*(5), 1517–1538.

Peus, C., Wesche, J. S., Streicher, B., Braun, S., & Frey, D. (2012). Authentic leadership: An empirical test of its antecedents, consequences, and mediating mechanisms. *Journal of Business Ethics, 107*(3), 331–348.

Puls, T. R., Ludden, L. L., & Freemyer, J. (2014). Authentic leadership and its relationship to ministerial effectiveness. *The Journal of Applied Christian Leadership, 8*(1), 55–75.

Sidani, Y., & Rowe, W. G. (2018). A reconceptualization of authentic leadership: Leader legitimation via follower-centered assessment of the moral dimension. *The Leadership Quarterly, 29*(6), 623–636.

Sivasubramaniam, N., Murry, W. D., Avolio, B. J., & Jung, D. I. (2002). A longitudinal model of the effects of team leadership and group potency on group performance. *Group and Organization Management, 27*(1), 66–96.

van Dijke, M., De Cremer, D., Mayer, D. M., & Van Quaquebeke, N. (2012). When does procedural fairness promote organizational citizenship behavior? Integrating empowering leadership types in relational justice models. *Organizational Behavior and Human Decision Processes, 117*(2), 235–248.

Xiong, H.-B. & Fang, P. (2014). Authentic leadership, collective efficacy, and group performance: An empirical study in china social behavior & personality. *An International Journal, 42*(6), 921–932. https://doi.org/10.2224/sbp.2014.42.6.921.

Yaniv, I. (2004). Receiving other people's advice: Influence and benefit. *Organizational Behavior and Human Decision Processes, 93*(1), 1–13.

Zhu, W., He, H., Treviño, L. K., Chao, M. M., & Wang, W. (2015). Ethical leadership and follower voice and performance: The role of follower identifications and entity morality beliefs. *The Leadership Quarterly, 26*(5), 702–718.

CHAPTER 5

# The Authentic Leadership of Daniel, Joseph, and David

*Julie Headley*

## Introduction

Although the concept of authentic leadership is a more modern concept, it can be used to interpret the actions of ancient Biblical leaders. In particular, Daniel, Joseph, and David were reviewed. The three men were key leaders written about in the Old Testament of the Bible, and each of them displayed components of the modern concept of authentic leadership. Walumbwa, Avolio, Gardner, Wernsing, and Peterson (2008) said that authentic leadership is composed of four components, "Self-awareness, relational transparency, internalized moral perspective, and balanced processing" (p. 101). These four components directly relate to the subcategories of authentic leadership presented in this book. Relational transparency is tied to honest relationships, internalized moral

J. Headley (✉)
School of Business and Leadership, Regent University, Virginia Beach, VA, USA
e-mail: julihe2@mail.regent.edu

Franklin, TN, USA



B. E. Winston (eds.), *Transparent and Authentic Leadership*, Christian Faith Perspectives in Leadership and Business,
https://doi.org/10.1007/978-3-030-61996-1_5

perspective is representative of an ethical foundation, and self-awareness is a genuine self-concept which promotes openness. Further, through an exegetical analysis, an example of Walumbwa et al.'s (2008) four factors of authentic leadership can be derived from the lives of the Biblical leaders Daniel, Joseph, and David. In particular, Daniel exemplified internalized moral perspective, Joseph demonstrated astute balanced processing, and David excelled at self-awareness and relational transparency. Contemporary leaders can learn valuable lessons of authentic leadership from these ancient, Biblical leaders.

## Authentic Leadership

The concept of authentic leadership gained notoriety at a summit in 2003 (Northouse, 2016). The concept was further developed into theory by Walumbwa et al. (2008). The authors said that there are four key tenants of an authentic leader, "Self-awareness…relational transparency…balanced processing…[and] internalized moral perspective" (Walumbwa et al., 2008, p. 95). Overarchingly, researchers do not agree on a single definition of authentic leadership (Northouse, 2016, p. 196), but George (2015) posited that a foundational element of authentic leadership is character.

Further, through a study comprised of 125 effective leaders, George, Sims, McLean, and Mayer (2007) concluded that research participants did not have specific leadership traits or styles in common. Rather, the values that effective leaders were guided by developed through adversity and experience. Instead of being negatively affected by adversity, the leaders utilized their adversity in order to learn and grow.

Through experience, leaders became self-aware. According to Luthans, Norman, and Hughes (2006), self-aware leaders are guided by their values, they identify and accept their strengths and weaknesses, and they trust their own decision making. This acceptance of strengths and weaknesses, according to Luthans et al. (2006, p. 89), positively correlates with a leader who tends to analyze information fairly. Further, the researchers proposed that leaders who practiced transparency in their relationships, in turn, created healthy boundaries where emotion and information could be shared (Luthans et al., 2006, pp. 89–90). Therefore, authentic leaders are self-aware, they exhibit balanced processing, they hold steadfast to their values, and they employ open communication and transparent relationships with others.

These assessments of authentic leadership support Walumbwa et al.'s (2008) four core tenants of authentic leadership, "Self-awareness, relational transparency, internalized moral perspective, and balanced processing" (p. 89)." The researchers defined authentic leadership as:

> A pattern of leader behavior that draws upon and promotes both positive psychological capacities and a positive ethical climate, to foster greater self-awareness, an internalized moral perspective, balanced processing of information, and relational transparency on the part of leaders working with followers, fostering positive self-development. (Walumbwa et al., 2008, p. 94)

Of the four tenants, the tenant of self-awareness is comprised of both an individual's perception of the world and how his or her perception influences personal values, decision-making, and perception of self (Ryan & Deci, 2003). Northouse (2016) postulated that self-aware leaders know themselves down to their very core, and this characteristic will compel other leaders to interpret them as authentic (pp. 202–203). What a leader decides to show of him or herself is a part of relational transparency. For example, is the leader the same person behind closed doors as he or she is in front of others (Ryan & Deci, 2003)? According to Northouse (2016), relational transparency means open communication with others—regardless of whether the shared feelings are positive or negative (p. 203). Ryan and Deci (2003) said that the balanced processing component of authentic leadership is related to how a leader approaches a situation unbiasedly. He or she is open to the information at hand before making a decision (Ryan & Deci, 2003). Further, he or she is willing to objectively listen to other opinions (Northouse, 2016, p. 203). Finally, Ryan and Deci (2003) said that internalized moral perspective is composed of internal governance and self-control.

An authentic leader's actions support his or her words. Authentic leaders have a clear understanding of who they are, understand their purpose, are self-disciplined, and are intrinsically motivated. Authentic leaders are trusted by others, and they hold transparent relationships with those around them. Their actions are born out of their values. Because of this, authentic leaders are not born; they develop over time. Three leaders in the Old Testament that displayed the four tenants of authentic leadership were Daniel, Joseph, and David.

## Daniel

Based on the Biblical account, Daniel exhibited elements of self-awareness, relational transparency, internalized moral perspective, and balanced processing throughout his life. The story of Daniel especially highlights his strength in the area of internalized moral perspective. Woolfe (2002) said, "His purpose was unwavering, and it carried him even when it did not seem to have a likely short-term payoff" (p. 30). This was distinctive about Daniel's life and leadership. While internalized moral perspective shines brightest among the elements of authentic leadership in Daniel's life, all four of the tenants are displayed and can provide an example of authentic leadership for modern day leaders.

### *Self-Awareness*

Daniel understood where his strength ended and where God's strength began. In Daniel chapter 2, King Nebuchadnezzar had a dream that he desperately wanted to be interpreted, but he refused to tell anyone what the dream entailed. He was planning to execute the wise men that could not tell him what his dream was, but Daniel asked for a little time. The king granted it, and Daniel went to his friends and told them to ask God for the secret. Daniel was keenly aware that his knowledge, wisdom, and very life depended on God. According to Woolfe (2002), Daniel worshipped God in the face of adversity. Thus, when his life was put on the line, he relied solely on God. God answered Daniel, and Daniel went to the king.

> Daniel replied, "There are no wise men, enchanters, magicians, or fortune-tellers who can reveal the king's secret. But there is a God in heaven who reveals secrets, and he has shown King Nebuchadnezzar what will happen in the future. Now I will tell you your dream and the visions you saw as you lay on your bed.'" (Daniel 2:27–28, New Living Translation)

Daniel was self-aware of his limitations and continually pointed credit back to God. Because of the situation and outcome, King Nebuchadnezzar promoted Daniel into leadership in his kingdom, and he worshipped the God of Daniel (2:47–49). In alignment with authentic leadership, Daniel did not choose his actions in order to gain power;

instead, he chose actions that were true to himself, that showed self-awareness of his strengths and limitations, and that were based on his relationship with God.

### *Relational Transparency*

Along with being self-aware, Daniel exhibited relational transparency with those around him. In particular, Daniel was completely transparent with those in leadership over him and all three kings that he served. Borek, Lovett, and Towns (2005) said that "Daniel learned to appeal to those in authority over him to effect desirable changes" (p. 195). The three kings referenced throughout the account of Daniel are King Nebuchadnezzar, King Belshazzar, and King Darius.

As a young boy, Daniel was open and transparent with King Nebuchadnezzar's Chief of Staff, Ashpenaz. Daniel refused the king's food and drink and asked Ashpenaz for only vegetables and water (Daniel 1:8). Daniel was transparent about who he was and who he was willing to be.

In Daniel Chapter 5, Daniel showed that he was comfortable with who he was and the God he served while speaking boldly to King Belshazzar.

> You are his successor, O Belshazzar, and you knew all this, yet you have not humbled yourself. For you have proudly defied the Lord of heaven and have had these cups from his Temple brought before you. You and your nobles and your wives and concubines have been drinking wine from them while praising gods of silver, gold, bronze, iron, wood, and stone – gods that neither see nor hear nor know anything at all. But you have not honored the God who gives you the breath of life and controls your destiny! So God has sent this hand to write this message. (Daniel 5:22–24)

In this pericope, Daniel took a bold, almost fatherly tone with Belshazzar. Before this monologue, Daniel had recounted how Nebuchadnezzar had not humbled himself before God. Now, Belshazzar was doing the same thing. Daniel did not mince words. He was aware that being so bold could cost him dearly. However, Daniel knew who he was, and he ultimately served his God before his King. After Daniel's interpretation of the writing on the wall and his stern warning to the king, Belshazzar placed Daniel as the highest leader in the kingdom.

In Daniel chapter 6, Daniel was under the rule of King Darius. At the urging of his high officials, Darius signed a decree that everyone in his kingdom should not pray or worship anyone or anything besides him for the next 30 days. Daniel responded by unabashedly praying to his God. Daniel knelt down as he always did and prayed with his windows open (Daniel 6:10). Daniel was aware of his circumstances and the consequences, but he prayed anyway. "Daniel was a man with unshakeable purpose. He worshipped the God he believed in despite the punishment he knew he would receive for it" (Woolfe, 2002, p. 29). Daniel knew the King could not overturn the decree to save his life, but he prayed anyway. Daniel knew what he was doing and was in control of his actions. As a result of his worship towards God, he was thrown into the lion's den, but God spared his life (Daniel 6). Darius was thrilled that Daniel survived, and he decreed for the people of his kingdom to worship Daniel's God. Daniel prospered under the reign of Darius (Daniel 6:25–28).

### *Balanced Processing*

Daniel also demonstrated balanced processing throughout his life and leadership. Daniel did not just assume the answer to things. He first and foremost sought God. When Daniel obeyed God, he had favor with others. For example, when Daniel refused to eat the king's meat, he charged the king's Chief of Staff to give him and his friends a chance for ten days (Daniel 1). Daniel was diplomatic in his request. Daniel's experiment with the vegetables and water was successful, and the Chief of Staff listened to Daniel's request (Daniel 1:15–16). Repeatedly throughout his life, Daniel's reputation preceded him. He was trustworthy (Hammer, 1976). As new kings took over the kingdom, they heard about Daniel and were referred to him when needs arose. Because of Daniel's consistency and balanced processing, people trusted him. "Daniel soon proved himself more capable than all the other administrators and high officers. Because of Daniel's great ability, the king made plans to place him over the entire empire" (Daniel 6:3). Daniel was a leader consistently identified and utilized by other leaders. He was loyal, steadfast, consistent, wise, and responsible.

### *Internalized Moral Perspective*

In the same way that Daniel showed self-awareness when he unashamedly prayed with the windows open (Daniel 6:10) knowing he would be arrested and sentenced to death, he also exhibited an internalized moral perspective. Daniel's actions supported his words. Throughout his life, Daniel continuously served his God only. The reader starts to see this unfold when Daniel is a young boy and refuses to eat the king's meat (1:8). Then, when Belshazzar offered Daniel lavish gifts, Daniel responded with, "Keep your gifts or give them to someone else, but I will tell you what the writing means" (Daniel 5:17). This is displayed again when Daniel prays to his God and worships his God only with his windows open (6:10). His allegiances were not hidden. He spoke of them, and he acted on them. When Daniel came out of the lion's den, he proclaimed that God had shut the mouths of the lions for he was innocent and had not wronged the king (6:22). Daniel stayed true to his core values and remained committed to God alone, even when faced with imminent death.

Daniel remained steadfast in who he was and that he served God before King. Yet, all three kings placed Daniel into positions of prominence. Something so distinguished Daniel that he was repeatedly placed into leadership positions not by one king or two kings, but by multiple kings. Borek et al. (2005) pointed out that, "Despite being falsely accused and thrust into a trial by ordeal, Daniel remained loyal to his leader" (p. 196). Thus, Daniel balanced first his commitment to God and second his loyalty to his leaders. Daniel was self-aware, he had a core set of values from which he made decisions, and he was consistent and transparent. Daniel displayed may components of authentic leadership. Authentic leaders are true to themselves and have a strong sense of morality and principles by which they live (Walumbwa et al., 2008). They are transparent and consistent. Daniel's trials, pursuit of God, and victories are lessons for leaders aspiring to live and lead with more authenticity.

## Joseph

At a young age, Joseph had dreams of leadership, but he did not yet have the maturity for it. As he grew, Joseph demonstrated traits of an authentic leader—self-awareness, relational transparency, balanced processing, and internalized moral perspective. Joseph demonstrated self-awareness in his interpretation of Pharaoh's dream (Genesis 41:1–36) and when he took over leadership in Egypt. He showed relational transparency with his brothers (45:1–15) and Pharaoh in adulthood. He exhibited astute balanced processing when he saved his brothers' and family's lives during the famine, and he showed internalized moral perspective as he stood his ground by refusing Potiphar's wife and honoring Potiphar's leadership and God's direction (39:7–18).

### *Self-Awareness*

When he was young, Joseph had very little self-awareness. Joseph did not express humility, and he did not read the emotions and feelings of others well. This is seen when Joseph repeatedly shared with his family how he dreamed that they would all bow down to him one day (37:5–11). However, Joseph matured, and from his adversity grew in self-awareness. Borek et al. (2005) said, "The Scriptures describe Joseph as one who developed his leadership credibility in the worst of conditions by making good decisions. The skills he developed in less-than-favorable conditions qualified him for the significant leadership responsibilities entrusted to him later" (p. 47). By the time Joseph had an audience with Pharaoh, Joseph expressed keen self-awareness. "The Pharaoh said to Joseph, 'I had a dream last night, and no one here can tell me what it means. But I have heard that when you hear about a dream you can interpret it'" (Genesis 41:15). Joseph responded that he could not, but God could. Like Daniel, Joseph was aware of where his ability ended and where God's ability began. Later, when Pharaoh tells Joseph that he is going to put him in charge of a multitude of items with significant responsibility, Joseph was confident that he could take everything on and do it successfully (41:37–49). Joseph's self-awareness and judgment were validated when his decisions and actions were successful.

### *Relational Transparency*

Joseph's relational transparency was on display in the account of Joseph revealing himself to his brothers during their time of need (Genesis 45:1–15). Egypt and the surrounding land were in a time of famine. Because of his foresight, Joseph could have victimized the people, but instead he chose to save them (Woolfe, 2002, p. 185). Joseph, as second in command of the kingdom, was in charge of divvying out Egypt's stored food. His family thought that Joseph was dead. They had no idea that he had risen into power and leadership in Egypt. Joseph's brothers traveled to Egypt to buy food for their family, and they did not recognize Joseph. However, Joseph recognized them. After a series of interactions, Joseph revealed that he was their long-lost brother. He cries with them and celebrates with a feast. Around this time, Joseph also disclosed to Pharaoh who his family was so that they could be taken care of in the kingdom. Joseph's transparency mended deep scars and saved his family's lives.

### *Balanced Processing*

In the same story accounted above about Joseph's relational transparency with his brothers, Joseph also demonstrated balanced processing. Woolfe (2002) said that, "His overall scheme was just and fair" (p. 186). Joseph could have been bitter, frustrated, and angry with his brothers. He could have been vengeful and wielded his power over them. However, instead of taking revenge, Joseph showed compassion (Woolfe, 2002, p. 62). Joseph saw the actions of his brothers, and he saw his actions and mistakes. Most importantly, Joseph saw the hand of God in the midst of it all—in both his terrifying tragedies and his triumphant victories. Joseph set aside any need for revenge. Instead, he made a decision that showed he was balancing the information and making a decision for a better future rather than a decision to avenge the past. Joseph said, "You intended to harm me, but God intended it all for good. He brought me to this position so I could save the lives of many people" (Genesis 50:20). Borek et al. (2005) said that Joseph, "Understood God used those situations to shape him into what God wanted him to be" (p. 49). Thus, Joseph saved his family and all of Egypt from famine (Laniak, 2004, p. 26). Joseph's balanced processing changed his life and the lives of all of his family.

When Joseph's family arrived in Egypt to re-settle there, Joseph again demonstrated balanced processing. He decided to tell Pharaoh the truth, that his family were shepherds (Genesis 46: 32). However, he instructed his family how to respond when asked what they do for a living. "Pharaoh will send for you. He'll ask, 'What do you do for a living?' You should answer 'We've taken care of livestock from the time we were boys. We've done just as our fathers did.'" (Genesis 46:33–34a). Joseph instructed them in this way because "It's the practice of the people of Egypt not to mix with shepherds. So Pharaoh will let you settle in the area of Goshen" (Genesis 46:34b). Joseph understood all sides of the situation and the cultural norms at hand, so Joseph gave direction based on his adept balanced processing.

### *Internalized Moral Perspective*

Joseph's internalized moral perspective started at a young age. When he was 17, he worked for his half-brothers. Even though they were the sons of his father, Joseph reported back to his father bad things that his half-brothers had been doing (Genesis 37:2), and his brothers sold him into slavery. Borek et al. (2005) addressed Joseph's moral perspective when they stated, "Even though he [Joseph] had been sold into slavery against his will, he served Potiphar with a pure heart. As Potiphar recognized Joseph was trustworthy, he gave him increased responsibility" (Borek et al., 2005, p. 52).

While serving Potiphar, Joseph again demonstrated his unshakeable morals. Friedman and Friedman (2004) said that, "Joseph remained an individual of great integrity and a man of faith" (p. 4). While in charge of Potiphar's house, Potiphar's wife came on to Joseph. She repeatedly pressured him to sleep with her. Joseph repeatedly refused, citing that he could not do such a thing to Potiphar and he could not sin in such a way against God (Genesis 37:8–10). Joseph did not waiver in his commitment to God and Potiphar. Nevertheless, Potiphar's wife lied and made up a story that Joseph had tried to rape her (39:11–18). As a result, Potiphar threw Joseph in prison, but God was still with Joseph. The prison warden put Joseph in charge of everything and did not worry about it (39:22). "Joseph proved himself to be a man committed to certain unalterable core values in life. These values guided him and helped him make wise and healthy decisions" (Borek et al., 2005, p. 53). Joseph had integrity, and he was trustworthy and responsible. Borek et al. (2005) said that, "Joseph was productive in life because he was connected to the source of life" (p. 51). He did not waiver from serving God, and God caused everything at Joseph's hand to prosper and succeed (39:23).

## David

David was a key leader in Israel's history whose life was recounted in the Old Testament. David repeatedly demonstrated astute self-awareness and relational transparency throughout his life. He excelled at identifying and expressing his emotions. He also showed that he could listen to multiple sides of a situation and make a decision through balanced processing. David depended on God and continually sought God, even when he feared and doubted. David was a beloved King whom Samuel called, "A man after God's own heart" (1 Samuel 13:14).

### *Self-Awareness*

David showed a significant amount of self-awareness throughout his life, especially as displayed in his writing in Psalms. While David was king, a man named Nabal was mean and angered David (1 Samuel 25). Nabal's wife, Abigail, hurried to meet David to try to save the life of her husband (25:23–38). She pleaded with David to spare him, calling Nabal a fool (v. 25). She apologized profusely and offered to take the blame (v. 24). Because of Abigail's request, David spared the lives of Nabal and his men.

> David replied to Abigail, 'Praise the Lord, the God of Israel, who has sent you to meet me today! Thank God for your good sense! Bless you for keeping me from murder and from carrying out vengeance with my own hands. For I swear by the Lord, the God of Israel, who has kept me from hurting you, that if you had not hurried out to meet me, not one of Nabal's men would still be alive tomorrow morning. (1 Samuel 25:32–34)

In this situation, David was fully aware of his intended actions (Smith, 1933). He was aware enough to hear Abigail's perspective and change his plan. In this, he also showed perceptive, balanced processing.

Along with showing an awareness of his emotions and the feelings of others throughout his life and leadership, David also wrote about how he felt. According to Meyer (1974), the Book of Psalms, authored mostly by David, is full of emotional and spiritual highs and lows. David praised God and displayed faithfulness, but he also experienced depression and doubt. David had the ability to identify, name, and describe his emotions and feelings. He was aware of how his emotions made him feel and act, and he was not ashamed of them. In Psalms 42–43, David speaks to his soul. He identifies his fear and doubt but makes a conscious decision to trust God anyway. One passage encapsulates the chapters well by stating, "Why am I discouraged? Why is my heart so sad? I will put my hope in God! I will praise him again – my Savior and my God!" (Psalm 42:5–6a). This example is an excellent lesson for contemporary organizational leaders. A leader does not need to diminish his or her feelings or push them away and not deal with them. Instead, a leader can identify his or her range of emotions and make a conscious decision of how to proceed.

### *Relational Transparency*

In a similar way that David was honest with himself, David was also transparent with others. Even after his son Absalom betrayed him, David loved him dearly and cared about his son's life. When he found out Absalom had died, David was devastated (Friedman & Friedman, 2004) and grieved deeply and openly. "The king was overcome with emotion. He went up to the room over the gateway and burst into tears. And as he went, he cried, 'O my son Absalom! My son, my son Absalom! If only I had died instead of you! O Absalom, my son, my son" (2 Samuel 18:33).

The death of Absalom was not the only time that David cried in front of others. David and Saul's son Jonathan were close friends (Woolfe, 2002). There came a time when Jonathan signaled to David that he needed to leave for his safety. When Jonathan and David had to say goodbye to one another, they both cried. "Both of them were in tears as they embraced each other and said good-bye (sic), especially David" (1 Samuel 20: 41b).

David expressed relational transparency in more ways than just crying in front of and with others. David was thrilled that the Ark of the Lord had blessed Obed-edom's house, and he went to transfer the ark from Obed-edom's house back to the City of David. David stopped to make a sacrifice to the Lord, and then, "David danced before the Lord with all his might, wearing a priestly garment. So David and all the people of Israel brought up the Ark of the Lord with shouts of joy and the blowing of rams' horns" (2 Samuel 6:14–15). Henry (1996) said that no one danced with David, but David danced joyfully and genuinely. David was not embarrassed or ashamed; he expressed his delight to the Lord in front of all to see.

### *Balanced Processing*

Throughout his life, David also demonstrated balanced processing. When he was a young man, David brought food to his brothers in battle (1 Samuel 17:17–18). While there, he offered to fight the Philistine giant named Goliath. His family was angry (v. 28), and Saul did not take him seriously (v. 33). However, David knew that they did not have all of the information. David knew that he had successfully defended his herd from both a lion and a bear. God had been with him before, and David trusted that God would be with him again. Thus, David weighed the information and still offered to fight Goliath. Friedman and Friedman (2004) said that David's approach to Goliath, "Demonstrated faith and humility" (p. 11). God was with David, and David successfully defeated Goliath (v. 50).

As an adult, David also demonstrated balanced processing. After David bore a son with Bathsheba, he was told that his son would not live (2 Samuel 12:14). David responded by crying, fasting, and praying fervently (v. 16). However, when his son died, David stopped mourning and quickly started participating in normal life activities again (v. 20). Bosworth (2011) said that this is an example of David's resilience in the midst of adversity. He understood that he had done all he could do, and he had pleaded with God. There was nothing else that could be done. When the decision had been made, and his son passed away, David stopped pleading with God and moved forward.

Another instance of balanced processing was when David and his men were living in Ziklag, and his wives and all of their possessions were stolen (1 Samuel 30). David and his men responded by going to the Amalekites and conquering them. David recovered everything he had lost. After they returned home, David planned to split the plunder between the warriors and those who will stay behind to keep everything safe. Henry (1996) said that this decision was just and kind for those who kept guard at home. The warriors complained that those who stay behind to protect the belongings do not deserve the plunder that they recovered. Taking all pieces of information and feelings from multiple sides into account, David said, "No, my brothers! Don't be selfish with what the Lord has given us. He has kept us safe and helped us defeat the band of raiders that attacked us. Who will listen when you talk like this? We share and share alike – those who go to battle and those who guard the equipment" (1 Samuel 30:23–24). Thus, David exhibited balanced processing and made a decree for regulation that was followed for a long time (v. 25).

### *Internalized Moral Perspective*

David's internalized moral perspective shined brightly in his interactions with King Saul. While Saul was hunting David to kill him, Saul ended up in a vulnerable position in a cave (1 Samuel 24). David had the chance to kill Saul, and David's men urgently encouraged him to do so. However, David refused. Instead, David cut a corner off of Saul's robe. Woolfe (2002) said that this act showed both David's power and compassion. After Saul had left the cave, David confronted him. David said, "For the

Lord placed you at my mercy back there in the cave. Some of my men told me to kill you, but I spared you. For I said, 'I will never harm the king – he is the Lord's anointed one" (1 Samuel 24:10b). Later, Saul began pursuing David again to kill him. David again had a chance to kill Saul. However, David said, "Don't kill him. For who can remain innocent after attacking the Lord's anointed one?" (1 Samuel 26:9). Instead of killing him, David took Saul's spear and water jug that had been laying near his head. When David was repeatedly given a chance to kill Saul and rule over Israel, David did not. David was more concerned about serving God, respecting God's anointing on Saul, and remaining innocent in God's eyes. "David had mercy on Saul, and was rewarded with a kingship" (Woolfe, 2002, p. 62). Further, David's mercy did not stop there. Many years after Saul had died David specifically went looking for a descendant of Saul. He found Mephibosheth, a grandson of Saul. He restored the inheritance of Saul to Mephibosheth, and Mephibosheth ate with David at his table from then on out (2 Samuel 9). In this instance, Woolfe (2002) said that "David's compassion was greater than his vengefulness" (p. 58). David's internalized moral perspective was life-giving and restorative.

## Lessons for Contemporary Leaders

While Daniel, Joseph, and David all displayed each of Walumbwa et al.'s (2008) four tenants of authentic leadership—self-awareness, relational transparency, balanced processing, and internalized moral perspective (Walumbwa et al., 2008)—each leader excelled in one area. From Daniel, modern leaders can learn about internalized moral perspective. Daniel knew who he was and what he believed. He had a core set of values from which he did not waiver (Woolfe, 2002). Daniel was unabashedly himself, and he served God even when threatened with imminent death. Daniel maintained his values and beliefs through trials and pressure from peers and those in authority. With every king Daniel served, Daniel did not change who he was or what he practiced. God honored Daniel, and he prospered under each king.

Joseph excelled at balanced processing. Because of his ability to see multiple sides of an issue, he saved the lives of his family (Laniak, 2004). Even amid a life-changing situation when Joseph was deeply wronged by his family, he was able to set aside any remaining anger and bitterness and see how God worked good out of the situation. At multiple points in his life, Joseph was a trusted leader and was given substantial responsibility. This was in part because Joseph was able to weigh what was at hand and make wise decisions. Of note is also Joseph's internalized moral perspective, especially demonstrated through the situation with Potiphar's wife. Joseph remained innocent before God, and God prospered Joseph everywhere he went.

As seen throughout the account of David's life and throughout the Psalms, David displayed an exceptional aptitude for the authentic leadership components of self-awareness and relational transparency. From his openly crying while saying goodbye to Jonathan to his unashamed dancing for God in the streets in front of all of his men, David was not afraid to be who he was, to serve God in front of others, and to be open and real with those around him. He was confident in his abilities but also dependent on the Lord. He was fully aware of God's strength within him. David was attuned to his emotions—his highs and his lows (Meyer, 1974). He could identify what he felt, understand it, and express it. At his core, David knew who he was and who he served.

Modern day leaders aspiring to become authentic leaders can follow the examples set by Daniel, Joseph, and David in the Bible. Leaders should focus on developing Walumbwa et al.'s (2008) four tenants of authentic leadership—self-awareness, relational transparency, balanced processing, and internal moral perspective. To glean additional self-awareness, modern leaders can take assessments, ask questions of others, and identify their strengths and weaknesses. A further lesson from David that modern leaders can learn from is to be boldly open with those around them while letting their core values shine through. Modern leaders can also study the life of Joseph to learn the art of balanced processing, understanding multiple sides of a situation, and strategic leadership. Finally, the life of Daniel provides a view into what a consistent life of devotion and service to God looks like. Thus, following the example of the three Biblical leaders, modern leaders hoping to develop authentic leadership should identify who they are, what their purpose is, and who they serve.

## Conclusion

Daniel, Joseph, and David all showed an aptitude for knowing their God-given strengths and abilities. Key to this awareness was an equal understanding of where human strength ended and where God's strength began. The three Biblical leaders demonstrated repeated dependence on

God. They were open with others about who they were, and they did not waver. Their actions were born out of their values, and they continually sought God for direction, guidance, and wisdom. Woolfe (2002) stated, "Even when their [Biblical leaders] visions seemed unrealistic, people followed them because of their integrity and honesty" (p. 2). Their authenticity drew others to them, and each man was placed into senior leadership in their kingdoms. The lives of these ancient leaders are ripe with lessons for contemporary authentic leaders. Daniel, Joseph, and David knew who they were, knew the God they served, and they authentically, unabashedly led from that awareness.

## References

Borek, J., Lovett, D., & Towns, E. L. (2005). *The good book on leadership: Case studies from the Bible*. Nashville, TN: Broadman & Holman Publishers.

Bosworth, D. A. (2011). Faith and resilience: King David's reaction to the death of Bathsheba's firstborn. *The Catholic Biblical Quarterly, 73*(4), 691–707.

Friedman, H., & Friedman, L. (2004). Biblical leadership: Insights for today's managers. *EJBO—Electronic Journal of Business Ethics and Organization Studies, 9*(1). Retrieved from http://ejbo.jyu.fi.

George, B. (2015). *Authentic leadership rediscovered*. Harvard Business School. Retrieved from http://hbswk.hbs.edu/item/authentic-leadership-rediscovered.

George, B., Sims, P., McLean, A. N., & Mayer, D. (2007). Discovering your authentic leadership. *Harvard Business Review*. Retrieved from https://www.homeworkmarket.com/sites/default/files/qx/15/04/13/05/article.pdf.

Hammer, R. (1976). *The book of Daniel*. Cambridge, UK: Cambridge University Press.

Henry, M. (1996). *Matthew Henry's commentary on the whole Bible*. Peabody, MA: Hendrickson Publishers.

Laniak, T. S. (2004). *Shepherds after my own heart: Pastoral traditions and leadership in the Bible* (D. A. Carson, Ed.). Downers Grove, IL: InterVarsity Press.

Luthans, F., Norman, S., & Hughes, L. (2006). Authentic leadership: A new approach for a new time. In R. J. Burke & C. L. Cooper (Eds.), *Inspiring leader* (pp. 84–104). New York, NY: Routledge.

Meyer, S. G. (1974). The Psalms and personal counseling. *Journal of Psychology and Theology, 2*(1), 26–30.

Northouse, P. G. (2016). *Leadership theory and practice* (7th ed.). Thousand Oaks, CA: Sage.

Ryan, R. M., & Deci, E. L. (2003). On assimilating identities to the self: A self-determination theory perspective on internalization and integrity within cultures. In M. R. Leary & J. P. Tangney (Eds.), *Handbook of self and identity* (pp. 253–272). New York, NY: Guilford.

Smith, J. M. P. (1933). The character of King David. *Journal of Biblical Literature, 52*(1), 1–11.

Walumbwa, F., Avolio, B., Gardner, W., Wernsing, T., & Peterson, S. (2008). Authentic leadership: Development and validation of a theory-based measure. *Journal of Management, 34*(1), 89–126. https://doi.org/10.1177/0149206307308913.

Woolfe, L. (2002). *The Bible on leadership: From Moses to Matthew—Management lessons for contemporary leaders*. New York, NY: AMACOM.

CHAPTER 6

# Principles of Transparent and Authentic Leadership from Scripture

*Patrick S. Millsap*

## Introduction

Antonakis and Day (2018) cautions our understanding of authentic and transparent leadership, having noted that authentic leadership is a spinoff theory from transformational and charismatic leadership. Authentic, ethical, and servant forms of leadership are connected, due to some elements that they share in common. One element is that they are all "loaded" in terms of how they are defined, which means that they include the outcome in their definitions. Also, the term is positively and morally valenced. Constructs, in science, should not be defined by their outcomes as this may lead to circular theorizing. It has been shown that transformational and authentic leadership are very highly correlated (Antonakis & Day, 2018, pp. 68–69). Given the preceding caveat, Yukl (2013)

P. S. Millsap (✉)
Mount Saint Mary's University, Los Angeles, Los Angeles, CA, USA
e-mail: patrickmillsap@cox.net



B. E. Winston (eds.), *Transparent and Authentic Leadership*, Christian Faith Perspectives in Leadership and Business,
https://doi.org/10.1007/978-3-030-61996-1_6

noted that authentic leadership is grounded in positive psychology and psychological theories of self-regulation. All theorists emphasize consistency in a leader's words, action, and values, with additional aspects that include positive leader values, leader self-awareness, and a trusting relationship with followers. Authentic leaders create high mutual trust through honesty, altruism, kindness, fairness, accountability, and optimism, with an emphasis on follower welfare and development. Authentic leaders have a high self-awareness about the values, beliefs, emotions, self-identities, and abilities, which allows them to make accurate assessments about who they are, as a reality, and what they believe. They do not seek leadership positions to gratify a need for esteem status, as a desire to be liked, admired, and to retain their position, which would be self-seeking. As a result, they are less defensive (Yukl, 2013, pp. 351–352).

Scripture is given by inspiration of God; therefore, it is authentic. Scripture is profitable for doctrine, reproof, correction and for instruction in what is right so that individuals may be perfect, or mature, and capable of doing good works 2 Timothy 3:16–17 (NKJV). The Old Testament is replete with stories that reveal God's authentic working and actions toward humanity to reveal a reality beyond our current perception, to awaken the individual to that which is truly authentic and of the kingdom of God. This chapter highlights Balaam, who was a prophet and leader in the Old Testament whose wisdom was sought after by many kings. Balaam is the opposite of what would be an authentic leader, but by way of apophatic teaching, much is learned through the story noted in Numbers as "*Balaam and his donkey.*" The story is a narration from the aspect of one watching and listening in, but who is not a participant. The text is reviewed through an inner texture treatment to break down the elements of the story.

Robbins (1996) noted that narrational inner texture, an element of socio-rhetorical criticism, or the narrational voice as a rhetorical device within the text gains acceptance as a reliable guide to the meaning of the text, because of the way the narrator tells the story (Robbins, 1996, p. 55). The narrator is perceived to be Moses, who is commonly accepted has the one who wrote the first five books of the Old Testament, also known as the Pentateuch (Thompson's Original and Complete System of Bible Study, Index 4226). Inner texture concerns relationships among word-phrase and narrational patterns that produce aesthetic patterns in the text. These intermingling patterns are the contexts for networks of signification that create meaning, and therefore, values in the concepts found in the text (Robbins, 1996, p. 46). Osborne (2006) noted that Old Testament allusions are utilized in the New Testament to convey meaning to readers, which may have had a greater impact at the time of the writing as a way of presupposing the reader's knowledge. He noted that an individual writer's traits, such as the Apostle Paul, the Apostle Peter, and the Apostle John, use a very high incidence of allusions. The allusion presupposes the original Old Testament context behind the allusion and not merely the allusion itself, which intensifies the thrust of the context (Osborne, 2006, pp. 167–168). The New Testament notes this, as there are scriptures that mention Balaam as a negative role model and not to follow his example.

Vanhoozer (1998) noted that speech acts, such as narration, could become the equivalent of the character's action at the level that may entail actual history. Texts not only display a world but communicate a way of perceiving that world, thus a possible training, or portraying, ways of being human (Vanhoozer, 1998, p. 227). The author also noted that there is a relation between authorial intentions and communicative action. Therefore, there needs to be a way to distinguish between "mapping intentions" and "meaning intentions." The first has to do with planning and plotting a course, and the second has to do with historical deeds and destinations. It is important to explain the author's intent in terms of action, what happened, versus what may happen, which is psychology and inference (Vanhoozer, 1998, p. 246). Moses, as noted, wrote the pericope to be reviewed, but the nature of its detail in terms of what was said, who is speaking, and the tone that is taken by each speaker is difficult to comprehend as having been heard specifically by him in person. Also, Balaam is traveling to see the enemy of Israel; therefore, Moses would not have been privy to the conversation between Balaam and his donkey. The narration also notes that there is no one else present during the exchange, except for the angel. Numbers 22:22 (NKJV) does mention two servants are traveling with him, but they are not part of the narrative, so we have no information about them. The conclusion is, therefore, one of faith. Moses wrote the narrative for the book of Numbers by the inspiration of God. The entire story of Balaam, who had been requested by Balak, the Son of Zippor, king of the Moabites, to curse Israel, is found in Numbers 22:01–24:25 (NKJV). The pericope consists of the verses in Numbers 22:22–22:35 (NKJV).

## Chronological, Historical, Narrative Context Before the Pericope: Numbers 22:22–22:35

As noted, the pericope consists of Numbers 22:22–22:35 (NKJV). Leading into the pericope, as a chronological sequence, is a narrated piece concerning Israel's defeat of Og, king of Bashan, and taking possession of his land. Israel then moves to camp in the plains of Moab on the side of Jordan across from Jericho (Numbers 21:33–35, 22:1, NKJV). Balak, the son of Zippor, was the king of the Moabites during this time and had heard and seen all that Israel had accomplished (Numbers 22:4, NKJV). He realized the severity of his situation and reached out to Balaam, the son of Beor, who was at Pethor, which was near the Euphrates River in the land of the sons of his people into bring him on-side for his cause. He noted that the Israelites were a people who had come from Egypt and that they were covering the earth and had now settled next to him in Moab, in a way that was in opposition (Numbers 22:5, NKJV). Pethor, or Pitru, is thought to have been about 400 miles from Moab, in Mesopotamia on the River Euphrates. The distance required an estimated three-week journey each way to both inform Balaam and return ("International Standard Bible Encyclopedia," 2019, p. 1).

The request from Balak was to have Balaam curse Israel, as he felt they were too mighty for him to oppose. He sent the elders of both Moab and Midian with a diviner's fee, or honor, to employ Balaam for the task of cursing Israel. Alter (2004) noted that the honor, or payment, would be lavish in value, he would also receive special raiment that would enhance his status as an authority figure (Alter, 2004, p. 11). He noted that whom Balaam blesses is blessed, and whom he curses is cursed, which reveals an authority that is given deference by kings (Numbers 22:6–7, NKJV). Thus, Balaam would be considered to be in the ranks of a highly paid, authoritative consultant that was brought into help the organization achieve success for a price. Balaam received the dignitaries and asked them to wait while he inquired of the Lord. As he goes to the Lord, the Lord asks him as to whom these men are. Balaam recounts the details of the request and that he has been requested to curse the Israelites so that once cursed Balak would be able to drive them out of the land. The narrative flows in such a way that Balaam does not seem to have an awareness of Israel having been delivered from the hand of Pharoah, in Egypt, by God's hand (Numbers 22:8–11, NKJV). God forbids Balaam to go with them and not to curse them, for he has blessed them (Numbers 22:12, NKJV). Balaam returns to the envoy and lets them know that God will not allow him to return to Moab with them. The messengers return to Balak and relay the message that Balaam has refused (Numbers 22:13–14, NKJV). Balak now sends princes to Balaam and asks him to come and let nothing hinder him from coming. The king states that he will honor him greatly and that he will do whatever Balaam instructs him to do, but to please come and curse these people for him (Numbers 22:15–17, NKJV). Each trip was approximately three-weeks to cover the 400 miles, so at least nine weeks had passed by this point in time from the initial inquiry. Also, Balak says that he will do whatever Balaam requires, but that excludes the act of cursing Israel; which is the task to be performed.

Balaam noted to the new group of envoys that through Balak were to give him his house full of silver and gold; he would be unable to go beyond the word of the Lord, his God, to do any more than what he had done. He then asked them to stay while he inquired of the Lord again. This time the Lord changes his mind and tells Balaam he may go with them, but that he may only speak that which the Lord gives him to speak. The caveat given is that "if the men come and call you, arise and go with them... The narration notes that Balaam rose in the morning, saddled his donkey, and went with the princes (Numbers 22:18–21, NKJV). Balaam did not wait for this final inquiry from the envoys. Instead, he made the next step. Small things are very important in the life of a leader, especially an authentic one. Moses is told at Horeb to smite the rock to give water to the Israelites (Exodus 17:6, NKJV). But, at Meribah, he is told to speak to the rock and instead smites the rock two times. The Lord notes that because Moses and Aaron did not believe God, to sanctify him in the eyes of the children of Israel, they would not be allowed to bring the congregation into the land (Numbers 20: 11–13, NKJV). God produces leaders in an authentic way that engages both the reality in the world and the reality that emanates and is imputed, from the kingdom of God. Authenticity is of great interest to God in the world, as is holiness (I Peter 1:16, NKJV). Holiness and authenticity have to do with integrity, very similar to the physical integrity of objects such as steel and diamonds. Integrity gives an individual the capacity to withstand both an inward and outward onslaught that endeavors to break down that integrity. Authenticity is something God desires in leaders, for it is from one's authenticity that individuals come to understand the kingdom of God, as a perception of reality. If a leader changes portions of God's instruction, then the outcomes change as well. Balaam had taken a step that he was not to take until the envoys initiated the first move. Therefore, something of Balaam's character and intention has been revealed in the opening verses of the chapter.

This completes the chronological, historical narrative intro leading up to the pericope, Numbers 22:1–21 (NKJV), which is given in a narrative form that follows chronological events as they occur. As noted, Moses is considered to be the author of the book of Numbers, and the dialogue is very specific and could not have been heard by him, as he was 400 miles away. It is the Spirit of God that has given him this narrative. The pericope follows the same narrative format as given in the preceding sequence, which is chronological, historical, and conversational.

## Inner Texture Treatment of Numbers 22:22–22:35

See Table 6.1.

## Pericope Applications for the Contexts of Leadership, Followership, and the Organization

There are several levels between leaders, followers, and organizational contexts in the story. Balak, the king of the Moabites, sends envoys to a hire Balaam, a powerful diviner whose ability to curse (hex) someone is well known. He believes he will be able to use Balaam to curse Israel and thus be able to control destiny though a technical manipulation in the realm of the spirit world through his ability to curse (Alter, 2004, p. 7). The envoys, who were diviners as well, fail to bring back Balaam to the king and he increases his request of "bestowing honor" on Balaam by sending princes to entice him to come to Moab. Balaam capitulates and saddles his donkey to go to Moab. Thus, the organizational side of the Moab group is complete. The donkey belongs to Balaam but is not an active participant in the enticement of Balaam. The donkey is a faithful

**Table 6.1** Numbers 22: 22–35

| *Text: Num. 22:22–35 (delivered in Narrator style—as one watching the action)*<br>*Version: New King James Version* | *Who is speaking* | *Who is spoken to & nature of communication* | *Purpose/corroboration*<br>*Version: New King James Version* |
|---|---|---|---|
| Num. 22:22 Then God's anger was aroused because he went,<br>and the angel of the LORD<br>took His stand in the way<br>↳ as<br>an adversary against him<br>And he was riding on his<br>donkey, and his two servants<br>*were* with him | Narrator | Description of the situation<br>Those involved are Balaam, the donkey, the angel, and two servants | The result of his going without being requested by those asking (Verse: 20) kindles God's anger because he went<br>The angel stands against him |
| Num. 22:23 Now the donkey saw the angel of the LORD standing in the way with His drawn sword in His hand<br>↳ and the donkey turned aside<br>out of the way and went<br>into the field<br>↳ So Balaam struck the<br>donkey to turn her back<br>onto the road | The Narrator explains what the donkey sees, which explains the donkey's logical response | Description of the situation and the action, which is known only to the donkey | Action: The donkey takes action without any communication from its master, Balaam, who is the leader in this scenario<br>Balaam's response to the donkey's perceived disobedience |
| Num. 22:24–25 Then the angel of the LORD stood in a narrow path between the vineyards, *with* a wall on this side and a wall on that side<br>↳ And when the donkey saw<br>the angel of the LORD, she<br>pushed herself against the<br>wall and crushed Balaam's<br>foot against the wall; | The Narrator explains the movement of the angel to block Balaam's progress<br>The donkey's gender is female<br>Balaam is physically injured | Description of the actions being taken by the angel | We do not, at this point in the story, know the donkey's reasoning. We can only surmise what may be occurring in the mind of an animal<br>Balaam's response is one of cruelty, but he is also in pain<br>Proverbs 12:10 notes that the righteous man regards the life of his |

(continued)

**Table 6.1** (continued)

| *Text: Num. 22:22–35 (delivered in Narrator style—as one watching the action)*<br>*Version: New King James Version* | *Who is speaking* | *Who is spoken to & nature of communication* | *Purpose/corroboration*<br>*Version: New King James Version* |
|---|---|---|---|
| ↳ so he struck her again | Balaam strikes the donkey again | | beast: but the tender mercies of the wicked are cruel. Balaam knows nothing of what is occurring in reality and only knows that what he wants is not being accomplished, so he is treating his follower, the donkey, harshly to derive obedience, which reveals the selfishness of an individual |
| Num. 22: 26–27 Then the angel of the LORD went further, and stood in a narrow place where there *was* no way to turn either to the right hand or to the left<br>↳ And when the donkey saw the angel of the LORD, she lay down under Balaam;<br>↳ so Balaam's anger was aroused, and he struck the donkey with his staff | The Narrator explains the angel's second move to block Balaam's | Descriptive of the action taken by the angel and by the donkey. The way is entirely blocked, and there is no further move to make, so the donkey lays down under its rider, Balaam | There are several levels of communication in play that are not openly discussed, but they are revealed in the narrative. First, the angel has not taken the life of Balaam but instead is blocking his way. Secondly, the donkey can see the angel, which could only have been given by God. As a result, there is a great deal to unravel at deeper levels of interpretation. Also, the leader-follower context applies to the relationship between Balaam and the donkey, the angel and God, and finally, the angel and the donkey – at this juncture of the narration |
| Num. 22:28–29 Then the LORD opened the mouth of the donkey, and she said to Balaam<br>↳ "What have I done to you, that you have struck me | God opens the mouth of the donkey to speak human language | Balaam | This is the first communication in the text that is not merely physical, with Balaam striking the donkey |

(continued)

**Table 6.1** (continued)

| *Text: Num. 22:22–35 (delivered in Narrator style—as one watching the action)*<br>*Version: New King James Version* | *Who is speaking* | *Who is spoken to & nature of communication* | *Purpose/corroboration*<br>*Version: New King James Version* |
|---|---|---|---|
| these three times?"<br>↳ And Balaam said to the donkey<br>"Because you have ↳ abused me. I wish there were a sword in my hand, for now, I would kill you!" | donkey<br>Balaam | donkey | The donkey is quoted as asking a question of its master (leader) that implies the need for an answer<br>Balaam noted that he had been mocked. The Hebrew (*Hithpael*) means to make a fool of or make sport of someone ("Transliteration: *alal*," 2019, p. 1)<br>This is the same man who is on his way to receive honors from a king. He is being thwarted by a domesticated animal, which has moved him to want to kill the animal, which would leave him on foot. This does not reveal authentic leadership |
| Num. 22:30 So the donkey said to Balaam,<br>"*Am* I not your donkey on which you have ridden, ever ↳ since *I became* yours, to this day? Was I ever disposed to do this to you?"<br>↳ And he said, "No" | donkey<br>Balaam | Balaam<br>donkey | A discourse between Balaam and his donkey, without mention of the strangeness of the exchange. Balaam simply replies, "No," in a logical manner<br>The logic of the donkey's statement is true in that it seems that the animal has been faithful to Balaam from the moment he obtained him. The animal has been disposed of or accustomed to obeying him. Jones (2019) noted that according to Ben Hart of the |

(continued)

**Table 6.1** (continued)

| *Text: Num. 22:22–35 (delivered in Narrator style—as one watching the action)*<br>*Version: New King James Version* | *Who is speaking* | *Who is spoken to & nature of communication* | *Purpose/corroboration*<br>*Version: New King James Version* |
|---|---|---|---|
| | | | Donkey Preserve in the United Kingdom, donkey's are trustworthy because they will stop and think rather than bolt, unlike horses. This is not a character flaw, but a character trait in donkeys (Jones, 2019, p. 1) |
| Num 22: 31–33 Then the LORD opened the eyes of Balaam, and he saw the angel of the LORD standing in the way, and his sword drawn in his hand<br><br>↳ and he bowed down his head, and fell flat on his face<br><br>And the angel of the LORD said unto him,<br><br>↳ Wherefore hast thou smitten thine ass these three times?<br><br>↳ behold, I went out to withstand thee, because *thy* way is perverse before me:<br><br>↳ "The donkey saw Me and turned aside from Me these three times | Lord opens Balaams eyes to the authentic reality<br><br>Balaam's response is one of contrition<br><br>angel<br><br>angel inquires as to the reason for his actions<br><br>This is followed by the angel's reasons for being against Balaam<br><br>angel notes that the donkey saves him | Reality is given to Balaam<br><br>No words yet had been spoken only a revealing<br><br>To Balaam<br><br>Inquiry<br><br>Reasons are given to Balaam<br><br>Balaam | Authenticity is based on a true perception based in reality<br><br>Balaam's response is authentic and genuine<br><br>Balaam's cruelty to the donkey is noted. The reason for the encounter is due to Balaam's perverse way. The connotation is that Balaam has been destructive or fully selfish in his way ("Yarat," 2019, p. 1), which are not traits of being authentic<br><br>The angel tells Balaam that if the donkey had not turned aside the three times, he would have killed Balaam and left the donkey alive. It is due to the donkey's |

(continued)

**Table 6.1** (continued)

| *Text: Num. 22:22–35 (delivered in Narrator style—as one watching the action)*<br>*Version: New King James Version* | *Who is speaking* | *Who is spoken to & nature of communication* | *Purpose/corroboration*<br>*Version: New King James Version* |
|---|---|---|---|
| ↳ If she had not turned aside from Me, surely I would also have killed you by now, and let her live" | | | authentic response that Balaam is still alive |
| Num. 22: 34–35 And Balaam said to the angel of the LORD,<br>↳ "I have sinned, for I did not know You stood in the way against me<br>↳ Now, therefore, if it displeases You, I will turn back" | Balaam | angel | Balaam's perverse way has been revealed. He notes that he was unaware, but that he will repent and turn back. This response is elicited by the donkey's actions as a follower |
| Then the angel of the LORD said to Balaam,<br>↳ "Go with the men, but only the word that I speak to you, that you shall speak"<br>So Balaam went with the princes of Balak | angel | Balaam | The angel gives Balaam a new task, which is to go with the princes to Moab but only to speak the word that is given to him. Balaam is not a prophet of God, but a diviner, but God will use him to bless Israel instead of cursing Israel, which is recorded in Numbers 23:36–24:25 |

follower of Balaam that is not corrupt or selfish. The angel is an emissary of God. As such, the angel in all respects is authentic, transparent and is holy or of integrity. The relationship with God is not mentioned but inferred in that the angel is an angel of the Lord. Israel is seen as a threat by Moab and is blessed by God, as noted by the angel, but is not an active participant in the story. Although the impetus for the story is Israel's arrival. The organizational side of those that fall on the side of the Lord are the angel and Israel.

Sanford (1950) noted that leadership occurs as part of an intricate relation between leaders and followers in a specific organizational context (Sanford, 1950). Kellerman (2008) noted that leadership and followership should not be just joined together, but that they should be thought of in tandem, or as inseparable, as one does not exist without the other (Kellerman, 2008, p. 239). The entire story of Balak and the Moabites, which is found in Numbers 22:01 to Numbers 24:25 (NKJV) and includes the pericope, is about seeing, or gazing, which is to have one's eyes opened to reality and is a trait of authentic leaders and followers (Alter, 2004, p. 8). Alter (2004) also noted that this implies the ability to not see as well. The thematic keyword of the entire episode is "to see," or *ra'oh*, or to gaze. Balak, the Moabite king, sees the vast multitudes of the Israelites and is afraid. Therefore, he endeavors to hire a diviner to curse the Israelites, which will solve his organizational problem. The diviner is enticed to come but is blind to his avarice and guile, but his beast of burden, a donkey, is not. The angel of the Lord sees everything clearly and allows an unveiling to take place for Balaam to see the reality his follower, the donkey, already sees (Alter, 2004, p. 8). The donkey is the lynch-pin of the story in that she is the first to be able to see the authentic reality that is taking place. She makes decisions based on the reality she sees that shows her concern for her leader or master. The opening of Balaam's eyes creates a different relationship between the two sides, which is dealt with in the remaining section that ends at Numbers 24:25 (NKJV). The application of the pericope, or what it means for authentic leadership and followership today, is given in three segments. First, is the application to the context of leadership; second, is the application to the context of followership; and third, is application to the organizational context, which affects the first two contexts.

## Context of Leadership

The application of the story of Balaam and his donkey is found in the New Testament in the form of apophatic teaching, which is to describe something as what it is not or giving a moral lesson in a way that describes what not to do (Apophatic Theology, 2019, p. 1). As noted above, the writings of the Apostles Peter, Paul and John employ narrative that is allusionary, or alluding to something, in nature, which occurs in 2 Peter 2:15 & 16 (NKJV) concerning the warning to false teachers and compares them to Balaam's folly. Peter notes that they have forsaken the right way and gone astray, following the way of Balaam, who loved the wages of righteousness. He was rebuked for his iniquity by a dumb donkey speaking with a human voice, which restrained his madness (2 Peter 2:15–16, NKJV). Balaam, as a prophet, diviner, and leader is not authentic but is a false teacher who thinks in terms of his own needs and not the needs of others. Balaam is a man of guile, which is associated with deceit and uncleanness (I Thessalonians 2:3, NKJV). He, therefore, is one who is considered to have perverted justice, by showing partiality, and taking bribes which has blinded (hence not able to see) the eyes of the wise and twisted the words of the righteous (Deuteronomy 16:19, NKJV). Romans 2:11 (NKJV) notes that there is no partiality with God; therefore, partiality would not exist in an authentic leader. Selfishness leads to blindness and lack of being able to see reality, both in the known world and spiritually. These traits are in opposition to authenticity, transparency, and integrity.

Jude 1:11 (NKJV) notes that those who are selfish and only serving themselves have crept into the body of Christ. These people are like Balaam in that they seek only personal profit. They are considered to be spots in the love feasts of the body of Christ, and feast without fear serving only themselves. They are like clouds without water, trees without fruit—that are twice dead and pulled up by the roots, and wandering stars for whom is reserved the blackness of darkness forever (Jude 1:12–13, NKJV). These are attributes of leaders that are not authentic or transparent, and they are compared specifically to Balaam in a negative way that reveals non-authentic, non-transparent leadership.

Yukl (2013), as noted above, stated that authentic leaders are not motivated by a desire to be liked and admired to retain their position. Instead, they are motivated by a desire for self-improvement and self-verification, which allows them to be less defensive and more open to learning from feedback and mistakes (Yukl, 2013, p. 352). Balaam punishes his donkey because he feels that the donkey has abused, or mocked, him (Numbers 22:24, NKJV). Alter (2004) noted that the first two beatings by Balaam were probably with a switch, but the third beating was performed with a staff. Balaam also states that if he had a sword he would kill the donkey (Alter, 2004, p. 13). These are punishments given in light of Balaam's selfish desires and not being open to self-improvement or self-verification; therefore, he is very defensive of his selfish position. Konopaske, Ivancevich, and Matteson (2018) defined punishment as presenting an uncomfortable or unwanted consequence for a particular behavior and is an increasingly used managerial strategy. Although it may suppress behavior if used effectively, it is considered to be a controversial method to be utilized by leaders. This method is only utilized after a careful and objective consideration of all the relevant aspects of the situation are known (Konopaske, Ivancevich, & Matteson, 2018, p. 165). Balaam utilizes punishment as a first response, which reveals that he is not in a state of mind where he is thinking about anything other than himself and how he is perceived.

The final scripture in the New Testament, concerning Balaam, is found in Revelations 2:14 (NKJV) and is speaking to the church at Pergamos, the compromising church, which is one of the seven churches written to in the book of Revelations. John notes that the Lord has a few things against the church and the first noted is that there are those in the church who hold the doctrine of Balaam, who taught Balak to put a stumbling block before the children of Israel, to eat food sacrificed to idols and to commit sexual immorality (Revelations 2:14, NKJV). Yukl (2013) noted that authentic leaders maintain the capacity to lead followers through their enhanced confidence, clarity of values, and integrity. As a result, followers have a personal identification with the authentic, transparent leader, as well as a social identification with the organizational group that allows for an indirect follower effect through follower self-concepts and self-identities that would be considered a form of mentoring (Yukl, 2013, p. 352). The authentic leader assists in creating an authentic relationship with followers, in an organizational context that is consistent with the leader's values as well as the follower's values. Riggio, Chaleff, and Lipman-Blumen (2008) noted that the theory of authentic leadership development (ALD) that acknowledges leadership development as an interactive process by leaders, followers and the context in which they find themselves embedded over time. Thus, authentic leaders are individuals who are self-aware, transparent, and ethical in the way they approach leadership in the organization (Riggio et al., 2008, p. 327). Therefore, the leader-follower process, in context, is continually in a transformational state of becoming authentic. These are important aspects for those desiring to develop in an authentic leadership that is transparent versus the inauthentic, closed, selfish leadership that Balaam practices. Gardner, Avolio, Luthans, May, and Walumbwa (2005) noted that authentic follower development is a result of the modeling done by authentic leaders, which produces higher levels of follower self-awareness and self-regulation that lead to positive follower development (Gardner et al., 2005, p. 346) Contrary to this conception de Zilwa (2016) noted that authentic followership involves relational interactions between the follower, leader, and the context and that authentic followership is a proactive process. This proactive process is initiated by the authentic follower and allows the follower to decide if they will or will not follow the leader. In this sense it is constructionist (de Zilwa, 2016, p. 311). The interrelation of leader, follower, and context are noted throughout this chapter and share possible new concepts of what these titles may mean in reality.

## Context of Followership

The follower in the story is the donkey. The donkey is attached to the Moab organizational group in that the donkey is the property of Balaam. But, the donkey is faithful to Balaam and not to Balaam's schemes with Balak, king of Moab. Therefore, the donkey is an authentic follower from the beginning of the story and is not associated with the negative attributes of Balaam, as noted above. Kelley (1992) noted five types of followers, which he exhibits on a grid that ranges from being active to being passive, as a horizontal axis, and being an independent, critical thinker to being a dependent, uncritical thinker on the vertical axis. The combination of variables on the two-axis gives the following results. (1) Passive follower, passive and dependent, uncritical thinking; (2) Conformist follower, active and dependent, uncritical thinking; (3) Alienated follower, passive and independent critical thinking; (4) Exemplary follower, active and independent, critical thinking; (5) Pragmatist follower, is situated in a mid-position amongst all the variables (Kelley, 1992). The donkey displays attributes of the exemplary follower, who is actively engaged, able to see reality, and act according irrespective of the leader. The donkey is also acting as a courageous follower, in that she is not following the unction of her leader, but is responding to the reality of the situation, as she perceives it. In her actions, she is revealing self-awareness and self-identity, but not selfishness. She perceives, or sees, the reality of the situation and is acting authentically. Chaleff (2009) noted that the courageous follower's role is to find ways leaders can receive the feedback they need. It helps if the follower links the information given to a positive outcome for the leader, which supplies motivation to the leader to follow the advice (Chaleff, 2009, p. 90).

As noted, the donkey, more than being exemplary, is exhibiting attributes of being a courageous follower. Courageous followership exhibits the following attributes: (1) participates in transformation; (2) constructively challenges counterproductive policies and organizational behaviors; (3) assumes responsibility for the common purpose of the organization; (4) supports both the leader and the group; and (5) takes moral action when needed (Chaleff, 2009, p. 40). The donkey initiates the transformation and in this respect becomes the authentic leader, who acts based on the reality exhibited, rather than the mere follower. She challenges the counterproductive policies at a cost three separate times; she also assumed responsibility for her actions in taking the existing punishment being delivered to her by the leader. She is supporting the minor group that consists of her and her leader in endeavoring to keep both of them safe. Finally, she takes moral action in ceasing to move forward and laying down, which did not support the leader in his quest to move forward at great risk. The donkey has acted in a way that reveals authentic followership. She has decided not to follow the leader in order to protect him. Avolio et al. (2004) noted that authentic followership is proactive, which reverses the conventional view that leader's influence and direct the follower's behavior (De Zilwa, 2016, p. 311) Not until the angel gives the donkey speech, Numbers 22:28 (NKJV), is there a revealing of the authentic reality of the situation, which allows the leader, Balaam, to enter the conversation.

The donkey receives the ability to speak in the narrative in a way that Balaam may converse with her. He is out of control, and she asks what she has done that he has beaten her three times (Num. 22:28, NKJV). Balaam's retort is that she has abused, or mocked him and that he would kill her if he had a sword. Her answer is authentic. She questions his logic, or his ability to see things clearly, by asking if she had ever done anything like this before. The rhetorical means of questioning allows Balaam to ponder his relationship with his follower, the donkey, and reply that this has never happened before (Num. 22:30, NKJV). This questioning is courageous in that the donkey is noting a history that is not congruent, authentically, with the incident that is taking place. Thus, the question of whether or not the donkey is acting authentically is answered by Balaam. She is acting in an authentic transparent manner, and Balaam is not. Num. 22:31 (NKJV) narrates the sequence where the angel opens Balaam's eyes to see what the donkey has been able to see, and thus, authentic reality is revealed to him. Balaam prostrates himself in the same position as the donkey, and the sword, which he would like to have had, is welded by the angel. He has come into an authentic, transparent reality that reveals what God is doing organizationally; which negates all other previous organizational interests. The ability of the authentic leader and follower to perceive reality through different means of perception is important for both authentic leadership and followership. Yukl (2013) noted that follower perception of leader authenticity might be influenced by follower perception of the situation. Trust may be undermined if the leader's actions do not appear to be congruent with authenticity (Yukl, 2013, p. 352). Balaam's actions are not authentic or genuine, but instead selfish. The donkey speaks to question Balaam's motives, and then the angel opens his eyes, only then is the authenticity of the situation revealed, perceived, or seen. Balaam has been allowed to gaze upon the real situation. This is brought about by the donkey's faithful leadership, instead of proper leadership on the part of Balaam. The donkey has acted from a position of followership, as a courageous follower. Authenticity, as noted above, implies self-awareness and self-perception. Application is for followers as well as leaders. Chaleff (2009) noted that all leaders are followers in some sense. But whether or not the leader is a positive role model, we still, as courageous followers, must prepare ourselves to become courageous leaders (Chaleff, 2009, p. 30). This assessment of being a courageous follower is closely linked to the concepts described concerning authenticity. He also noted that leaders and followers are joined in the context of organizational purpose (Chaleff, 2009, p. 3). Aligning the leadership-followership-organizational context through time is an on-going process of transformation. The individual who desires to become an authentic leader must be open to the organizational context as an important part of leadership process.

## The Organizational Context

As noted, authentic leadership and followership are embedded in the context of an organization, which has an organizational intention, purpose, and culture. An organizations intention and purpose is a part of the company's vision and mission. Suffice to say organizations are made up of individuals that fall into the category of leader or follower in the organization, and in some sense many individuals may occupy both roles simultaneously. The organizational context, for this chapter, will focus on organizational culture. The pericope notes two specific organizational cultures or groups. The first is the Moab group, which consists of Balak, king of Moab, the envoys and the princes, along with Balaam who has been summoned to perform on their behalf against the Israelites. The second group is that of the Lord, the angel, and Israel as represented by the angel. The donkey is with Balaam and is attached to him in such a way that she is protective of him alone and therefore does not belong expressly to either group; therefore she has no hidden, or selfish, agenda.

Hiebert (2008) noted that the levels of culture range from surface culture, which is sensory and contains behaviors, signs, and rituals, through belief systems, which are explicit, down to core worldview themes that retain epistemology and are implicit (Hiebert, 2008, p. 33). Ashkanasy, Wilderom, and Peterson (2011) noted that in an organization conversation between the "we" and the "us," of those involved in the organization, set up dynamic processes of listening and responding, thus the organization's responses are always contextualized by the organization's cultural meanings. Therefore, organizational culture and identity dynamics are intertwined, which is similar to that noted above in the leadership-followership process (Ashkanasy et al., 2011, pp. 345–347). Authentic leadership-followership is pre-loaded, as noted above, in that the term is also the outcome, which is to say that authentic leadership-followership implies an outcome that is morally good (Antonakis & Day, 2018, p. 68). That being said the attributes, as noted above, of an authentic leader or follower lean toward positive outcomes from both leaders and followers. Thus, the authentic, transparent organizational culture should also lead to positive, moral outcomes for all stakeholders involved.

The conversation in organizational culture between the "we" and the "us" of those involved in the organizational context should be similar to the I/Thou relationship. Buber (1937) noted that there is a radical difference between a person's attitude to other human beings and their attitude to things. The attitude to other people should be a relation between persons, and to things it is a connection of objects. In this relationship, the "I" of the first individual encounters the "Thou" of the other, whereas concerning things, the "I" encounters the "It." In the I/Thou relation the "I" meets the other, which has no boundary, and can only be known in relation to oneself. Whereas the I/It relationship presupposes a single center of consciousness, the "I," and the person may dispose of the "it" in any fashion it desires (Buber, 1950, pp. vi–vii). Authentic leadership is inherently an I/Thou exchange. In organizational culture, to remain authentic, those involved need to work to maintain and I/Thou exchange in the "we" and the "us" dynamic. If the conversational exchange, and therefore the relationship, becomes an I/It exchange than the possibility of creating an authentic organizational culture, which would be necessary for authentic leaders and followers, would be slim. As an application, the I/Thou exchange is necessary for the "we" and "us" exchange, for both leaders and followers, in authentic organizational culture. Knowledge of this fact for those who desire to create an authentic organizational context and culture is preeminent.

## Conclusion

Authentic leadership, followership, and organizational contexts, or cultures, may exist as a subset of other forms of leadership, followership, and organizational structures. Antonakis and Day (2018) noted that authentic leadership is closely associated with both servant and transformational leadership. The concept of being authentic, transparent, and having integrity are embedded in both servant and transformational leadership (Antonakis & Day, 2018, pp. 68–69). As a result, many forms of leadership may improve by using models of authentic leadership within their main leadership focus. Yukl (2013) noted that LMX theory has several conceptual weaknesses that limit its utility, but that it can improve by a using a clear description of the way a leader develops different dyadic relationship (Yukl, 2013, p. 224). It may well be that further study of authentic leadership and authentic followership as it applies to other forms of leadership may assist our understanding of the human dynamics of trust, openness, integrity, perception of the other, and transparency that are inherent in authentic leadership. Also, by studying biblical constructs, such as Balaam and his donkey, we are allowed to view, historically, what authentic leadership is not and what authentic followership may look like. Apophatic teaching may allow for strong examples of what would be categorized as inauthentic leadership, which may extend our meaning and understanding of the category. It is recommended that further study of leadership and followership in scripture be continued to verify different leadership models that would either be authentic or inauthentic to gain a deeper understanding of leadership models in scripture.

## References

Alter, R. (2004, Autumn). Balaam and the ass: An excerpt from a new translation of the five books of moses. *The Kenyon Review, 26*(4), 6–32. Retrieved from https://www.jstor.org/stable/4338644.

Antonakis, J., & Day, D. V. (2018). *The nature of leadership* (3rd ed.). Los Angeles: Sage Publication.

Apophatic Theology. (2019). Retrieved from https://search-credoreference-com.ezproxy.regent.edu/content/entry/cupdct/apophatic_theology/0.

Ashkanasy, N. M., Wilderom, C. P., & Peterson, M. F. (2011). *The handbook of organizational culture and climate* (2nd ed.). Thousand Oaks, CA: Sage Publications.

Avolio, B., Gardner, W., Walumba, F., Luthans, F., & May, D. (2004). "Unlocking the mask: A look at the process by which authentic leaders impact follower attitudes and behaviors", *The Leadership Quarterly, 15*(6), 801–823.

Buber, M. (1937). *I and Thou*. Edinburgh, Scotland: T. & T. Clark.

Buber, M. (1950). *I and Thou*. Edinburgh, Scotland: T. & T. Clark.

Chaleff, I. (2009). *The courageous follower: Standing up to & for our leaders* (3rd ed.). Oakland, CA: Berrett-Koehler Publishers.

De Zilwa, D. (2016). *The strengths and capacities of authentic followership.Leadership and Organizational Development Journal, 37*(3), 310–324. Retrieved from https://doi-org.ezproxy.regent.edu/10.1108/LODJ-01-2014-0010.

Gardner, W. L., Avolio, B. J., Luthans, F., May, D. R., & Walumbwa, F. (2005). "Can you see the real me?" A self-based model of authentic leader and follower development. *The Leadership Quarterly, 16*(3), 343–372. https://doi.org/10.1016/j.leaqua.2005.03.003.

Hiebert, P. G. (2008). *Transforming worldviews: An anthropological understanding of how people change*. Grand Rapids, MI: Baker Academic.

Jones, C. (2019). *Are donkey's stubborn?* Retrieved from https://animals.mom.me/donkeys-stubborn-3410.html.

Kellerman, B. (2008). *Followership: How followers are creating change and changing leaders*. Boston, MA: Harvard Business Press.

Kelley, R. E. (1992). *The power of followership: How to create leaders people want to follow and followers who lead themselves* (1st ed.). Retrieved from http://library.regent.edu/record=b1387655.

Konopaske, R., Ivancevich, J. M., & Matteson, M. T. (2018). *Organizational management and behavior* (11th ed.). New York: McGraw-Hill.

Mock (Abuse). (2019). Retrieved from https://www.blueletterbible.org/lang/lexicon/lexicon.cfm?Strongs=H5953&t=KJV.

Osborne, G. R. (2006). *The hermeneutical spiral: A comprehensive introduction to biblical interpretation* (2nd ed.). Downers Grove, IL: InterVarsity Press.

Perverse. (2019). Retrieved from https://www.blueletterbible.org/lang/lexicon/lexicon.cfm?Strongs=H3399&t=KJV.

Pethor. (2019). Retrieved from https://biblehub.com/topical/p/pethor.htm.

Riggio, R. E., Chaleff, I., & Lipman-Blumen, J. (2008). *The art of followership: How great followers create great leaders and organizations*. San Francisco, CA: Josey Bass.

Robbins, V. K. (1996). *The tapestry of early Christian Discourse: Rhetoric, society, and ideology*. New York: Routledge.

Sanford, F. H. (1950). Authoritarianism and leadership: A study of the follower's orientation to authority. *Institute for Research in Human Relations*. Retrieved from https://psycnet.apa.org/record/1952-00818-000.

Vanhoozer, K. J. (1998). *Is there a meaning in this text? The Bible, the reader, and the morality of the literary knowledge*. Grand Rapids, MI: Zondervan.

Yukl, G. (2013). *Leadership in organizations* (8th ed.). Boston: Pearson.

CHAPTER 7

# Toward a Model of Judicious Transparency That Builds Trust Within Organizations

*Daniel Holmquist*

## Introduction

The general public has been demanding greater transparency in leadership and from leaders themselves, whether in politics, business, nonprofits, or even in the smallest and most localized of organizations. Researchers have been examining the nature of transparency in leadership and increasing understanding of how transparency works in leadership and organizational life. Practitioners have been pursuing greater transparency in their leadership, yet they have also been seeking to understand how certain situations might influence different levels of transparency, and then how this might impact the building of trust and creating an open and honest organizational culture.

D. Holmquist (✉)
School of Business and Leadership, Regent University, Chesapeake, VA, USA
e-mail: daniho3@mail.regent.edu

Essex Fells, NJ, USA



B. E. Winston (eds.), *Transparent and Authentic Leadership*, Christian Faith Perspectives in Leadership and Business,
https://doi.org/10.1007/978-3-030-61996-1_7

One of the constructs of authentic leadership theory has been relational transparency, referring to leaders who present their true selves to their followers, building trust through self-disclosure, open and honest communication, and self-management of emotions (Northouse, 2016; Walumbwa, Avolio, Gardner, Wernsing, & Peterson, 2008; Yukl, 2013). This relational transparency relates closely to another construct, self-awareness, which refers to strong and stable acceptance of self-identity, with a clear and consistent awareness of one's values, beliefs, emotions, and abilities (Northouse, 2016; Walumbwa et al., 2008; Yukl, 2013). Authentic leadership theory describes transparency as a principled commitment to an authentic expression of self to others; yet, this description of transparency focuses directly on the person of the leader without much accounting for other variables such as followers' levels of comfort with personal transparency or situational constraints to achieve organizational goals. Rather than viewing authentic leadership as simply a leadership style, Sidani and Rowe (2018) proposed a model of authentic leadership based upon a follower-centered legitimization process.

Discursive leadership theory understands organizations as discursively constructed through leaders influencing of work-related conversations to strategically guide their organizations (Eisenberg, Trethewey, LeGreco, & Goodall, 2017; Fairhurst & Putnam, 2004). Leaders function as storytellers who manage meaning and sensemaking and establish social and communication norms (Fairhurst, 2011). In the practice of discursive leadership, leaders play a powerful role in the daily discourse throughout their organizations and in communicating organizational mission, vision, and strategy. Discursive leadership would describe leadership transparency in terms of leader commitment to organizational realities, not in terms of a personalized principle as in authentic leadership theory. Although not purely utilitarian in approach, discursive leadership transparency would be guided by how leaders would desire to influence perception, build necessary trust, and construct a social reality for their organizations.

The principled, personal, and almost absolute transparency of authentic leadership theory appears in opposition to the managed, situational, and strategic transparency of discursive leadership theory. However, leaders must utilize both types of transparency in leading people and their organizations. This conceptual paper introduces a new concept of *judicious transparency*, a wise, discerning, astute, and sensible transparency, that seeks to bring together these seemingly opposite understandings of transparency to build organizational trust and honest relationships. One way to accomplish this will be through the use of political skill, a social competency in which leaders effectively influence others for positive personal and organizational outcomes (Bowen, Ferris, & Kolodinsky, 2010; Ferris et al., 2005 Harris, Kacmar, Zivnuska, & Shaw, 2007). This chapter examines the concepts of transparency within both authentic leadership theory and discursive leadership theory. Then, through comparison and contrast, and the introduction of the use of political skill, this chapter introduces a new conceptual model of judicious transparency and suggests avenues for future research into judicious transparency.

### *Authentic Leadership Theory*[1] *and Transparency*

Although the concept of authenticity in leadership could be traced back to at least the ancient Greeks (Harter, 2002), modern interest in authentic leadership as a theory of leadership surfaced about 2003–2005 (Walumbwa et al., 2008). Since then, research into Authentic Leadership Theory (ALT) and its theoretical development has grown. Authentic leaders possess a high degree of self-awareness and self-acceptance and are guided by strong personal positive core values; because of their integrity and transparency, followers readily identify with them, grant them legitimacy, and perceive them to be optimistic, confident, and worthy of trust (Sidani & Rowe, 2018; Yukl, 2013).

Various definitions of authentic leadership have been proposed, but Walumbwa et al. (2008) have provided the most widely accepted definition:

> A pattern of leader behavior that draws upon and promotes both positive psychological capacities and a positive ethical climate, to foster greater self-awareness, an internalized moral perspective, balanced processing of information, and relational transparency on the part of leaders working with followers, fostering positive self-development. (p. 94)

[1] Much of the discussion of authentic leadership is taken from my article "Authentic Leadership Theory: Enhancements from 1 Peter 5:1–5," by D. B. Holmquist, 2018, *Theology of Leadership Journal, 1,* 88–97. Copyright 2018 by Daniel B. Holmquist. Adapted with permission.

In their research and development of the Authentic Leadership Questionnaire to measure authentic leadership, Walumbwa et al. (2008) defined authentic leadership's four constructs: (a) self-awareness, (b) relational transparency, (c) balanced processing, and (d) internalized moral perspective. Self-awareness refers to an awareness of how one makes sense of the world and attributes meaning, and how this process impacts one's view of self (Walumbwa et al., 2008). Self-aware individuals grow in their understanding of their strengths and weaknesses through exposure to, and experience with, others and observing their impact upon them. Relational transparency refers to the presentation of one's true self to others, building trust through open disclosure. Those who exhibit relational transparency can also control their emotions and measure them appropriately depending on the situation (Walumbwa et al., 2008). Balanced processing refers to the ability to gather relevant information from a variety of sources, analyze the data objectively, and then make a decision (Walumbwa et al., 2008). This processing includes intentionally seeking out alternate viewpoints from one's own. Internalized moral perspective refers to the consistency of decision making based upon internal moral standards and values. Those possessing deep personal self-regulation will guide themselves based upon moral convictions even in the face of pressures from colleagues, other leaders, society, and even organizational culture (Walumbwa et al., 2008).

In using this formulation of authentic leadership, researcher have not only discovered its value but have also noted areas in need of further examination, all of which could bear upon the notion of transparency. For example, Sendjaya, Pekerti, Härtel, Hirst, and Butarbutar (2016) studied the relationship between moral reasoning and moral action among managers using ALT. Their analysis revealed the "absence of a direct relationship between moral reasoning and authentic leadership, and an absence of a direct relationship between authentic leadership and moral action" (Sendjaya et al., 2016, p. 135). Their findings have suggested that additional moral components interact with moral antecedents, moral outcomes, and even self-concepts of authentic leadership. ALT has not fully explored or explained how moral components, capacities, motivation, and courage function within all of the constructs of authentic leadership, including relational transparency (Northouse, 2016; Sendjaya et al., 2016).

Desired outcomes that flow from authentic leadership and the relational transparency involved include follower empowerment, relational improvement, and organizational citizenship behavior (Ilies, Morgeson, & Nahrgang, 2005). More could be studied regarding these positive outcomes; and yet, researchers have offered advice to improve ALT. O'Connell (2014) described how authentic leadership combined with intercultural competencies could shape global leaders who will be more effective with vision because of their integrity; certainly, cultural dynamics would play a significant role in relational transparency. Berkovich (2014) offered practical improvements to ALT and the training of leaders that would move the theory away from its pure functionalism of being true-to-self and toward greater attendance to others, attitudes, and relationships.

Others have pointed out ALT's dependence upon modern positive psychology and its functionalist focus. Harter (2002) indicated that the concept of authenticity originated at least as far back as the ancient virtue philosophy of the Greeks. However, Walumbwa et al. (2008) noted that in the development of ALT, authenticity has been conceptualized more so by modern psychology. As a result of these two source streams (virtue philosophy and positive psychology), ALT ended up blending the concepts of self-awareness, self-acceptance, and self-development with modern moral notions of authenticity. ALT could benefit from further research into ancient virtue philosophy, possibly leading to a re-assessment and re-incorporation of external standards and higher-order morality into the theory to balance out the over-emphasis upon modern psychology for defining the constructs of ALT (Gardner, Avolio, Luthans, May, & Walumbwa, 2005). Such improvements might deepen the ALT construct of relational transparency beyond its association with positive psychology.

ALT focuses upon leaders, their self-expression, and their authentic seeking of personal and social identification from their group members. These foci produce organizations with positive ethical climates and build up the psychological capacities of leaders and followers (Yukl, 2013). As part of authenticity in ALT, relational transparency builds trust and dependability, and it establishes credibility and legitimacy (Ilies et al., 2005; Sidani & Rowe, 2018; Walumbwa et al., 2008); however, ALT demonstrates an almost exclusive internal orientation of leadership transparency. This internal orientation may prove insufficient in promoting honest relationships.

### *Discursive Leadership Theory and Transparency*

Discursive leadership refers to leaders' abilities during various interaction processes to influence work-related conversations, the meanings that emerge, and the norms that become established (Clifton, 2012; Eisenberg et al., 2017). This includes the "social, linguistic, and cultural aspects of leadership" (Eisenberg et al., 2017, p. 282) as they play out in conversational interaction for social construction of reality (Cooren, Taylor, & Van Every, 2006; Robichaud & Cooren, 2013). Practically, discursive leadership is about leaders as storytellers and speakers who "use communication strategically to guide ... sense making [sic] and interpretation of organizational realities" (Eisenberg et al., 2017, p. 282). In their influential article that began the stream of research into organizations as discursive constructions, Fairhurst and Putnam (2004) explored the complex relationship of discourse and organizations. They found three organizational orientations: (a) already formed and having discourse clearly reflect the form, (b) in the process of becoming and in the process of discourse forming, and (c) grounded in action and practices of intertwined discursive forms. Fairhurst and Putnam (2004) argued that all three organizational orientations occur in organizations simultaneously and that discourse should be studied from multiple perspectives.

Fairhurst (2007) differentiated her approach to studying leadership from the psychological approach, although they act like two lenses from which to view leadership. The psychological approach has focused upon the internal processes and individual characteristics of leaders and followers, whereas the discursive approach, a second lens, has examined the social and communicative aspects between them. In 2008, she expanded on the book and highlighted key distinctives of studying discursive leadership, namely, studying the basic elements of discourse, the importance of both text and context, and the understanding of reflexive agency in conversations (Fairhurst, 2008).

In describing the basics of discursive analysis, Fairhurst (2011) identified two notions of how meaning gets constructed: (a) *little d* discourse, referring to daily interactions and the choices made in carrying on conversations; and (b) *big D* discourse, referring to larger organizational culture narratives reflected in conversations. Discursive views of leadership analyze communication and reflect on what is happening based on social theories (Clifton, 2006). Discursive leadership itself involves the framing of events, people, and situations in the context in order to manage meaning (Fairhurst, 2009, 2011). Clearly, the strategic choices that leaders make in their communication regarding framing and management of meaning relates to the topics and levels of transparency, as well as, the communication choices of followers.

Ten years after introducing discursive leadership theory, Putnam and Fairhurst (2015) reviewed the foundational research in agency theory and sense-making theory that led to their theory of organizations as discursive construction, as well as, the large and varied stream of research that has flowed out from their proposal since 2004. As one example that relates to the topic of leadership transparency, Cooren and Sandler (2014) presented a ventriloquism metaphor to explain the notion of how people mobilize figures, concepts, values, and emotions in such a way that they incarnate themselves in other people's discourses. Continuing with this metaphor, Cooren and Sandler (2014) demonstrated how various forms of ventriloquism manifest themselves in conversations and express a personified reality of communication. This metaphor of ventriloquism relates to motives behind transparency or non-transparency, as well as, the processes and effectiveness of transparent communication.

The most researched area of discursive leadership relates to the everyday performance of leadership; within this everyday communication, issues surrounding leadership transparency are managed strategically. Regarding *little d* discourse, Nielsen (2009) examined how managers interpret the daily experiences and observations of employees and then relate these to corporate contexts and realities. Gadelhina (2016) described leadership in terms of the multiple small interactions that constitute the reality of doing leadership by providing intelligible formulations of reality. Clifton (2012) conducted an analysis of transcripts of natural conversations and explained discursive leadership in terms of influencing the management of meaning from a privileged position; however, he noted that in reality, the process of managing meaning remains a distributed process.

Regarding *big D* discourse, Nielsen (2009) showed how the communication interaction strategies of managers demonstrated leadership by framing and managing language and meaning for larger organizational purposes. Tonkiss and Skelcher (2015) highlighted the importance of framing as a discursive leadership resource, but also of gaining a discursive advantage through structuration and institutionalization. Ilie (2017) analyzed interviews and press conferences of several CEOs in order to examine how discursive leadership works to construct and re-construct organizational cultural identity in times of transition and change; in other words, how discursive leadership works to navigate internal and external challenges of corporate values and competitiveness.

In discursive leadership theory, the focus of transparency exists beyond the individual leader in the social and organizational realities and processes. Transparency will be conditioned by the strategic management of communication and the framing of meaning within an organizational narrative. This does not mean that this approach to, or a framework of, transparency is false or misleading, or even contrary to ethical behavior. Rather, transparency is not an absolute ideal end in itself, but a tool for structuring reality, managing change, developing organizational culture, and promoting values. Yet, it remains unclear how discursive leadership would promote honest relationships within an organization.

### *Comparison and Potential Integration of Transparency Approaches*

Transparency is about openness and honesty. At first glance, the concept of relational transparency from authentic leadership theory would seem to be at odds with any concept of transparency within discursive leadership theory because of the potential for playing language games to manage meaning for others. However, the two different approaches to transparency could be combined, or integrated, to develop a more robust understanding of transparency in leadership. An integrated model of judicious transparency could address situational factors that call for different levels of prudence in transparency, and lead to the building of more profound trust and honesty as a result.

Table 7.1 shows a comparison between authentic leadership and discursive leadership on five aspects of transparency; distinctions appear sharper than typically practiced for comparison. The inner being of the leader serves as the source of transparency in authentic leadership theory, while in discursive leadership theory the leader acting as an agent serves as the source of transparency; although both the internal and external components of leadership will be used as sources of transparency in practice. In authentic leadership theory, the basis or foundation of transparency is a matter of principle, whereas in discursive leadership theory sense-making serves as the basis of transparency. Authentic leadership theory views the purpose of transparency to express who leaders are personally; discursive leadership theory views the purpose of transparency to guide others and the organization strategically. No limitations on transparency

**Table 7.1** Comparison of transparency approaches

| *Transparency aspect* | *ALT transparency* | *DLT transparency* |
|---|---|---|
| Source | Leader (internal) | Leader (as agent) |
| Basis | Principle | Sense-making |
| Purpose | Personal expression | Strategic guide |
| Limitations | None | Organizational realities |
| Desired outcome | Trust (open disclosure) | Trust (reliable communication) |

*Note* ALT refers to authentic leadership theory; DLT refers to discursive leadership theory

would exist in principle (though some would in practice) within authentic leadership theory, although within discursive leadership theory the organizational realities would provide the boundaries for transparency. Finally, both authentic leadership and discursive leadership theories seek relational and organizational trust, the former through open disclosure and the latter through reliable communication. Throughout this comparison, the two approaches to transparency are not necessarily mutually exclusive on any of the five transparency aspects. Both approaches could be used to create positive ethical organizational climates, and if they were integrated into a concept of judicious transparency could build even greater trust and honest relationships within organizations.

### *Political Skill*

Political skill could provide the bridge between the two approaches to transparency, paving the way for integration in theory and practice. Bowen et al. (2010) differentiated the concept of political skill from the concept of organizational politics, the latter being almost exclusively associated with negative self-serving organizational realities and experiences. Political skill, on the other hand, refers to the social competencies of understanding people and organizations to effectively influence others for positive outcomes (Ferris et al., 2005; Harris et al., 2007).

Ferris et al. (2008) identified four distinct factors of political skill: (a) social astuteness, (b) interpersonal influence, (c) networking ability, and (d) apparent sincerity. As a competency, leaders with political skill can adjust the manifestations of their thinking, emotions, and behaviors as needed to influence people and the organization through collaborative, partnership-like methods, which fits with both authentic leadership and discursive leadership. Bowen et al. (2010) compared characteristics of political skill with characteristics of servant leadership and put forth the new concept of a politically skilled servant leader. Whitman, Halbesleben, and Shanine (2013) underscored the value of self-regulation as a key underlying component of political skill. In addition, many of the characteristics of political skill also fit with authentic leadership, such as emotional intelligence, self-awareness, integrity, trustworthiness, sincerity, and being genuine and honest.

Understanding political skill as the exercising of informal power, Kurchner-Hawkins and Miller (2006) suggested that the use of political skill can foster collaboration for the attainment of shared organizational objectives, which, incidentally, is often the purpose in using discursive leadership. A constructive and strategic political approach for politically skilled leaders would involve four capabilities: (a) understanding power and its value to achieve goals, (b) understanding themselves, (c) awareness of the political situation within the organization and outside the organization, and (d) ongoing development of their interpersonal skills (Butcher & Clarke, 2008). Political skill involves the positive use of power to unite the personal concerns of authentic leadership theory with the organizational concerns of discursive leadership theory.

### *A Conceptual Model of Judicious Transparency*

Judicious transparency would combine some of the views of transparency from both authentic leadership theory and discursive leadership theory and would subsume two aspects of transparency from authentic leadership theory under those of discursive leadership theory. Holding transparency as a high ethical value in itself, yet understanding situational limitations, judicious transparency refers to the wise, discerning, astute, and sensible use of transparency.

Table 7.2 shows the comparison of transparency approaches between authentic leadership theory and discursive leadership theory as in Table 7.1, with the added model of judicious transparency. Judicious transparency would retain both source aspects of transparency, the inner leader and the leader as an agent. It would also retain both bases of transparency, principle, and sense-making. Judicious transparency would be less concerned with the value of personal expression of authenticity

**Table 7.2** Comparison of transparency approaches including judicious transparency

| *Transparency aspect* | *ALT transparency* | *DLT transparency* | *Judicious transparency* |
|---|---|---|---|
| Source | Leader (internal) | Leader (as agent) | Leader (internal)<br>Leader (as agent) |
| Basis | Principle | Sense-making | Principle<br>Sense-making |
| Purpose | Personal expression | Strategic guide | Strategic guide |
| Limitations | None | Organizational realities | Organizational realities |
| Desired outcome | Trust (open disclosure) | Trust (reliable communication) | Trust (open disclosure)<br>Trust (reliable communication) |

*Note* ALT refers to authentic leadership theory; DLT refers to discursive leadership theory

through transparency and would subsume this purpose under the purpose of strategic guidance. Although transparency carries high intrinsic value, in judicious transparency it would not retain the near absolute status it does with authentic leadership theory but would be subject to the limitations of organizational realities. Finally, judicious transparency would retain both aspects of trust building, through open disclosure and reliable communication.

## Future Research

Future research into the concept of judicious transparency should seek to clarify the eight aspects of transparency listed in Table 7.2. Qualitative investigations could examine how each of these components of transparency operates, their antecedents, and their conditional constraints. Interviews with leaders and followers on trust building and judicious transparency would likely prove very helpful because this is often the chief desired outcome of transparency. Case studies could provide insight into how judicious transparency works in practice and offer rich descriptions of judicious transparency. Authentic leadership theory has developed quantitative instruments that measure relational transparency but discursive leadership, being such a young theory, has not yet moved beyond qualitative inquiry in the flow of research; consequently, mixed method studies involving both of these theories could supply a greater understanding of the concept of judicious transparency. Hopefully, as a result of such qualitative exploration, researchers could develop and validate instruments to measure judicious transparency.

## Conclusion

With the demand for greater and greater transparency from leaders and organizations throughout the USA and the world comes the need for a more refined and robust understanding of the nature and practice of transparency. Calls for transparency can seem like demands for absolute openness and honesty, but transparency that builds relational trust, organizational trust, and that leads to a culture of trust will attend to each organization's unique context, people, and situations in order to determine the appropriate level and type of transparency. This concept paper introduced a new model of transparency, namely judicious transparency. This type of transparency will lead to more satisfying honest relationships. In developing this concept of judicious transparency, the concepts of transparency in authentic leadership theory and discursive leadership theory were compared, contrasted, and combined in such a way to offer a potentially stronger and more productive understanding of transparency. Judicious transparency refers to the wise, discerning, astute, and sensible use of transparency that seeks to build trust in organizations. It includes the aspects of (a) leaders being the source of transparency both in terms of their character and in terms of their actions, (b) the bases of transparency comprising both principled and sense-making notions, (c) the purpose of transparency functioning as a strategic guide, (d) the limitations of transparency being the actual organizational realities, and (e) the chief desired outcome being trust gained through open disclosure and reliable communication. Hopefully, future research into judicious transparency will further clarify these aspects of transparency and establish operational definitions to guide ongoing research efforts. Ultimately, judicious transparency may provide a path forward for a world clamoring for improvements in transparency and honest relationships.

## References


Berkovich, I. (2014). Between person and person: Dialogical pedagogy in authentic leadership development. *Academy of Management Learning & Education, 13*(2), 245–264.

Bowen, M. G., Ferris, G. R., & Kolodinsky, R. W. (2010). Political skill, servant leadership, and workplace spirituality in the creation of effective work environments. In R. A. Giacalone & C. L. Jurkiewicz (Eds.), *Handbook of workplace spirituality and organizational performance* (2nd ed., pp. 126–142). New York, NY: Routledge.

Butcher, D., & Clarke, M. (2008). *Smart management: Using politics in organizations* (2nd ed.). Houndmills, UK: Palgrave Macmillan.

Clifton, J. (2006). A conversation analytical approach to business communication: The case of leadership. *Journal of Business Communication, 43*(3), 202–219.

Clifton, J. (2012). A discursive approach to leadership: Doing assessments and managing organizational meanings. *Journal of Business Communication, 49,* 148–168.

Cooren, F., & Latour, B. (2010). *Action and agency in dialogue: Passion, incarnation, and ventriloquism.* Amsterdam, The Netherlands: John Benjamins.

Cooren, F., & Sandler, S. (2014). Polyphony, ventriloquism, and constitution. *Communication Theory, 24*(3), 225–244.

Cooren, F., Taylor, J. R., & Van Every, E. J. (Eds.). (2006). *Communication as organizing: Empirical and theoretical explanations in the dynamic of text and conversation.* Mahwah, NJ: Erlbaum.

Eisenberg, E. M., Trethewey, A., LeGreco, M., & Goodall, H. L. J. (2017). *Organizational communication: Balancing creativity and constraint* (8th ed.). Boston, MA: Bedford/St. Martin's.

Fairhurst, G. T. (2007). *Discursive leadership: In conversation with leadership psychology.* Thousand Oaks, CA: Sage.

Fairhurst, G. T. (2008). Discursive leadership: A communication alternative to leadership psychology. *Management Communication Quarterly, 21*(4), 510–521.

Fairhurst, G. T. (2009). Considering context in discursive leadership research. *Human Relations, 62*(11), 1607–1633.

Fairhurst, G. T. (2011). *The power of framing: Creating the language of leadership.* San Francisco, CA: Jossey-Bass.

Fairhurst, G., & Putnam, L. (2004). Organizations as discursive constructions. *Communication Theory, 14*(1), 5–26.

Ferris, G. R., Blickle, G., Schneider, P. B., Kramer, J., Zettler, I., Solga, J., ..., Meurs, J. A. (2008). Political skill construct and criterion-related validation: A two-study investigation. *Journal of Managerial Psychology, 23*(7), 744–771.

Ferris, G. R., Treadway, D. C., Kolodinsky, R. W., Hochwarter, W. A., Kacmar, C. J., Douglas, C., & Frink, D. D. (2005). Development and validation of the political skill inventory. *Journal of Management, 31,* 126–152.

Gadelhina, G. (2016). *Discursive leadership in technological change* (Doctoral dissertation). Retrieved from ProQuest Dissertations (Order No. 10590449).

Gardner, W. L., Avolio, B. J., Luthans, F., May, D. R., & Walumbwa, F. (2005). "Can you see the real me?" A self-based model of authentic leader and follower development. *The Leadership Quarterly, 16*(3), 343–372.

Harris, K. J., Kacmar, K. M., Zivnuska, S., & Shaw, J. D. (2007). The impact of political skill on impression management effectiveness. *Journal of Applied Psychology, 92*(1), 278–285.

Harter, S. (2002). Authenticity. In C. R. Snyder & S. J. Lopez (Eds.), *Handbook of positive psychology* (pp. 382–394). London, UK: Oxford University.

Holmquist, D. B. (2018). Authentic leadership theory: Enhancements from 1 Peter 5:1–5. *Theology of Leadership Journal, 1*(1), 88–97.

Ilie, C. (2017). Discourses of leadership change or changes of leadership discourse? *Journal of Economic Development, Environment and People, 6*(4), 6–17.

Ilies, R., Morgeson, F. P., & Nahrgang, J. D. (2005). Authentic leadership and eudaemonic well-being: Understanding leader–follower outcomes. *The Leadership Quarterly, 16*(3), 373–394.

Kurchner-Hawkins, R., & Miller, R. (2006). Organizational politics: Building positive political strategies in turbulent times. In E. Vigoda-Gadot & A. Drory (Eds.), *Handbook of organizational politics* (pp. 328–351). Cheltenham, UK: Edward Elgar.

Nielsen, M. F. (2009). Interpretative management in business meetings: Understanding managers' interactional strategies through conversation analysis. *The Journal of Business Communication, 46*(1), 23–56.

Northouse, P. G. (2016). *Leadership: Theory and practice* (7th ed.). Los Angeles, CA: Sage.

O'Connell, P. K. (2014). A simplified framework for 21st century leader development. *The Leadership Quarterly, 25*(2), 183–203.

Putnam, L., & Fairhurst, G. (2015). Revisiting "organizations as discursive construction" 10 years later. *Communication Theory, 25*(4), 375–392.

Robichaud, D., & Cooren, F. (2013). *Organization and organizing: Materiality, agency, and discourse.* London, UK: Routledge.

Sendjaya, S., Pekerti, A., Härtel, C., Hirst, G., & Butarbutar, I. (2016). Are authentic leaders always moral? The role of Machiavellianism in the relationship between authentic leadership and morality. *Journal of Business Ethics, 133*(1), 125–139.

Sidani, Y., & Rowe, W. G. (2018). A reconceptualization of authentic leadership: Leader legitimation via follower-centered assessment of the moral dimension. *The Leadership Quarterly, 29*(6), 623–636.

Tonkiss, K., & Skelcher, C. (2015). Abolishing the audit commission: Framing, discourse coalitions and administrative reform. *Local Government Studies, 41*(6), 861–880.

Walumbwa, F. O., Avolio, B. J., Gardner, W. L., Wernsing, T. S., & Peterson, S. J. (2008). Authentic leadership: Development and validation of a theory-based measure. *Journal of Management, 34*(1), 89–126.

Whitman, M. V., Halbesleben, J. R., & Shanine, K. K. (2013). Psychological entitlement and abusive supervision: Political skill as a self-regulatory mechanism. *Health Care Management Review, 38*(3), 248–257.

Yukl, G. (2013). *Leadership in organizations* (8th ed.). Upper Saddle River, NJ: Prentice Hall.

CHAPTER 8

# Peter: An Authentic and Transparent Leader

*Andrew Morgan*

## Introduction

Ask any group of undergraduate biblical studies students their opinion on who in the New Testament is the greatest example of a leader, and after accounting for Jesus and the Apostle Paul, the name Peter will undoubtedly enter into the conversation. This should not come as a surprise given the fact that within the four gospels, after the name of Jesus, no name is mentioned more than Peter's; no other disciple is recorded as speaking more than Peter; and Jesus is recorded as speaking to no disciple more than to Peter (Lockyer, 1972). However, sharing the historical stage with Jesus and being referred to often in the gospel accounts does not make Peter a leader. A determination of leadership attributes requires an examination of Peter's life through the lens of leadership theory. The following pages consider genuine self-concepts and present the disciple Peter as an authentic and transparent leader and offer an understanding of transparency and authenticity in leadership applicable in the twenty-first century.

A. Morgan (✉)
School of Business and Leadership, Regent University, Chesapeake, VA, USA
e-mail: andrmo1@mail.regent.edu



B. E. Winston (eds.), *Transparent and Authentic Leadership*, Christian Faith Perspectives in Leadership and Business,
https://doi.org/10.1007/978-3-030-61996-1_8

### *Why Authentic and Transparent Leadership*

Northouse (2016) stated that "authentic leadership represents one of the newest areas of leadership research" (p. 195). Yet, an acknowledgment of the opportunity for examining a new area of leadership is not enough motivation to invest in the reading of this book. Terrible calamity and globally recognized failures in leadership have left people searching for leaders they can trust, "leaders who are honest and good" (Northouse, 2016, p. 195), who are perceived as authentic in their leadership. Yes, authentic leadership is a new area of academic study, but more than an academic exercise, the search for authentic leaders rises from a demand for leaders who are honest and engender trust through specific behavior. So what exactly are people searching for in an authentic leader? This chapter offers a response to that question by examining authentic leadership within the frameworks of first an intrapersonal perspective, then an interpersonal perspective, and finally, a developmental perspective (Northouse, 2016, p. 196), which will include a focused examination of relational transparency. Referring to a unified consideration of these three frameworks, Lawler and Ashman (2012) noted that "despite each having a slightly different focus, certain themes recur within these approaches which merit consideration" (p. 331). To aid in understanding the frameworks and perspectives, the life and leadership example of Jesus' disciple Peter is used to illustrate the theoretical concepts of authentic leadership.

### *Intrapersonal Perspective*

An intrapersonal perspective of authentic leadership was put forward by Shamir and Eilam (2005) and summarized by Northouse (2016) to incorporate a "leaders' self-knowledge, self-regulation, and self-concept" (p. 196). Shamir and Eilam (2005) acknowledged "that there is no single accepted definition of authentic leadership" (p. 395). They suggested an authentic leader would possess "self-knowledge and a personal point of view, which reflects clarity about their values and convictions" (Shamir & Eilam, 2005, p. 396). They stated further that an authentic leader would identify "strongly with their leadership role, expressing themselves by enacting that role, and acting on the basis of their values and convictions" (Shamir & Eilam, 2005, p. 396). From this intrapersonal perspective, Shamir and Eilam (2005) suggested that an authentic leader would understand and act upon what they felt to be their "'true' or 'real' self" (p. 397). In summarizing Shamir and Eilam's (2005) intrapersonal perspective of authentic leadership, Northouse (2016) suggested that authentic leaders "exhibit genuine leadership, lead from conviction, and are originals, not copies" (p. 196). The three authentic leadership aspects of, genuine leadership, lead from conviction, and are originals, not copies will be examined and illustrated through biblical accounts of the disciple, Peter.

### *Genuine Leadership*

Authentic leaders are genuine; they "do not fake their leadership. They do not pretend to be leaders just because they are in a leadership position" (Shamir & Eilam, 2005, p. 396). The disciple Peter had a leadership position among Jesus' disciples. Note that Peter (at the time referred to as Simon) and his brother Andrew, along with James and his brother John, were the first disciples to be called by Jesus (Mark 1:16–20). Also note concerning leadership position that Peter and the other three appear named at the beginning of the recorded lists of disciples (Matthew 10:2–4; Mark 3:16–19; Luke 6:14–16; Acts 1:13). In Matthew's account, he stated, "These are the names of the twelve apostles: first, Simon (who is called Peter) and…" (Matthew 10:2, NIV). Note that Matthew, in his account, delineated Peter as 'first.'

Also of interest are the apparent inner circle positions of Peter, James, and John. Jesus invited them into situations that the other disciples were not asked to join. Jesus invited these three to join him when he raised Jairus' daughter from the dead (Mark 5:37–42; Luke 8:50–55). Jesus invited them to come apart and support him as he prayed in the Garden of Gethsemane (Matthew 26:36–39; Mark 14:32–36). They were present at Christ's transfiguration (Matthew 17:1–2). All of these examples can be presented as evidence of Peter's leadership by his positional authority. There were other examples to prove that Peter's leadership was not fake (Shamir & Eilam, 2005, p. 396), not restricted to his position (Shamir & Eilam, 2005, p. 396). Peter was the first and only disciple to get out of the boat and walk on the sea like Jesus (Matthew 14:22–31). Peter's leadership was evidenced by his bold statement that "even if I have to die with you, I will never disown you" (Matthew 26:35; Mark 14:31, NIV). The verse concludes with the phrase, "and all the other disciples said the same" (Matthew 26:35, NIV), further evidencing how Peter was a leader of the disciples. Peter lead and the others followed. And this was genuine, not fake, as was evidenced when Peter drew his sword in defence when the armed party came to arrest Jesus (John 18:10). Peter put his words into action and proved his leadership was not fake or limited to position only.

### *Lead from Conviction*

Authentic leaders "do not take on a leadership role or engage in leadership activities for status, honor or other personal rewards. Rather, they lead from a conviction" (Shamir & Eilam, 2005, p. 396). Shamir and Eilam (2005) describe such a "eudaimonic activity for authentic leaders" (p. 397), meaning the leader's "activities are congruent with their deeply held values" (p. 397). Eudaimonically motivated leaders care not only for self-actualization but have a greater good in mind and desire to make a difference (Shamir & Eilam, 2005, p. 397). Leading from conviction is evidenced by a clear and confident response and direction as needed. Followers note when authentic leadership is evidenced by conviction. Consider, for example, Peter in response to Jesus' question to the disciples about whom the people were saying Jesus (the Son of Man) was. The disciples replied, "Some say John the Baptist; others say Elijah; and still others, Jeremiah or one of the prophets" (Matthew 16:14, NIV). Then when Jesus pressed his disciples as to whom they thought he was, Peter responded by stating, "You are the Messiah, the Son of the living God" (Matthew 16:16, NIV). This clear evidence of Peter's conviction regarding the Christ was responded to by Jesus, who said, "Blessed are you, Simon son of Jonah, for this was not revealed to you by flesh and blood, but by my Father in heaven" (Matthew 16:17, NIV). Then as an affirmation of the importance of such conviction of leaders, Jesus declared, "I tell you that you are Peter, and on this rock I will build my church, and the gates of Hades will not overcome it" (Matthew 16:18, NIV). This example of Peter's declaration and Jesus' response offers a promise that nothing can overcome such faith when congruent with deeply held convictions. Authentic leaders lead from convictions such as Peter's.

### *Are Originals, not Copies*

Authentic leaders "are originals, not copies" (Shamir & Eilam, 2005, p. 397). Shamir and Eilam (2005) clarified, stating, "this does not mean that they are necessarily unique or very different from each other in their personality traits" (p. 397). Instead "the process through which they have arrived at these convictions and causes is not a process of imitation" (p. 397). This attribute of authentic leaders arises out of personal experiences that shape and form values to be true for this individual. Even though societal and other pressures will impact their values, authentic leaders are noted as originals and not copies because "they have made these values and conviction highly personal through their lived experiences, experienced emotions, and an active process of reflection on these experiences and emotions" (Shamir & Eilam, 2005, p. 397). Foundational to this aspect of authentic leadership was Shamir and Eilam's (2005) understanding of Bennis (1992), who argued that a leader must own their leadership perspective. Bennis (1992) stated that "you cannot borrow a point of view any more than you can borrow someone else's eyes. It must be authentic, and if it is, it will be original, because you are original" (p. 122). A leader's "point of view does not have to be dramatically different from the point of view of others who hold or held that position, but it has to be personal in the sense that it has developed from personal experiences, personal reflection and personal learning" (Shamir & Eilam, 2005, p. 397).

Consider Peter as an original, not a copy. The Acts of the Apostles record the account of Peter's arrest and appearance before the Sanhedrin. He was asked to explain by what power, what name, what conviction he had been healing and preaching. Just as Jesus responded to Nicodemus and said, "you are Israel's teacher, and you do not understand these things" (John 3:10, NIV), Peter could have addressed the members of the Sanhedrin and asked why they did not understand how he was healing and preaching. They were each a copy, a product of a legalistic religious framework. Peter was a man of faith who adhered to this religious framework. It was this framework that assisted Peter to recognize Jesus as Master (Luke 5:5) and respond in obedience to instructions on how to catch fish (Luke 5:5–6), and then to respond in obedience to the call to leave his profession of fishing and become a fisher of men (Luke 5:10). As Peter stood before the Sanhedrin, he stood out from the conformity of legalistic religion as an original because of his convictions regarding the deity of Jesus Christ. Peter's religious convictions stood out as original because of his faith that had developed from personal experiences, personal reflection, and personal learning while living and ministering with Jesus. The members of the Sanhedrin noted the courage and boldness of Peter as he addressed them (Acts 4:13), and these religious leaders took note that Peter had been with Jesus (Acts 4:13). Peter was seen as an authentic leader, original in his values and convictions.

### *Interpersonal Perspective*

An interpersonal perspective of authentic leadership was put forward by Eagly (2005) who considered authentic leadership as relational. Northouse (2016) described this relational, interpersonal perspective of authentic leadership as resulting "not from the leader's efforts alone, but also from the response of followers" (p. 196). Northouse (2016) highlighted the reciprocal process involved in this interpersonal perspective of authentic leadership where "leaders affect followers and followers affect leaders" (p. 196). Eagly (2005) argued "that authenticity must be acknowledged by followers for it to produce positive outcomes," (p. 461) thus highlighting the relational aspect of authentic leadership. In this interpersonal perspective of authentic leadership, Eagly (2005) presented two components that distinguish relational authenticity. The first relational component detailed how "leaders endorse values that promote the interests of the larger community and transparently convey these values to followers" (Eagly, 2005, p. 461). The second component of relational authenticity detailed how "followers personally identify with these values and accept them as appropriate for the community in which they are joined to the leader" (Eagly, 2005, p. 461).

The newly forming community of Christ-followers in the few years after Christ's resurrection and ascension found themselves needing to attend to cultural values that were affecting matters of faith and practice in Christian communities. Chapter 15 of the Acts of the Apostles provides an account of how the Council in Jerusalem was asked to decide on a matter of acceptable Christian community practice. After "much discussion, Peter got up and addressed them" (Acts 15:7, NIV). Peter, in his address, evidenced an interpersonal perspective of authentic leadership by attending to relational authenticity. He stated:

> Brothers, you know that some time ago God made a choice among you that the Gentiles might hear from my lips the message of the gospel and believe. God, who knows the heart, showed that he accepted them by giving the Holy Spirit to them, just as he did to us. He did not discriminate between us and them, for he purified their hearts by faith. Now then, why do you try to test God by putting on the necks of Gentiles a yoke that neither we nor our ancestors have been able to bear? No! We believe it is through the grace of our Lord Jesus that we are saved, just as they are. (Acts 15:7–11, NIV)

Peter's relational authenticity featured the two components of Eagly's (2005) relational authenticity concept. First, Peter presented and endorsed values that promoted the interests of the broader community. He not only transparently but convincingly conveyed values to the Council in Jerusalem who followed his recommendations. Second, aligning with Eagly's (2005) relational authenticity, the followers whom Peter addressed personally identified with the values for which he argued, and they accepted them as appropriate for the community. Followers acknowledged Peter's authenticity, and it produced positive outcomes—ensuring unity in Christian communities.

### *Developmental Perspective*

The third theoretical concept of authentic leadership considered in this chapter is the developmental perspective (Northouse, 2016, p. 196). Walumbwa, Avolio, Gardner, Wernsing, and Peterson (2008) introduced this developmental perspective of authentic leadership. The developmental perspective of authentic leadership suggested: "authentic leadership is something that can be nurtured in a leader rather than as a fixed trait" (Northouse, 2016, p. 196). Walumbwa et al.'s (2008) conceptual framework of a developmental perspective of authentic leadership had four distinct, yet related components: (a) self-awareness, (b) internalized moral perspective, (c) balanced processing, and (d) relational transparency. Before examining these four components, it is appropriate to note Walumbwa et al.'s (2008) definition of authentic leadership, stated as "a pattern of leader behavior that draws upon and promotes both positive psychological capacities and a positive ethical climate, to foster greater self-awareness, an internalized moral perspective, balanced processing of information, and relational transparency on the part of leaders working with followers, fostering positive self-development" (p. 94). The following will outline Walumbwa et al.'s (2008) four components of authentic leadership as per their developmental perspective, and will illustrate these components of authentic leadership by featuring biblical accounts of the disciple Peter.

### *Self-Awareness*

Authentic leaders are self-aware. Walumbwa et al. (2008) referred to self-awareness as "demonstrating an understanding of how one derives and makes meaning of the world and how that meaning-making process impacts the way one views himself or herself over time" (p. 95). They stated that self-awareness "refers to showing an understanding of one's strengths and weaknesses and the multifaceted nature of the self, which includes gaining insight into the self through exposure to others, and being cognizant of one's impact on other people" (Walumbwa et al., 2008, p. 95). From Walumbwa et al.'s (2008) work it is appreciated how a leader's meaning-making process and recognition of their strengths and weaknesses, and how their personhood and leadership impact others and assists a leader in becoming self-aware and authentic.

In the life of Peter, were examples of him being or becoming self-aware. Consider first, Peter's interaction with Jesus at the Last Supper when Jesus washed the disciples' feet (John 13:1–17). When Jesus approached Peter, water basin in hand, a towel wrapped around him, Peter asked the question, "Lord are you going to wash my feet?" (John 13:6, NIV). Jesus responded, explaining, "You do not realize now what I am doing, but later you will understand" (John 13:7, NIV). Evidencing his present understanding and meaning-making, Peter retorted, "No, you shall never wash my feet" (John 13:8, NIV). To which Jesus answered, "Unless I wash you, you have no part with me" (John 13:8, NIV). In consideration of this answer, Peter's meaning-making and view of himself caused him to blurt out, "Then, Lord, not just my feet but my hands and my head as well!" (John 13:9, NIV). In this statement, was Peter evidencing self-awareness of his weaknesses and his need for Jesus' cleansing? Was he aware of his personhood through exposure to Jesus and how the impact of his weaknesses needed attention?

Another example of Peter's authentic leadership evidenced by self-awareness is seen in chapter 16 of the Acts of the Apostles. The Jerusalem based Christ-followers in the period just after Christ's resurrection and ascension were engaged in a social ministry that involved a controversial daily distribution of food, especially among needy widows (Acts 6:1). In response to this concern, the "Twelve" (Acts 6:2, NIV), which included Peter, gathered together with other disciples to discuss what should be done. Through a sense-making process, a consideration of strengths and weaknesses, and an awareness of their impact on others, the disciples argued that "It would not be right for us to neglect the ministry of the word of God in order to wait on tables" (Acts 6:2, NIV). The reasoned proposal was to "choose seven men" (Acts 6:3, NIV) "who are known to be full of the Spirit and wisdom" (Acts 6:3, NIV) and "turn this responsibility over to them" (Acts 6:3, NIV) so that the disciples could continue to give their "attention to prayer and the ministry of the word" (Acts 6:4, NIV). In this example, we see how Peter and the disciples evidenced authentic leadership through self-awareness.

### *Internalized Moral Perspective*

In outlining this next developmental perspective of authentic leadership, Walumbwa et al. (2008) referred to Ryan and Deci (2003) and described internalized moral perspective as "an internalized and integrated form of self-regulation" (p. 95). An internalized moral perspective is a form of self-regulation that "is guided by internal moral standards and values versus group, organizational, and societal pressures" (Walumbwa et al., 2008, pp. 95–96). Internalized moral perspective "results in expressed decision making and behavior that is consistent with these internalized values" (Walumbwa et al., 2008, p. 96) rather than succumbing to a group, organizational, or societal pressures.

An example of an internalized moral perspective and expressed decision-making as opposed to succumbing to a group, organizational, or societal pressures is observed in the engagement of Peter with the Sanhedrin after the witnessing of a miracle. Peter had said to a disabled man, "In the name of Jesus Christ of Nazareth, walk" (Acts 3:6, NIV), and the man was miraculously healed. Crowds gathered, and Peter preached, taught, and explained that Jesus Christ was the fulfillment of prophecy and that faith in Jesus could bring healing and life. The temple guards arrested Peter and John, who was with him, and the next day they were brought before the Sanhedrin for questioning. Peter's internalized moral perspective guided his response, and he spoke with bold self-regulation consistent with his internalized values. Peter and his authentic response was a threat to the religious leaders and so the Sanhedrin "commanded them not to speak or teach at all in the name of Jesus" (Acts 4:18, NIV). However, Peter, firm in his internalized moral perspective and guided by internal moral standards and values rather than standards and values of the religious leaders, refused to succumb to the pressure. Peter evidenced his authentic leadership through his internalized moral perspective and refuted the requirement of the Sanhedrin and stated, "Which is right in God's eyes: to listen to you, or to him? You be the judges! As for us, we cannot help speaking about what we have seen and heard" (Acts 4:19–20, NIV).

### *Balanced Processing*

Balanced processing, a developmental perspective of authentic leadership, "refers to leaders who show that they objectively analyze all relevant data before coming to a decision" (Walumbwa et al., 2008, p. 95). Walumbwa et al. (2008) noted further that authentic leaders utilizing balanced processing "also solicit views that challenge their deeply held positions" (p. 95). Individuals desiring to develop as authentic leaders are encouraged to balance their processing by seeking other views that challenge their own deeply help positions and then objectively analyze all relevant data before coming to a decision.

A few examples from the life of Peter previously presented in this chapter are worthwhile returning to as they highlight this authentic leadership attribute of balanced processing. Recall how chapter 15 of the Acts of the Apostles provided an account of the Council in Jerusalem who was asked to decide on a matter of acceptable Christian community practice. The issue at hand was the position held by some believers who belonged to the party of the Pharisees (Acts 15:5) who argued that Gentile believers in Jesus Christ "must be circumcised and required to keep the law of Moses" (Acts 15:5, NIV). Note that "the apostles and elders met to consider this question. After much discussion, Peter got up and addressed them" (Acts 15:6–7, NIV). Through the "much discussion" (Acts 15:7, NIV) did Peter engage in balanced processing, allowing his deeply held positions to be challenged as he analyzed all the relevant data before he stood to offer his opinion?

Recall also how Peter and John were arrested, after the healing of the disabled man, and were brought before the Sanhedrin. They were commanded, "not to speak or teach at all in the name of Jesus" (Acts

4:18, NIV). "On their release, Peter and John went back to their own people and reported all that the chief priests and the elders had said to them" (Acts 4:23, NIV). Peter reasoned through his reporting and subsequent prayer with the Jerusalem believers. They reviewed together their deeply held positions, and Peter analyzed all the relevant data, including a review of the prophetic words of David from Psalm 2:1–2 (Acts 4:25–26). They considered how the actions of Herod and Pontius Pilate also fulfilled what God by his "power and will had decided beforehand should happen" (Acts 4:28, NIV). From this balanced processing involving consideration of deeply held positions and the views of others, Peter's authentic leadership resolve was strengthened, and he sought the Lord's enabling to speak further with great boldness (Acts 4:29). Note also in Acts chapter 5 how Peter and the other apostles did speak boldly and performed other miracles in the name of Jesus. Once again, they were arrested and reminded by the Sanhedrin that they were given "strict orders not to teach in this name" (Acts 5:28, NIV). To which Peter infamously responded, "We must obey God rather than men!" (Acts 5:29, NIV). Peter was then forced into a period of balanced processing and the consideration of other viewpoints when he was punished by flogging for his deeply held positions. And he decided to rejoice for he "had been counted worthy of suffering disgrace for the Name" (Acts 5:41, NIV). What a lesson for individuals desiring to develop as authentic leaders. Peter offered an example of how to objectively analyze relevant data, allow other views to challenge deeply held positions, and then come to a decision.

### *Relational Transparency*

The final developmental perspective of authentic leadership presented is what Walumbwa et al. (2008) titled relational transparency. Relational transparency refers to "presenting one's authentic self (as opposed to a fake or distorted self) to others" (Walumbwa et al., 2008, p. 95). Regarding the work of Kernis (2003), Walumbwa et al. (2008) identified relational transparency behavior which "promotes trust through disclosures that involve openly sharing information and expressions of one's true thoughts and feelings while trying to minimize displays of inappropriate emotions" (p. 95). Walumbwa et al.'s (2008) definition of relational transparency involved an individual presenting and disclosing their true self to others through sharing appropriate thoughts and feelings while curbing or minimizing inappropriate emotional displays of their thoughts and feelings.

The accounts of the disciple Peter provide ample illustrative material to consider this developmental perspective of authentic leadership. Peter offers examples of relational transparency that show his ability to disclose his true self to others through sharing appropriate thoughts and feelings, as well as his developmental opportunities where Peter displayed inappropriate emotional responses, thoughts, and feelings. Peter was passionate and demonstrative. But how developed was his authentic leadership attribute of relational transparency? Consider first Peter's calling as recorded in Luke's gospel. Jesus was crowed around by those seeking to hear him speak at the shore of the Lake of Gennesaret (Luke 5:1). Seeing a boat, Jesus got in and asked the owner, Peter, to put out a little from shore (Luke 5:3). The people then sat down on the shore while Jesus addressed them from the boat (Luke 5:3). After Jesus finished speaking, he remained in the boat and told Peter where to let down his nets. Peter rebuked Jesus saying, "We've worked hard all night and haven't caught anything" (Luke 5:5, NIV), but tempered his response to Jesus with obedience and a qualifying statement saying that "because you say so, I will let down the nets" (Luke 5:5, NIV). This exchange contained emotions, thoughts, and feelings. Peter's response may have been an appropriate way for a fisherman to respond to a carpenter. Luke records a miraculous catch of fish with so many fish that the boat began to sink (Luke 5:7). How Peter responded next brings into question Peter's appropriate emotional display. Luke recorded that Peter "fell at Jesus' knees and said, 'Go away from me, Lord; I am a sinful man!'" (Luke 5:8, NIV), a seemingly emotional response, expressing thoughts and feelings. Whether appropriate or inappropriate is left for interpretation.

Also consider Peter's relational transparency through what is recorded by John in connection with Jesus' arrest. Jesus and his disciples had left the city of Jerusalem, crossed the Kidron Valley, and entered an olive grove (John 18:1). It was there, during the night, that some officials from the chief priests and Pharisees, together with a detachment of soldiers, approached Jesus (John 18:3). Jesus identified himself to the group and peacefully asked that they let the men who were with him go (John 18:8). It was then that "Peter, who had a sword, drew it and struck the high priest's servant, cutting off his right ear" (John 18:10, NIV). It is not understood that, there in the dark, Peter had carefully and precisely aligned his sword to ensure only a superficial wound of removing an ear would result from his strike on the high priest's servant. Rather, Peter wielded his sword to lop off the man's head, but missing his neck, struck his skull, his blade glancing off, removing the man's ear. Peter's emotions, thoughts, and feelings drove him to respond as he did. The question regarding relational transparency is whether Peter, at that moment, promoted trust through disclosures that involve openly sharing information and expressions of his true thoughts and feelings while trying to minimize his displays of inappropriate emotions. Perhaps not. He certainly presented his authentic self to others. A developmental perspective of authentic leadership, suggests that Peter had a growth opportunity regarding relational transparency.

Peter's thrice denial of his Lord offers another consideration of his relational transparency. Recall that relational transparency behavior should promote "trust through disclosures that involve openly sharing information and expressions of one's true thoughts and feelings while trying to minimize displays of inappropriate emotions" (Walumbwa et al., 2008, p. 95). How did Peter evidence relational transparency involving his presenting and disclosing his true self to others through sharing appropriate thoughts and feelings while curbing or minimizing inappropriate emotional displays of his thoughts and feelings?

An authentic leadership relational transparency examination of Peter's denial of Jesus must first commence with Jesus' prediction of Peter's denial. Mark recorded Jesus telling his disciples, "you will all fall away" (Mark 14:27, NIV), to which only Peter is recorded as responding. Peter declared, "Even if all fall away, I will not" (Mark 14:29, NIV). Aligning with Walumbwa et al.'s (2008) relational transparency, Peter was presenting his authentic self (p. 95). Did Peter have something of a "distorted self" (Walumbwa et al., 2008, p. 95)? He openly shared information and expressed his "true thoughts and feelings" (Walumbwa et al., 2008, p. 95). But whether he was unaware of his display of emotion or whether he was aware and was "trying to minimize displays of inappropriate emotions" (Walumbwa et al., 2008, p. 95), is not known. Jesus offered an interpretation of Peter's relational transparency when he responded to Peter and said, "Truly I tell you, today—yes, tonight—before the rooster crows twice you yourself will disown me three times" (Mark 14:30, NIV). In Peter's transparency, did he hold a distorted view of himself as evidence of his inappropriate display of emotions? "Peter insisted emphatically, 'Even if I have to die with you, I will never disown you'" (Mark 14:31, NIV). He was certainly authentic and transparent! However, aligning with Walumbwa et al.'s (2008) developmental perspective of relational transparency, Peter showed inappropriate emotional displays of his thoughts and feelings.

Later in Mark's gospel, is the account of the three times Peter did deny Jesus. First, a servant girl of the high priest took note of Peter after Jesus' arrest and declared, "You also were with that Nazarene, Jesus" (Mark 14:67, NIV). But Peter denied it, saying, "I don't know or understand what you're talking about" (Mark 14:68, NIV). In stating this, his first denial, Peter gave evidence of his lack of relational transparency through an inappropriate emotional display, denying his true thoughts and feelings, and offered a fake or distorted self in response to the servant girl's question. A short time later, the servant girl pointed out Peter again and said, "This fellow is one of them" (Mark 14:69, NIV). Again Peter denied it. Just as in his first denial, Peter once again gave evidence of his lack of relational transparency through inappropriate response.

The third time Peter denied Jesus, he did not show expressions of his true thoughts, and he gave evidence of his lack of relational transparency through an inappropriate and emotional display. When challenged by those standing around him, because he had been recognized as a Galilean, Peter "began to call down curses, and he swore to them, 'I don't know this man you're talking about'" (Mark 14:71, NIV). The scripture states that after this third denial, "Immediately the rooster crowed the second time. Then Peter remembered the word Jesus had spoken to him: "Before the rooster crows twice you will disown me three times." And he broke down and wept." (Mark 14:72, NIV). At that moment Peter saw his authentic self and realized his relational transparency behavior and how, through his disclosures, he did not express his true thoughts and feelings but rather displayed inappropriate emotions and responses. In this time of denial, Peter evidenced his lack of authentic leadership from the developmental perspective of relational transparency.

## Summary

Through the lens of authentic leadership theory, the disciple Peter's life and his genuine self-concepts present illustrations of an intrapersonal perspective of authentic leadership, an interpersonal perspective of authentic leadership, and a developmental perspective of authentic leadership. Additional exploration of the relational transparency aspects of the developmental perspective of authentic leadership allowed an appreciation of how, in the person of Peter, both appropriate and inappropriate examples of relational transparency existed. In summary, Peter offered an example through which authentic and transparent leadership may be appreciated and considered for application today.

## References


Bennis, W. G. (1992). *On becoming a leader*. Wilmington, MA: Addison-Wesley.

Eagly, A. H. (2005). Achieving relational authenticity in leadership: Does gender matter? *Leadership Quarterly, 16*(3), 459–474.

Kernis, M. H. (2003). Toward a conceptualization of optimal self-esteem. *Psychological Inquiry, 14*, 1–26.

Lawler, J., & Ashman, I. (2012). Theorizing leadership authenticity: A Sartrean perspective. *Leadership, 8*(4), 327–344.

Lockyer, H. (1972). *All the apostles of the bible: Studies in the characters of the apostles, the men Jesus chose and the message they proclaimed*. Grand Rapids, MI: Zondervan.

Northouse, P. G. (2016). *Leadership: Theory and practice* (7th ed.). Thousand Oaks, CA: Sage.

Ryan, R. M., & Deci, E. L. (2003). On assimilating identities to the self: A self-determination theory perspective on internalization and integrity within cultures. In M. R. Leary & J. P. Tangney (Eds.), *Handbook of self and identity* (pp. 253–272). New York, NY: Guilford.

Shamir, B., & Eilam, G. (2005). "What's your story?" A life-stories approach to authentic leadership development. *The Leadership Quarterly, 16*(3), 395–417. https://doi.org/10.1016/j.leaqua.2005.03.005.

Walumbwa, F. O., Avolio, B. J., Gardner, W. L., Wernsing, T. S., & Peterson, S. J. (2008). Authentic leadership: Development and validation of a theory-based measure. *Journal of Management, 34*(1), 89–126. https://doi.org/10.1177/0149206307308913.

CHAPTER 9

# Social Media Use by the Modern Leader

*Alicia L. Peltier*

## Introduction

In the 1920s, religious leaders added the use of radio broadcasts to share the Gospel of Jesus Christ (Newport, 2020). Ministry efforts later expanded to television broadcasts, showing viewers all over the world what congregants experienced weekly during Sunday services. Nearly 100 years later, the reach of religious leaders has extended even more by using social media. Social media is electronic communications used to connect people or a community of people using an online forum ("social media," n.d.) Before 2020, social media appeared as the next televangelist forum for the modern church (Stetzer, 2015). Considering 45% of mankind uses social media (Kemp, 2019), a pastor who uses online platforms can reach a large body of people for the sake of authentic fellowship while maintaining relevancy when sharing the Gospel ("Is Social Media…," 2017). Stetzer (2015) likened ministry avoidance of social media to a pastor who does not use a microphone when preaching to

A. L. Peltier (✉)
School of Business and Leadership, Regent University, Virginia Beach, VA, USA
e-mail: alicpel@regent.edu





B. E. Winston (eds.), *Transparent and Authentic Leadership*, Christian Faith Perspectives in Leadership and Business,
https://doi.org/10.1007/978-3-030-61996-1_9

a large congregation, indicating that such avoidance is a response that is not easy to understand.

When considering the online presence of ministry, Scott-Lundy (2017) discussed ministry branding as an important opportunity for churches to show authenticity, unity, and relevance. The social media accounts of churches display authenticity when leaders share the truth on their social platform, relay unity as it relates to working with other community leaders, and show relevance when using their accounts (Coman & Coman, 2017). For example, if a church works hard to promote a proper self-image of its leader, then it matters what the leader offers to followers online (Coman & Coman). A positive online posture helps leaders avoid keyboard warrior status—one who attacks every post they find disagreeable in an abusive manner ("keyboard warrior," n.d.)—causing people to feel gentleness versus abuse when the leader posts a message. Another way positive online posture is viewed by followers is when ministry leaders share humorous content such as short videos prepared by Christian comedians. Such posts help demonstrate the scientifically proven Christian proverb that indicates laughter is medicine for the body (University of Maryland Medical Center, 2005; King James Version Proverbs 17:2–24). It is important to note that in times of peril, the online presence of ministry also requires proper social presence, especially as it relates to the complexities of ministering with distancing between the physical church and its congregants.

Social media use took a new turn in 2020 when the Coronavirus (COVID-19) pandemic struck the world (Newport, 2020). Before the pandemic, ministry leaders often posted to social media outlets at least once a week for Sunday morning church service. At the onset of the pandemic, social distancing (Center for Disease Control and Prevention, 2020) began and churches were instructed by government leaders to close their physical doors (The Office of Governor Larry Hogan, 2020). Therefore, online weekly services began to include internet Bible study sessions and small group meetings. Social distancing led to pastoral sermons becoming more intimate as leaders sat behind their home office desks to deliver their messages. Their mission included using social media to help members understand how to manage a pandemic while maintaining a Biblically principled life. Social media was also used by pastoral leaders from across the nation who gathered in unity to teach other leaders how to manage their churches during the pandemic. For example, one pastoral collaborative outreach session called "Pastoring During a Pandemic," was hosted on Facebook Live on April 27, 2020, by Bishop

Joseph W. Walker, III, pastor of Mount Zion Baptist Church in Nashville, TN (Mount Zion Baptist Church, 2020). The session was titled "Grace for a New Space," and began with Bishop Walker introducing the session to its viewers, ultimately letting the viewers know, "...we need to hear the truth around COVID and its impact upon an underserved community...." (Mount Zion Baptist Church, 2:32). He also said, "...we need to hear the truth in how we can protect ourselves and protect our families; it's incredibly important" (Mount Zion Baptist Church, 2:39). Bishop Walker explained how some churches lacked the skills to use innovative methods to maintain relevancy. His opening statement was transparent in showing even leaders sometimes lack information in uncertain times; however, he explained that leaders need to understand how to exhibit flexibility during a time where mobility was limited. In the series opener, Bishop Walker hosted a well-respected panel of ministry leaders from all over the nation to share in the discussion, including Pastor John K. Jenkins, Sr., pastor of First Baptist Church of Glenarden in Upper Marlboro, MD, Bishop T. D. Jakes, pastor of The Potters House in Dallas, TX, Bishop Paul S. Morton, Sr., founder of Full Gospel Baptist Church Fellowship, International, Atlanta, GA, Dr. Craig L. Oliver, Sr., pastor of Elizabeth Baptist Church in Atlanta, GA, Pastor Keion Henderson of Lighthouse Church in Houston, TX, Pastor Terrance Johnson of Higher Dimension Church in Houston, TX, Elder Decari Middlebrooks, executive director of Mount Zion Baptist Church's Virtual Church, and Dr. Stephanie Walker, MD, MPH, of Mount Zion Baptist Church (Mount Zion Baptist Church, 2020). Bishop Walker prompted each leader with different questions regarding how church leaders could work to help the church maintain authenticity, relevancy, and unity during the pandemic, especially as it related to moving forward with the mission of the church while using technology. While engaging thousands of online viewers, each leader expressed their thoughts regarding strategies for reaching church members while taking care of self during the current climate of COVID-19. The leaders could agree that while traditional leadership qualities may remain unchanged, modern leaders require innovation and technical savviness to better serve their churches, including the use of social media platforms.

While the tech savvy pastor uses modern technology for the sake of spreading the Gospel, it is important that additional thought goes into the transparency and authenticity of each post and act made online. Stetzer (2015) mentioned three ways modern leaders damage their efforts when using social media. When the pastor uses social media to gain notoriety and fame, engages in conflicts, or shares false news, he has crossed the line from sharing the Gospel to hurting it (Stetzer). When the pastor works to increase his influence instead of spreading the gospel, participates in online arguments over politics or football, or shares speculation versus the truth, the integrity associated with him could inadvertently shed an unpleasant view on the Gospel, especially if the video goes "viral."

When a video or post goes "viral," it is deemed a dream or nightmare, depending on several factors. The factors include the creator of the content, what the content represents, and whom the content reaches (Moreau, 2018). Viral, a word stemming from the word 'virus,' or an infectious agent, is what happens to a post when there is a spike in emotion based on the shared content (Moreau). The emotional response causes the recipient of the content to want to share the feelings they experienced with others (Moreau). When a pastor has online content that goes viral, the obvious desire is it is a dream, where the content is shared massively to spread positive, Godly information. However, a misstep by the pastor can cause a nightmare, where negative, ungodly information escapes her grasp. If the leaders in "Pastoring During a Pandemic" chose to speak rhetoric instead of truth, then the authenticity and transparency required for Christian leaders could be at stake. By them speaking the truth, they cultivated transparency and authenticity (Men, 2014) where followers eagerly await additional Biblical guidance.

In the era of social media, building and protecting the reputation of leaders and organizations are progressively becoming a more important task for Christian leaders. The high level of importance is due to the public, which places unseen levels of high hopes in leaders and their companies to exhibit "openness, visibility, transparency and authenticity" (Men, 2014, p. 254). Christian leaders are no exception. Leaders, including Christian leaders, know they have influence over followers and have a mandate of required transparency and authenticity based on the values associated with their belief system.

### *Transparency and Authenticity*

Yukl (2006) described leadership as the development of follower influence. The role of leaders helps create an atmosphere that influences the attitudes, behavior, and motivation of followers (Men, 2014). Part of leader influence includes transparency. Men described transparency in three sections. First, the information shared by the leader is clear and substantial without keeping followers guessing. Next, the leader does not simply make organizational decisions; instead, the decision-making process includes both the leader and the stakeholders. Further, transparent leaders show accountability through the words they communicate, how they behave, and their actions. While a transparent leader may share either positive or negative information online, being authentic also increases the odds of a positive outcome (Cooper, Scandura, & Schriesheim, 2005).

Authentic leadership is a leadership type that helps shape the perception and behavior of followers. Walumbwa, Avolio, Gardner, Wernsing, and Peterson (2008) posited that authentic leadership births itself out of a climate of increased organizational scandals and malfeasance in management. The negative associations organizations experience due to the damaging behavior of some of their public figures required a foundational need for a leadership style based on values—the authentic leadership style (Men, 2014). The value-based leadership style of authentic leadership seeks to "train and develop leaders who will proactively foster positive environments and conduct business in an ethical, socially responsible manner" (Cooper et al., 2005, p. 476). In the online environment, leaders who are transparent with an authentic leadership style have a strong basis in their values.

### *Value-Based Leadership*

Winston (2002) discussed leaders who base their methods on values, mentioning the idea of having values as a leader is nothing new. Winston argued that values are timeless and necessary. As a value-based leader, the Christian leader seeks the Holy Text for everything in life, including how to function online. While the daily operations of the Christian leader mimic non-Christian leaders, the way they handle business operations is different. In operating, a Christian leader seriously considers the Biblical commandment to live a life of worship through prayer (1 Timothy 2:1–2), seeking God (Psalm 105:4), and spreading the Gospel (John 3:16). A life of worship never ceases unless the Christian chooses another way of living or passes from this life to a life eternal (Galatians 6:8). Therefore, the value-based Christian leader ensures their values are front and center when using an online platform by living a life of worship.

### *Leading with Agapao*

Living a life of worship is not fulfilled without the demonstration of love. Agapao love is "...the cornerstone of the servant leadership/follower relationship..." (Patterson, 2003, p. 8). The manner through which Christian leaders benefit followers is by loving them with Agapao, which is also considered friendly love by Winston (2002). When a leader shows Agapao, they know how to handle people carefully, recognizing the four rights – the right location, the right time, the right gifts and abilities, and the right purpose (Winston). Such leaders also show love both socially and morally (Sachdeva & Prakash, 2017).

With an online platform, the right location is virtually based and the right time is anytime within a 24-hour day; however, the right gifts and abilities of followers along with the right purpose are consistent whether in the virtual or physical world. Therefore, it is imperative that Christian leaders exhibit authenticity and transparency in leadership when using social media.

Social media has seen extensive growth in the last 20 years, and Christian leaders could use mentors to help them sculpt their online persona. While leaders may use any historical or modern reputable leader as an influence, Christian leaders can find clarity on how God views His leaders in the Bible. Paul is an excellent example of how a leader is authentic and transparent in building leader trust in followers while also sharing the Gospel socially.

## Paul as an Authentic and Transparent Leader

The phrases 'terrorist' and 'man of God' are at least two descriptions of Paul during his lifetime. The placement of Paul's days of terror is in Chapters 7–8 in the book of Acts. His days of Godly influence are in Acts 9 through the Epistles.

### *A Young Terrorist: Saul*

If a person met Paul during his Christian journey, they might not have believed that he was once a terrorist of people who loved God (Acts 7–8). After the persecution of Stephen, many believers of Christ experienced persecution at the hand of young Saul (Acts 8:1). Saul penalized Christians due to their beliefs (Acts 8:3). He would abruptly disrupt the homes of people by taking them to a new home in the prison (Acts 8:1–3). Saul was not kind to the people of God. Instead, he harmed those who loved the Lord. He was not ashamed of his behavior and was authentic to his role and transparent in what he was doing, even though it was all for the wrong reason.

As Saul continued to enjoy his malicious behavior (Acts 9:2–3), it all had to come to a stop. The day his life changed was the day he met Jesus Christ on the road to Damascus (Acts 9:2–4). His meeting of Christ was not by chance but by design. Saul lost his natural vision to gain spiritual insight, and through three days of fasting, praying, and baptism, Saul regained his physical sight when Jesus instructed Ananias to lay hands on Saul (Acts 9). Then, Saul addressed his spiritual view (Acts 9). While not being accepted by the disciples, the apostles uplifted and supported him (Acts 9). Even though Saul changed, those who knew of his past had trouble accepting him as a man who loved Jesus Christ.

### *A Mature Leader: Saul also Known as Paul*

The construction of the early church included the works of Saul and his friend, Barnabas (Acts 11:25–30). During this time, Saul began to answer to the name, Paul (Acts 13:9). Also during this time, Paul spread the Gospel and worked to groom disciples of the Gentiles. While working, Paul was incarcerated (Acts 16), put out of towns, and chased by persecutors (Acts 14:8–27). Paul remained consistent as a Christian leader while building the early church in Corinth and Ephesus (DeSilva 2004). Through it all, Paul was authentic and transparent about who he was and whom he had become. After demonstrating his role and sharing his vision with his followers, and then his followers buying into his vision (Acts 20), the impact of Paul was significant in the early church (DeSilva).

### *Proper Use of Power*

From 'Saul to Paul' in Acts reads like a feel-good movie. However, Paul's influence throughout his life affected many people in both good and bad ways. In most of his written journey, he had a level of influence that followed with both sound and unsound decisions. Ivancevich, Konopaske, and Matteson (2014) discussed the steps to making a good decision, where the leader must first recognize a problem exists. The behavior of the leader impacts not only the leader but the organization as well

(Ivancevich et al.). The influence of Saul and Paul showed how power and influence could help or hurt people, and the person with decision-making power has the responsibility to lead followers in a way where they interact with one another and the leader to achieve the vision of the organization (Ivancevich et al.).

The Epistles written by Paul were letters that were meant to share the Gospel by using handwritten content. Once the messages left the hand of the writer, Paul could not change any of its content. Paul had an expectancy that more than one person would read his thoughts, as he wrote his messages to the early church in different locations. What Paul may not have expected was how the people of Corinth interpreted his letter in 1 Corinthians once received. The church was growing and subgroups developed after Paul left Corinth (Barentsen 2018). These subgroups did not experience Paul's written message the way he hoped. Barentsen posited Paul's letter appeared ineffective as conflict broke out after the church reviewed its contents. His leadership was questioned (Barentsen), yet through his hurt and pain, he creatively worked steadily through the situation to regain trust of his congregation once again through his subsequent writing. Overall, Paul's work ended up being quite impactful, where he built the trust of his followers, even after his challenging past and then challenging letter. He is a good example of an authentic and transparent leader, as his values came across to his followers in his written works and still come across today. Modern leaders can look to his example and see how even the most well-intended messages are misunderstood, yet a well-intended leader knows how to recover from a setback to better relay the truth in a more creative manner.

### *Best Practices for Modern Leaders*

The example of Paul reminds leaders of how transparency, authenticity, and value-based leading is a thing of the past that has staying power today. Reasons for business failures, such as proud leaders, scandal-based falls, limited innovation and creativity in the working environment, and neglected followers show why Paul's example is relevant today. Paul was an involved leader who was quite thoughtful and creative in demonstrating Christian behavior through his social outlets of writing letters. When modern leaders write social media comments or post new statuses or videos, they intend to share the information with their audience. Like Paul's letters, once the posts or video leaves the control of the preparer, the content cannot be changed ("Think Before You...," 2018). Even though a poster can remove the posted information, the content can be copied and shared ("Think Before You..."). Like Paul, modern leaders who use social media have an expectancy that more than one person will read their thoughts (or view their content). However, unlike Paul, if the content is not value-based, the work of the leader will not build the trust of followers. Paul had become an authentic and transparent leader, where he found roots in value-based leadership. His values came across to his followers in his written works and still comes across today. The Bible will always be relevant as the true and Holy Word of God. Christian leaders are expected to share it. If Christian leaders desire to remain consistent, transparent and authentic when using social media, then they should also consider the leadership promptings of the Beatitudes and be sure their work posted online is value-based.

### *The Beatitudes*

The Beatitudes, a portion of the famous Sermon on the Mount delivered by Jesus Christ in Matthew 5:3–10 (NKJV), is another creative way to teach modern leaders how to practice transparency and authenticity in their organizations and online (Winston, 2002). If an organization has a problem that needs solving, then creativity is the solution. If a leader has issues, then the Beatitudes is the answer.

The body of statements known as the Beatitudes help bond God with His people. The statements are a wealth of resources to help build value in modern leaders who want to exhibit transparency and authentic leadership traits (Winston, 2002) while using social media as a resource. Using each of the Beatitudes as a reference, Christian leaders have a template for the desired leadership traits. As a reference, the Beatitudes are as follows (Matthew 5:3–10):

> Blessed are the poor in spirit, for theirs is the kingdom of heaven.
> Blessed are they who mourn, for they shall be comforted.
> Blessed are the meek, for they shall inherit the earth.
> Blessed are they who hunger and thirst for righteousness, for they shall be satisfied.
> Blessed are the merciful, for they shall obtain mercy.
> Blessed are the pure of heart, for they shall see God.
> Blessed are the peacemakers, for they shall be called children of God.

> Blessed are they who are persecuted for the sake of righteousness, for theirs is the kingdom of heaven (NKJV).

### *Be Teachable*

Matthew 5:3 listed the first beatitude, which is, "Blessed are the poor in spirit, for theirs is the kingdom of heaven" (NKJV). Winston (2002) discussed how leaders who think more of themselves than they should are not teachable. Leaders who desire the teachable status should (Winston):

- Welcome help from others
- Seek advice from followers
- Think less of 'self' and more of others
- Use their influence for good
- Treat all followers equitably.

Christian leaders seek to be teachable so they will open themselves to receiving knowledge from any reputable knowledge based in Biblical principles (Winston, 2002). When seeking advice from followers, the teachable leader helps the follower feel included and worthy (Winston). Christian leaders who post content online that may not sit well with the Body of Christ should be open to receive criticism from those who deal with the output. Together, the leader and the followers can find solutions to different challenges.

de Jong and Den Hartog (2007) focused on employees working in an environment that is creative. A creative environment leads to an increase in innovation. When leaders allow employees to feel included, they tend to feel free to express new ideas and ways to make their work more beneficial. Therefore, if Christian leaders desire to be teachable, they ultimately enable followers to grow in creative spaces as free thinkers (Hatch & Cunliff, 2013) leading to innovative content to share with others.

### *Provide Follower Care*

"Blessed are those who mourn for they shall be comforted" (NKJV) reads from the pages of the Bible in Matthew 5:4 and helps leader evaluate how they treat their followers. Winston (2002) discussed how the mourning leader is one who cares for others as if they were mourning one who is deceased. In other words, the leader-care runs deeply. On social media, the face of people and organizations are what is viewed by followers. Some leaders with influence and status, use their platform to reach their followers and show follower-appreciation. For example, sometimes organizations and entertainers alike offer followers free tickets or products for merely being a loyal follower. People with influence show followers they care on social media, even though they may be culturally, socially, and economically far apart. As a Christian leader, follower-care is exhibited on social media by:

- Posting encouraging videos to let followers know they are considered
- Responding to a few followers in the comments to let them know that they are heard
- Relating to followers with follow-up content
- Showing respect for followers by understanding everyone online is not the same
- Protecting followers from abusive behavior in the comment section (Winston, 2002).

The leader's role when providing follower-care is essential to have a group of people who understand the vision of the organization.

### *Exhibit Controlled Discipline*

Matthew 5:5 reads, "Blessed are the meek for they shall inherit the earth" (NKJV). Winston (2002) discussed how the follower is not the one who should remain in control; instead, leaders are responsible for remaining in control. If the leader is in control, then the follower is soon to follow. A leader exhibits controlled discipline when she is (Winston):

- Trustworthy when recommending reading and/or posts online
- A pillar of strength amid online chaos
- Calm in demeanor when responding to disorderly followers
- Operating with selfless anger when having to address follower issues.

When a leader has uncontrolled discipline online, they inadvertently encourage uncontrolled follower behavior and potentially damaging results to the organization (Winston).

### *Seek What Is Right*

Matthew 5:6 reads, "Blessed are they which do hunger and thirst after righteousness, for they shall be filled" (NKJV). The hunger and thirst mentioned in this Beatitude do not reference actual food and drink. Instead, it references leaders who desire to do what is right for followers and the organization (Winston, 2002). A leader knows he is seeking what is right when he (Winston):

- Acts equitable by using Scripture as guidelines for leading
- Uses disciplinary methods that help, not hurt
- Seeks to work with other organizations for the greater good
- Creates atmospheres that benefit all stakeholders.

A leader should seek what is right, placing the organization and followers before himself. Humane orientation occurs when a leader has a considerable amount of concern for the well-being of his followers (Yukl, 2013). Creating humane orientation online may seem like a hard thing to do; however, when the leader limits self-concerns and increases follower concerns, humane orientation appears. A humane-orientated environment appears when the leader is value-based, showing kindness, compassion, and love (Yukl). Humane orientation is found in the Bible when a leader uses the Beatitudes as a basis for follower treatment.

### *Be Merciful*

The instruction to be merciful is found in Matthew 5:7, where it reads, "Blessed are merciful, for they will be shown mercy" (NKJV). Winston (2002) discussed how organizational problems are primarily system based. Winston shed light on how infrequent followers are at fault when organizational challenges arise. Therefore, Christian leaders show mercy by (Winston):

- Determining why there is an issue with a follower
- Training followers how to act in love instead of immediately deleting them
- Use controlled discipline instead of posting online in anger
- Exhibit mercy to nurture innovation.

When leaders are merciful towards followers, the followers are more likely to share their problems and help solve issues (Winston, 2002), and assist with innovation. For example, a chef on Facebook used to post pictures of the food he prepared. His followers began to ask for the recipes. Some were belligerent when making their request; however, the chef did not immediately delete the disrespectful followers. Instead, he explained in a video what his vision was regarding his recipes, which was to sell a cookbook. The chef later wrote and sold a cookbook with successful sales and reviews. When new followers joined his Facebook page and asked for recipes, his loyal followers referred them to his website where they could purchase his book. When new followers posted negative comments, the chef's loyal followers defended him. His loyal followers were some of the same people who were initially negative toward him, but due to the mercy he showed them, they later became his advocates, sending business his way.

### *Be Pure*

"Blessed are the pure in heart, for they shall see God" (NKJV) is found in Matthew 5:8. Being pure in the heart is recognizing the purpose of 'self' (Winston, 2002). The leader knows his role and understands what is required of him. A pure leader exists when he (Winston):

- Understands who he is
- Recognizes long-term thinking overrides short term thinking
- Constantly reminds followers of the vision of the organization
- Accomplishes the goal of follower comprehension of his role.

When Christian leaders are in charge, their followers should see a pure heart where they see God in the leader, and the leader's role is not ambiguous. Moura, Orgambidez-Ramos, and Goncalves (2014) describe role ambiguity as a scenario where a follower does not understand what is going on regarding the leader or themselves. The role ambiguity causes the follower to feel stressed and unsure (Moura, Orgambidez-Ramos, & Goncalves). When the follower begins to feel stressed and uncertain, they are more likely to disengage with the leader (McCraty, Atkinson, and Tomasino, 2003). When followers start to disconnect with people of influence online, it indicates that they are not pleased with the efforts of the leader and desire to be in another environment or with another leader (Ivancevich, Konopaske, and Matteson, 2014).

### *Be a Peacemaker*

"Blessed are the peacemakers, for they shall be called the children of God" (NKJV) is the Beatitude that instructs the leader to foster an atmosphere where conflict disperses in a quick manner (Winston, 2002). That leader becomes a peacemaker (Winston), even if the conflict is virtual. The value in a peacemaker is vital; therefore, to be a peacemaker, a leader must (Winston):

- Recognize conflict is imminent
- De-escalate the situation quickly
- Maintain a peaceful environment
- Use conflict resolution models.

A peaceful atmosphere is often temporary yet is required for a leader to facilitate peace continually.

### *Expect Persecution*

Matthew 5:10 reads, "Blessed are those who are persecuted because of righteousness, for theirs is the kingdom of God" (NKJV). Winston (2002) shared how others often persecute leaders who are effective at doing their job to damage performance levels of the effective leader. Loyal online followers can become disgrunted persecutors in the midst of a disagreeable situation. To address the idea of dealing with persecution as a leader, the leader should (Winston):

- Get used to defending their position
- Recognize Godly rules and worldly rules do not match

- Expect resistance to leadership methods
- Be ready for the blessing of innovation.

Winston (2002) discussed how leaders who use the Beatitudes for business matters should anticipate persecution, so it is wise for them to expect it. Winston provides the Christian leader with positive words, letting the leader know that anytime she follows the Scripture, she can expect to live an overall good life. The Christian leader can even see where Paul exhibited the characteristic of the Beatitudes.

## The Beatitudes as Demonstrated by Paul

In Galatians 1:12, Paul says, "For I did not receive it from a man, nor was I taught it, but it came through the revelation of Jesus Christ" (NKJV). Paul implied that a human being did not teach him, so how could he be considered teachable, like expected in the Beatitudes? Winston's (2002) expressions regarding being *teachable* were not limited to one component of learning. Paul said he received "...through the revelation of Jesus Christ" (NKJV). Remember his encounter with Jesus on the road to Damascus where he went blind (Acts 9)? Remember the three days of fasting and praying that ceased once Jesus permitted Ananias to lay hands on Paul so he could receive his sight once again? Paul used his revelatory experiences to learn more about the Gospel of Jesus Christ so he could "think less of 'self' and more of others" and use his influence for good. For the rest of his life, Paul provided *follower care* and *exhibited controlled discipline*, especially after the work, beatings, and dangerous journeys he encountered along the way (2 Corinthians 11:23–29). Paul *sought what was right* in the faith (2 Timothy 4:7–8) and *exhibited mercy* towards his brothers in Christ as he viewed God's mercy in high regard (Romans 9:15–18). Paul knew the challenges with the idea of *being pure*, although he made every attempt to do what was right (Philippians 3:12). DeSilva (2004) discussed how forms of *peacemaking* remained on Paul's radar considering he wrote a letter to Philemon, a Christian leader, on behalf of his runaway slave, Onesimus. The desire of Paul did not focus on class or status; instead, he focused on the reconciliation of the relationship between the master and the follower (Philemon). As Paul sent Onesimus back to Philemon (Philemon 12), he also sent his heart. Peace was the desire of Paul. *Persecution* is understood two-fold by Paul. He was once a persecutor of Christians (Acts 7) who later dealt with persecution for being a Christian (Acts 14 & 2 Corinthians 11:23–29).

Considering the content of the Beatitudes, modern Christian leaders can refer to Paul, as he exhibited transparency and authenticity. The Christian leader can hold on to the promises of the blessed statements for Godly, value-based leadership. In the online environment, the leaders can demonstrate Godly behavior to known and unknown followers.

## Summary

Cultivating transparent and authentic leadership in Christian leaders is possible when the leader has a desire to do things God's way. Transparent and authentic leadership is especially important when leaders use social media. Without social media use, Christian leaders can appear behind the times. COVID-19 showed congregants whether their churches were ready to minister full-time online when the doors of the physical church closed. Leaders who were ready to use social media during the pandemic did not impede the progress of spreading the Gospel of Jesus Christ.

Further, using social media without the consideration and application of the Beatitudes as an organizational guide can hurt the leader if they do not exercise the proper control over their influence. The influence of the life of Paul is a positive example for modern leaders. Value-based leadership along with the leadership guidelines of the Beatitudes shows Christian leaders how to be transparent and authentic leaders in and out of the virtual world.

## References

Barentsen, J. (2018). The social construction of Paul's apostolic leadership in Corinth. *HTS Teologiese Studies/Theological Studies, 74*(4), 13. https://doi.org/10.4102/hts.v74i4.5191.

Center for Disease Control and Prevention. (2020). *Social distancing, quarantine, and isolation*. Retrieved from https://www.cdc.gov/coronavirus/2019-ncov/prevent-getting-sick/social-distancing.html.

Coman, I. A., & Coman, M. (2017). Religion, popular culture and social media: The construction of a religious leader image on Facebook. *Essachess, 10*(2), 129–143. Retrieved from http://www.essachess.com/index.php/jcs/article/view/392/438.

Cooper, C. D., Scandura, T. A., & Schriesheim, C. A. (2005). Looking forward but learning from our past: Potential challenges to developing authentic leadership theory and authentic leaders. *The Leadership Quarterly, 16*(3), 475–493. Retrieved from https://www.journals.elsevier.com/the-leadership-quarterly.

de Jong, J. P. J., & Den Hartog, D. N. (2007). How leaders influence employees' innovative behavior. *European Journal of Innovation Management., 10*(1), 41–53. https://doi.org/10.1108/14601060710720546.

DeSilva, D. A. (2004). *An introduction to the new testament: Contexts, methods & ministry formation.* Downers Grove: IVP Academic.

Dictionary. (n.d.). Keyboard warrior. In *Dicitionary.com dictionary*. Retrieved April 30, 2020, from https://www.dictionary.com/browse/keyboard-warrior.

Hatch, M. J., & Cunliff, A. L. (2013). *Organization theory: Modern, symbolic, and postmodern perspectives.* Oxford, UK: Oxford University Press.

Is Social Media Hurting the Church? (2017, October 19). Retrieved from https://www1.cbn.com/cbnnews/us/2017/october/is-social-media-hurting-church-leaders-this-pastor-says-yes.

Ivancevich, J. M., Konopaske, R., & Matteson, M. T. (2014). *Organizational Behavior & Management* (10th ed.). New York, NY: McGraw Hill.

Kemp, S. (2019, January 30). *Digital 2019: Global internet use accelerates.* Retrieved from https://wearesocial.com/blog/2019/01/digital-2019-global-internet-use-accelerates.

McCraty, R., Atkinson, M. & Tomasino, D. (2003). Impact of a workplace stress reduction program on blood pressure and emotional health in hypertensive employees. *The Journal of Alternative and Complementary Medicine, 9*(3), 355–369. Retrieved from https://www.Raven-vauseconsulting.co.uk/userfiles/file/Hypertension%20Study.pdf.

Men, L. R. (2014). Internal reputation management: The impact of authentic leadership and transparent communication. *Corporate Reputation Review, 17*(4), 254–272. https://doi.org/10.1057/crr.2014.14.

Merriam-Webster. (n.d.). Social media. In *Merriam-Webster.com dictionary*. Retrieved April 30, 2020, from https://www.merriam-webster.com/dictionary/social%20media.

Moreau, E. (2018). *What does it mean to go viral online?: A piece of content can spread just like a virus.* Retrieved from https://www.lifewire.com/what-does-it-mean-to-go-viral-3486225.

Mount Zion Baptist Church. (2020, April 27). *Pastoring During a Pandemic: Grace for a new space.* https://www.facebook.com/mtzionnashville [Facebook update]. Retrieved from https://www.facebook.com/mtzionnashville/videos/2544310472336765/.

Moura, D., Orgambidez-Ramos, A, & Goncalves, G. (2014). Role stress and work engagement as antecedents of job satisfaction: Results from Portugal. *Europe's Journal of Psychology, 10*(2), 291–300. https://doi.org/10.5964/ejop.v10i2.714.

Newport, F. (2020, April 6). *Religion and the COVID-19 virus in the U.S.* Retrieved from https://news.gallup.com/opinion/polling-matters/307619/religion-covid-virus.aspx.

Patterson, K. A. (2003). *Servant leadership: A theoretical model* (Order No. 3082719). Available from Dissertations & Theses @ Regent University; ProQuest Central; ProQuest Dissertations & Theses Global; ProQuest One Academic. (305234239). Retrieved from http://eres.regent.edu:2048/login?url=https://search-proquest-com.ezproxy.regent.edu/docview/305234239?accountid=13479.

Sachdeva, S., & Prakash, A. (2017). Journey to the heart of servant leadership: Narratives in the indian context. *Journal of the Indian Academy of Applied Psychology, 43*(1), 20–33. Retrieved from http://eres.regent.edu:2048/login?url=https://search-proquest-com.ezproxy.regent.edu/docview/1874354254?accountid=13479.

Scott-Lundy, A. (2017, April 20). *Church branding*. Retrieved from https://ministry.acst.com/church-branding/.

Stetzer, E. (2015). *Five mistakes pastors make on social media.* Retrieved from https://www.christianitytoday.com/edstetzer/2015/november/five-mistakes-pastors-make-on-social-media.html.

The Office of Governor Larry Hogan. (2020, March 30). As COVID-19 *Crisis escalates in capital region, governor Hogan issues stay at home order effective tonight*. Retrieved from https://governor.maryland.gov/2020/03/30/as-covid-19-crisis-escalates-in-capital-region-governor-hogan-issues-stay-at-home-order-effective-tonight/.

Think Before You Post: Do's and Don'ts of Social Media for College and Beyond. (2018). Retrieved from https://hullnews.augusta.edu/2017/10/31/think-before-you-post-dos-and-donts-of-social-media-for-college-and-beyond/.

University of Maryland Medical Center. (2005). University of Maryland School of Medicine study shows laughter helps blood vessels function better. *ScienceDaily*. Retrieved from www.sciencedaily.com/releases/2005/03/050309111444.htm.

Walumbwa, F. O., Avolio, B. J., Gardner, W. L., Wernsing, T. S., & Peterson, S. J. (2008). Authentic leadership: Development and validation of a theory-based measure. *Journal of Management*, *34*(1), 89–126. Retrieved from https://journals.sagepub.com/home/jom.

Winston, B. E. (2002). *Be a Leader for God's Sake.* Regent University School of Business & Leadership, VA.

Yukl, G. A. (2006). *Leadership in organizations* (6th ed.). Upper Saddle River, NJ: Prentice-Hall.

Yukl, G. A. (2013). *Leadership in organizations* (8th ed.). Upper Saddle River, NJ:Prentice-Hall.

CHAPTER 10

# Effective Followership Impacting Transparent Leadership

*Emmanuel Mamaril*

## Introduction

"That lack of transparency, I think, is not appropriate" said United States (U.S.) Senator Jack Reed, during a U.S. Senate subcommittee hearing that occurred in July 2019 with Federal Aviation Administration officials regarding the ongoing hearings for the reinstatement of Boeing's 737 Max airplanes following the deadly crashes of two its 737 Max airliners (Krishner, 2019). The first Boeing 737 Max airliner crash occurred in October 2018 when Lion Air Flight 610 crashed only a few minutes after takeoff from Jakarta, Indonesia, and resulted in the death of 189 people (Gelles, 2019). The second Boeing 737 Max airliner crash happened a few months later in March 2019 when Ethiopian Airlines Flight 302 also crashed minutes after takeoff and led to the deaths of the 157 passengers and crew that were onboard (Gelles, 2019). In July 2019, U.S. Senate subcommittee members questioned the lax and limited oversight

E. Mamaril (✉)
School of Business and Leadership, Regent University, Houston, TX, USA
e-mail: emmamam@mail.regent.edu



B. E. Winston (eds.), *Transparent and Authentic Leadership*, Christian Faith Perspectives in Leadership and Business,
https://doi.org/10.1007/978-3-030-61996-1_10

from the Federal Aviation Administration regarding Boeing's interim fix and corrections after the first Boeing 737 Max airliner crash. A better response from this government agency possibly could have prevented the second crash from occurring in March 2019. Instead, the Federal Aviation Administration was one of the last agencies to ground the airplane (Krishner, 2019).

After the crashes, a multi-agency task force investigated the events leading up to the incidences. It determined that Boeing employees knew months before the first deadly 737 Max crash that there was a cockpit alert that was not working as the company intended (Johnsson & Schlangenstein, 2019). However, Boeing failed to inform international buyers of the 737 Max airliner of this cockpit alert issue and did not disclose this information to the Federal Aviation Administration (Johnsson & Schlangenstein, 2019). The cockpit alert issue involved the Maneuvering Characteristics Augmentation System (MCAS) that served as a new feature in the 737 Max airliner's control system (Gelles, 2019). The investigation indicated that "Boeing failed to adequately explain to regulators how MCAS worked" (Gelles, 2019). Indonesian investigators came to the same conclusion and faulted Boeing for not providing information to pilots and their crews on how to override the MCAS in the event of a software malfunction (Gelles, 2019).

Boeing's Chief Executive Officer, Dennis Muilenburg, received criticism regarding the lack of transparency and disclosure of pertinent information regarding the MCAS as well has how Muilenburg issued statements after the second 737 Max crash (Matthews, 2019). After the March 2019 crash, Muilenburg continued to defend the safety of the planes via the social media platform Twitter (Matthews, 2019). Aside from those statements issued on Twitter, Muilenburg and other Boeing leadership remained silent and did not share or communicate any additional information on the actions the company would take to address the issues that led to the two plane crashes (Matthews, 2019). The continued lack of transparency by Boeing and its leadership, coupled with its defensive posture, caused the public to perceive that Boeing was more interested in making a profit than ensuring the safety of airline passengers (Matthews, 2019).

Boeing's poor decision making regarding its failure to disclose the issues with the MCAS control system could have been prevented if Boeing's leadership team listened to complaints by employees regarding concerns with the 737 Max airplane. For instance, in 2016, a chief technical pilot who took part in the 737 Max program expressed worries that the MCAS had several serious issues (Gelles, 2019). Also, a senior engineer at Boeing filed an internal complaint this past year that the company willingly rejected the incorporation of a safety system with the MCAS to keep costs down that could have reduced the likelihood of the crashes from occurring (Gelles, 2019).

The tragic events of the two deadly Boeing 737 Max airplane crashes that claimed the lives of over 300 people illustrate the need for transparency and transparent leadership. If Boeing leadership properly disclosed and were open about the issues regarding the MCAS control system to federal agencies, buyers, and airline crews, then proper mitigations and contingencies could have been implemented to respond to the MCAS malfunction. Additionally, even though it appeared that the concerns expressed and brought up by Boeing employees about the MCAS issues were not taken into consideration, their actions emphasized the importance of followers being able to influence leaders' behaviors and efforts to help with better decision making. If Boeing's leadership looked into the complaints and concerns raised by Boeing employees regarding the 737 Max airplane, it could have prevented the plane crashes from occurring.

Boeing's missteps that led to hundreds of lives being loss illustrates the importance of honest and trusting relationships and the need to examine further how followers can effectively influence and contribute to leadership transparency (Ramazzina, 2017; Shahzadi, John, Qadeer, & Mehnaz, 2017). Therefore, this chapter approaches the concept of transparent leadership from the context of followership and explores the connection between followership and transparent leadership. The organization of this chapter begins with defining the term transparency and its value to individuals and organizations. I then briefly discuss the importance of honest and trusting leader-follower relationships. Next, I discuss the concept of transparent leadership and provide an overview of the concept of followership. Based on the available literature regarding the topics of transparency, honest leader-follower relationships, transparent leadership, and followership, I propose a question regarding followership's impact on transparent leadership.

To help answer this research question, I apply an exegetical analysis of the Biblical story involving the Prophet Nathan and his criticism of King David found in the Biblical book of 2 Samuel Chapter 12. Using Robbins' (1996) socio-rhetorical analysis, I analyze the social and cultural texture of the selected Biblical text to provide support to the relationship between effective followership contributing to transparent leadership. Lastly, I discuss how the conduct, behaviors, and actions of the Prophet Nathan can serve as an exemplar to contemporary leaders that stresses the need to develop and empower effective follower transparency to help improve leader transparency.

## Transparency Defined

The term transparency, in its most straightforward and literal definition, involves the ability to see through (Bennis, 2009). Transparency becomes associated with words such as openness, candor, and visibility (Bennis, 2009; Bernstein, 2015). The term also becomes related to ideas of honesty, truthfulness, and being free from lies, deceit, and corruption (Das Neves & Vaccaro, 2013; Ingram, 2009). From an organizational communication perspective, the concept of transparency involves actions that allow for the "free flow of information among stakeholders" (Bennis, Goleman, & O'Toole, 2008, p. 4). This flow of information applies to all stakeholders. The term stakeholders include those internal to the organizations such as leaders and followers as well as external to the organization such as society and the greater public (Essandoh et al., 2017).

While the concept of transparency consists of the disclosure and free flow of information, Forssbaeck and Oxel (2014) posited that transparency goes beyond the simple transfer of data between senders and receivers. Instead, those engaging in transparency must ensure that the information disclosed is timely, accurate, credible, and is of value to the person or persons receiving the information (Essandoh et al., 2017; Forssbaeck & Oxel, 2014). Additionally, Parris, Dapko, R. Arnold, and D. Arnold (2016), in their systematic review of the literature regarding the concept of transparency, determined a lack of consensus for a universal definition for this term. Therefore, for this chapter transparency becomes defined as the actions of individuals to ensure free-flowing communication and disclosure of timely, accurate, and trustworthy information that becomes perceived as valuable to both internal and external stakeholders who want to or have a right to know (Bennis et al., 2008; Das Neves & Vaccaro, 2013; Essandoh et al., 2017; Forssbaeck & Oxel, 2014). Next, I discuss the value of transparency and its importance to individuals and organizations.

### *Valuing the Concept of Transparency*

Applying the described definition of transparency, researchers and practitioners advocate for its use as a means to improve individual and organizational accountability, collaboration, creativity, knowledge sharing, and innovation (Bernstein, 2015; Parris et al., 2016). Also, increased transparency has been viewed as a solution to help counter corruption and ethical lapses and improved compliance with legal regulations (Essandoh et al., 2017; Estlund, 2011; Parris et al., 2016). Improved transparency with those external stakeholders outside the organization has even been linked to higher customer satisfaction and increased likelihood of meeting corporate social responsibility goals (Parris et al., 2016).

Additionally, improved transparency internal to the organization has resulted in improved individual and organizational performance (Berggren & Bernshteyn, 2007; "Deloitte Ethics & workplace survey," 2008; Parris et al., 2016; Scott, 2016). For example, Berggren and Bernshteyn (2007) observed from their case study of a software firm that transparency helped increase efficiencies and served as a fundamental driver to improved individual and organizational performance. Specifically, when the software firm's corporate leaders were transparent and communicated to their organizational followers regarding the organization's strategy, it aligned individual employee goals to the organization's overall strategy (Berggren & Bernshteyn, 2007).

Also, Berggren and Bernshteyn (2007) noted that transparency helped improve person-job fit because the software firm communicated job descriptions that focused on the strengths of the employees filling the position rather than forcing an employee "to fit a job role that is rigidly defined" (p. 414). Estlund (2011) furthered these findings and posited that improved workplace transparency resulted in a better developed and more educated workforce who become better equipped to make decisions and remain in compliance with mandatory legal regulations. Although research has provided support to the benefits associated with transparency and why organizations should place value in the concept, there are also disadvantages with its use (Bennis, 2009; Bernstein, 2015; Essandoh et al., 2017).

Bernstein (2015) indicated that in theory, transparency proves beneficial, but implementing transparency in practice is a bit more complicated. Bernstein (2015) continued by stating that the same openness associated with transparency "that at time can increase accountability, collaboration, knowledge sharing, innovation and productivity can also undermine it" (p. 1). Bennis (2009) explained as to why transparency can also undermine the benefits associated with it because of the difficulty associated with granting and distributing access to information. In other words, the more transparency individuals and organizations engage in, the less privacy and decreased amounts of confidentiality become perceived as "annoying, embarrassing, infuriating, and even dangerous" (Bennis, 2009, p. 7).

Essandoh et al. (2017) furthered Bennis' (2009) observations and indicated that too much or complete transparency could lead to individuals feeling micromanaged. Employees in these types of situations can feel exposed, vulnerable, and not in control (Essandoh et al., 2017). The overemphasis on transparency can result in decreased creativity, inability to problem solve, and breed feelings of mistrust (Essandoh et al., 2017). Therefore, more transparency is not necessarily the best option (Bernstein, 2015). Instead, organizational leaders should implement strategic and smarter transparency (Berggren & Bernshteyn, 2007; Bernstein, 2015) that strikes the right balance between privacy and openness. By using focused and strategic transparency, vice complete transparency leaders encourage its use but also ensure that boundaries exist that determine appropriate access to information that helps better identify those receivers of the information who need and have a right to know from those who do not (Essandoh et al., 2017). One way to help strike the appropriate balance and achieve strategic transparency is through honest and trusting leader-follower relationships.

### *Honest and Trusting Leader-Follower Relationships*

Despite the disadvantages associated with transparency, when used in a smart, strategic, and balanced manner, it helps ensure organizations and its members capitalize on its benefits. However, the underlying theme of transparency involves the development and maintenance of honest and "trusting relationships" (Crumpton, 2011, p. 126) between leaders and followers. McGowan (2009) indicated that the term honest can be perceived in many ways. However, D. Cherrington and Cherrington (1993) argued that the concept is not difficult to define and stated that "honest means to be free from deceit and fraud, to be open and above board in your transactions, and to be fair and just in how you treat others"

(p. 32). Additionally, those who are honest do not spread rumors, they do not make false statements and impressions that they know are untrue, and they do not steal (Cherrington & Cherrington, 1993). Most importantly, honest people "follow the rules they have agreed to accept" (Cherrington & Cherrington, 1993, p. 32).

Scarnati (1997) emphasized the importance of honesty and argued that it serves as a keystone and foundational element to achieve "productive human interaction" (p. 1). Scarnati (1997) posited that the value associated with honesty born from transparency in leader-follower relationships is that it provides a sense of security among followers. Additionally, honesty not only improves a sense of security among followers but it also leads to improved teamwork, creativity, performance, productivity, job satisfaction, and morale (Asacker, 2004; Strong, Ringer, & Taylor, 2001). These positive outcomes associated with honesty help support Scarnati's (1997) assertion of it being a key leadership behavior. Grover (2014) further provided support to the importance of leader honest by stating that "people want their leaders to be honest and to work for the overall good" (p. 48). When followers view leaders as honest and transparent it helps engender a sense of trust (Krot & Lewkicka, 2012).

The concept of trust becomes generally defined as "the willingness of one party to be vulnerable to the actions of another party" (Krot & Lewicka, 2012, p. 224). Parris et al. (2016) asserted that "trust is an antecedent and consequence of transparency. Transparency is necessary to create a sense of trustworthiness and accountability" (p. 224). In this context, trust becomes defined as the willingness of an individual to "assume the risk that goes along with taking action based on the reliance of another" (Parris et al., 2016, p. 224). According to Crumpton (2011), this trust becomes the responsibility of organizational leaders. A way for leaders to develop and maintain this trust, they "must be transparent in how information gathering and decisions are made" (Crumpton, 2011, p. 126). The observation that leader transparency contributes to the formation of honest and trusting relationships with followers illustrates the importance of transparent leadership. The concept of transparent leadership becomes discussed next.

### *Transparent Leadership*

Transparent leadership becomes associated with the term "open leadership" (Kerfoot, 2004, p. 33). Baum (2005) provided a more detailed description and described transparent leadership as "a leader who believes in telling the whole truth" (p. 42). The leadership style also encompasses the ability to prioritize people's needs and concerns for the greater good of the organization (Salvatico, 2006). Goldsmith and Wheeler (2007) summarized these two descriptions of transparent leadership and characterized transparent leaders as being able to "show their humanity and share information" (p. 20). Bennis (2008) described transparent leadership as a leader with "candor, integrity, honesty, ethics, clarity, full disclosure, legal compliance, and all that enables us to deal fairly with each other" (p. 19). Schwarz (2010) built on Bennis' (2008) description and indicated that transparent leaders productively share what they are thinking and ensure that people understand their thought processes, especially when "the stakes are high [and] views differ greatly" (p. 56). Scott (2016) expands on the idea of productively sharing information and discussed that transparent leaders explain the rationale of their decisions to their followers by engaging in conversations with them to further develop rapport, understanding, and trust.

Despite these descriptions of transparent leadership, Buell (2008) argued that the literature lacks a formal definition for the term. Additionally, transparent leadership often becomes associated with the leadership style of authentic leadership. Authentic leaders, similar to transparent leaders, exhibit "core values of honesty, altruism, kindness, fairness, accountability, and optimism" (Yukl, 2013, p. 361). However, Yukl (2013) stated that "authentic leadership is based on positive psychology and psychological theories of self-regulation" (p. 361). Ehret (2016) provided support to Yukl's (2013) definition and defined authentic leaders as individuals who are genuine, self-aware, and remain "true to themselves and their beliefs" (p. 11).

Authentic leaders lead by aligning their actions with the mission, vision, purpose, and values of the organization (Ehret, 2016). They also hold themselves accountable and personally responsible for their actions and the outcomes associated with those actions (Ehret, 2016). Based on Yukl (2013) and Ehret's (2016) definitions of authentic leadership, this type of leadership style primarily focuses on individual self-awareness and self-regulation. While authentic leadership can result in greater trust and transparency and thus becomes related to transparent leadership for this manuscript, they are considered different leadership concepts. Therefore, transparent leadership becomes defined as the productive sharing of essential and valuable information with stakeholders through engaging in open and honest dialogue and conversation that helps build trusting relationships (Schwarz, 2010; Scott, 2016).

Although leaders play an important role in building trust and organizational transparency (Crumpton, 2011), leaders only serve as one contributing factor. Followers also play an important role in establishing trust and transparency within organizations (Ramazzina, 2017; Shahzadi et al., 2017). Salvatico (2006) reinforced the role of followers in developing transparent leadership stating that "transparent leadership can only be achieved if it is truly embraced and consistently practiced throughout the entire organization" and by all individuals from the leaders to the followers (p. 1019). This assertion becomes supported by Bennis (2009), who indicated the need to make transparency "less dependent on the will of leaders" (p. 7). While the existing research has focused on leader transparency; Shum, Gatling, Book, and Bai (2019) examined follower transparency and its antecedents. These antecedents included follower personality traits of agreeableness and conscientiousness and peers who also exhibited high levels of transparency (Shum et al., 2019). Shum et al. (2019) studied emphasized how followers also value and can contribute to organizational transparency. Therefore, the next section discusses the importance of followership and its relation to transparent leadership.

## The Importance of Followership

The topic of leadership becomes widely researched and written about and primarily leader-centric in its approach (Uhl-Bien, Riggio, Lowe, & Carsten, 2014; Yukl, 2013). The interest in the topic of leadership becomes supported by people associating leaders as individuals "who blaze new paths and boldly goes where no one has gone before" (Ramazzina, 2017, p. 70). Additionally, it does not help that in Western culture, "being a follower connotes weakness, passivity or mindlessness" (Chaleff, 1996, p. 16). As well as being associated with words such as "low status [and] unimaginative" (Agho, 2009, p. 159). However, leadership only serves as one part of the critical relationship because, without any followers, there are no leaders (Chaleff, 1996; Kirchhubel, 2010). Additionally, Uhl-Bien et al. (2014) stated that "the significance of following for leadership means that our understanding of leadership is incomplete without an understanding of followership" (p. 84). Therefore, it becomes crucial to view followers as the complement to leaders and value their importance (Currie, 2014).

Followers, in the simplest terms, become defined as those assigned to or directly report to individuals in formal positions of authority or perceived informal leadership positions (Ehret, 2016). Followers also become referred to as subordinates, team members, and direct reports (Manning & Robertson, 2016). Followership becomes "described as the ability of individuals to competently and proactively follow the instructions and support the efforts of their superior to achieve organizational goals" (Agho, 2009, p. 159). Similarly, Kirchhubel (2010) described followership as "'managing upwards' or 'leading from the middle'" (p. 18). In other words, followership involves the ability of followers to willingly cooperate with those in positions of authority to accomplish the organization's mission and goals. (Kirchhubel, 2010). These definitions of followership both capture characteristics that make up effective followers.

Manning and Robertson (2016) indicated that effective followership becomes dependent upon the independence and autonomy that followers have to exercise critical thinking, initiative, and problem-solving and how passive or active they are. Therefore, effective followership becomes comprised of followers who are independent, apply critical thinking, and are engaged in their approach (Manning & Robertson, 2016). The four qualities that make up effective followers are "self-management, commitment, competence and focus, and courage" (Manning & Robertson, 2016). Additionally, Manning and Robertson (2016) argued the interdependent relationship between leaders and followers. In other words, leaders' actions and behaviors not only impact followers' conduct, but followers' actions and behaviors also affect leaders' conduct (Manning & Robertson, 2016; Riggio, Chaleff, & Lipman-Blumen, 2008; Uhl-Bien et al., 2014). For example, Shahzadi et al. (2017), in their quantitative study that employed a cross-sectional survey research design, found that effective followership positively impacted leaders' perceptions of trust.

The premise of followership focusing on the interdependent relationship between leaders and followers that allows followers the ability to impact leader and leadership processes supports the possible connection regarding effective followership affecting leader transparency. Based on this premise, the question arises of how does effective followership influences leader transparency? Lowe (2005) argued that if leaders want to communicate a point better to deliver the message in a story. Therefore, to help answer the proposed research question and to explore the relationships between followership and transparent leadership the next section examines the Biblical story of the Prophet Nathan's rebuke of King David and applies an exegetical analysis using Robbins' (1996) socio-rhetorical analysis method to analyze the text and help answer the research question.

## Social and Cultural Texture Analysis: Nathan's Rebuke of King David

Robbins' (1996) socio-rhetorical analysis provides an approach on how to interpret the meaning of a text. The socio-rhetorical analysis approach examines literature through five viewpoints or what the method calls textures (Robbins, 1996). One of the views or textures is the social and cultural texture where the text becomes reviewed taking into account the perspective of the social and cultural thoughts, practices, beliefs, and perceptions that help define the greater society during the time of when the text was written (Robbins, 1996). This section will conduct a social and cultural texture analysis of Nathan's rebuke of King David using the Biblical passage from the book of 2 Samuel Chapter 12. It will particularly explore the conversionist religious worldview, the reciprocity associated with dyadic contracts, the social and cultural viewpoint of honor during the era of King David, and the challenge-response social communication method (Robbins, 1996). However, before applying this analysis, a background of King David's affair with Bathsheba is first provided as it serves the reason for Nathan's rebuke.

### *King David and Bathsheba*

The Old Testament section of the Bible in the Biblical book of 2 Samuel, Chapter 11 tells of the story of King David's affair with Bathsheba. King David was the appointed ruler of the kingdom of Israel, and one day from the roof of his home, he saw a woman bathing (2 Samuel 11:2, English Standard Version). King David sent one of his servants to find out the identity of the woman. He found out that the woman's name was Bathsheba and that she was married to one of King David's soldiers, Uriah, who was currently away from the kingdom fighting a battle with the rest of King David's army (2 Samuel 11:3, ESV). Despite King David knowing that Bathsheba was married, he still ordered his servant to bring

Bathsheba to him (2 Samuel 11:4, ESV). This action resulted in King David and Bathsheba's affair and caused Bathsheba to become pregnant with King David's child (2 Samuel 11:5, ESV).

The story continues with King David's attempt to cover up his affair by first ordering Bathsheba's husband, Uriah, to return from the battlefield to have Uriah sleep with Bathsheba to make it appear that Bathsheba was pregnant with Uriah's child (2 Samuel 11:8, ESV). However, Uriah refused to go home to his wife because he did not think it was fair that he enjoys the company of his wife while his fellow soldiers were still engaged in battle (2 Samuel 11:11, ESV). At which point, King David sends Uriah back to the battlefield with a note to his commander, Joab, essentially sentencing Uriah to death (2 Samuel 11:14–15, ESV). After Uriah's death, King David took Bathsheba to be his wife (2 Samuel 11:27, ESV). The story continues with God observing King David's actions and being displeased with King David's behavior (2 Samuel 11:27, ESV). At this point, God sends the Prophet Nathan to help correct King David's actions and realize the consequences of his misconduct (2 Samuel 12:1).

## God's Intervention: A Conversionist Religious Response to the World

A worldview is a means of seeing the world, which helps define how one understands it (Kim, Fisher, & McCalman, 2009). Robbins (1996) starts the social and cultural texture analysis by first examining the worldview of the text and how does religion respond to that worldview. There are seven religious responses to the world, one of which is the conversionist response (Robbins, 1996). The conversionist religious answer is that the world is corrupt because people are unethical and immoral (Robbins, 1996). Therefore, to save the world, its people must be saved (Robbins, 1996). However, people only become saved from their unethical and immoral behaviors through divine or supernatural intervention (Robbins, 1996). The conversionist worldview does not believe that salvation becomes achieved through ordinary means, but only through extraordinary assistance (Robbins, 1996).

This religious response aligns well with the selected Biblical passage of 2 Samuel Chapter 12, verse 1, when God sends Nathan to speak to King David. King David's affair with Bathsheba and his subsequent cover-up by having Bathsheba's husband killed supports the conversionist viewpoint that people are unethical and immoral. The conversionist's response to such behavior is that King David needs the help of God to save himself from his destructive habits (Robbins, 1996). So from a conversionist viewpoint, God sent Nathan to speak with King David represents God's intervention and the supernatural assistance that King David requires to be rescued from his unethical behaviors (Robbins, 1996).

Ancient Israel's conversionist worldview. According to Malamat (2001), the conversionist worldview is applicable during the period of King David, given the long history of reliance on God by the people of Israel. Throughout the history of Israel, God has intervened and provided His assistance (Malamat, 2001). God's intervention could be traced back to the Biblical book of Exodus when God assisted the Israelites to freedom from being slaves to Egyptian rulers and how God helped the Israelites reach the Promised Land (Malamat, 2001). From the longstanding history between God and Israel, it is understandable why ancient Israel would find the conversionist worldview acceptable. This socially acceptable conversionist viewpoint also was deeply engrained in King David. Despite King David's immoral actions of having an affair and murder, it was not until God intervened through Nathan did he realize the error in his ways and admitted, "I have sinned against the Lord" (2 Samuel 12:13, ESV). Nathan's remarks illustrate again the reliance that King David has on God and provides further support to the conversionist religious response to the world. The relationship between King David and God becomes explored next through Robbins' (1996) dyadic contract concept.

### *Reciprocity and Dyadic Contracts*

Molm (2010) defines reciprocity as an exchange that involves the provision and return of benefits between parties. The idea of reciprocity lays the foundation regarding Robbins' (1996) dyadic contract concept. Dyadic contracts are informal agreements between two individuals founded under the notion of reciprocity (Robbins, 1996). The dyadic contract between two individuals only becomes enforced through the mutual benefits that each individual receives from partaking in the contract (Robbins, 1996). The continued back and forth of given, received, and return of mutual benefits develops trust between the two individuals (Molm, 2010). Applying the dyadic contract concept to the relationship between King David and God highlights specifically the patron-client dyadic contract.

King David and God's patron-client contract. The patron-client dyadic contract is an agreement between two entities of different statuses (Robbins, 1996). As mentioned earlier, the Israelites have a strong reliance on God due to their conversionist worldview (Malamat, 2001; Robbins, 1996). One can conclude that the Israelites reliance on God makes God their provider or patron. Applying the patron-client contract to God and King David defines roles where God is the patron, and King David is the client (Robbins, 1996). Despite the difference in statuses between God and King David, the concept of reciprocity still applies (Robbins, 1996). An example of King David and God's patron-client contract includes when God appointed David to be King of Israel (2 Samuel 12:8, ESV). Following the principle of reciprocity, since King David received the benefit from God of being appointed king, he returned the benefit and created a temple in Jerusalem to show gratitude and praise to God (McConkie & Boss, 2001). The patron-client contract between King David and God could be summarized when God, through Nathan said to King David:

> I anointed you king over Israel...And I gave you your master's house and your master's wives...And if this were too little, I would add to you as much more. Why have you despised the word of the Lord, to do what is evil in his sight? (2 Samuel 12:8–9, ESV)

This statement shows that God will continue to provide for King David as long as he follows God's rules and laws. However, when King David broke God's laws and committed adultery and murder through his affair with Bathsheba and the killing of her husband Uriah, it caused a violation in King David and God's patron-client contract. King David's immoral actions started a negative exchange between him and God, which resulted in God issuing a negative consequence to King David through the death of King David's firstborn son (2 Samuel 12:14, ESV). This negative consequence of losing his firstborn son greatly impacted King David and is discussed next.

*Cultural Concept of Honor*

Robbins (1996) defines honor as a social and cultural topic that is related to an individual's status in life. Honor is also associated with how an individual values oneself (Aslani et al., 2016). During the period of King David, honor was something that was earned or born into (Okaiwele,

2009; Robbins, 1996). Robbins describes "ascribed honor" as a way that status or reputation happens to in an individual as a result of birthright or being given this status by someone in a position of power (p. 76). The definition of ascribed honor applies to how God, an entity in a powerful position, gave status or honor to David by appointing him the King of Israel. The concept of honor or status during ancient Israel was also something that can be challenged. God challenged King David's honor or status when He caused his firstborn son to die as a result of King David's misconduct. The death of King David's firstborn son was a challenge to King David's honor because, in ancient Israel, firstborn sons had a right to inherit the worldly possessions and legacies of their fathers (Carmichael, 2008; Davis, 2008). Since King David's firstborn son died, that caused uncertainty regarding who would inherit King David's kingdom and who would carry on his lineage. Nathan also challenged King David's honor or status when he confronted him about his affair with Bathsheba. Nathan's challenge of King David's honor becomes explored through the social communication of challenge-response or riposte (Robbins, 1996).

*Challenge-Response*

Since the concept of honor or status was highly valued and associated to one's identity and self-worth, it was a subject of social communication that took place during ancient Israel (Aslani et al., 2016; Robbins, 1996). The challenge-response interaction was a social exchange between individuals that shared the same honor or status (Robbins, 1996). In this social interaction, individuals would send messages through words or actions to question the honor or condition of the other (Neyrey, 1998; Robbins, 1996). The interactions would typically take place in a public setting to embarrass the individual being challenged (Neyrey, 1998; Robbins, 1996). The challenge-response exchange would first begin with an individual who would issue the challenge, then the individual being challenged would receive the challenge, and then respond to the challenge (Neyrey, 1998; Robbins, 1996). An example of the challenge-response social exchange becomes shown when Nathan confronts King David of his unethical and immoral behaviors.

Nathan challenges King David. When God sent Nathan to see King David, Nathan physically entered the space of King David and, in that action, issued a challenge (Robbins, 1996). Nathan continued his challenge by telling King David a story about a rich man who had an abundance of livestock. However, despite having so many animals, the rich man decided to take and butcher a poor man's only pet lamb (2 Samuel 12:1–7, ESV). Nathan, after telling this story, then accused King David of being the rich man in the story who did such a horrible deed by slaughtering the only possession that the poor man owned and loved (2 Samuel 12:7, ESV). Nathan also questioned King David's actions by stating, "Why have you despised the word of the Lord, to do what is evil in his sight?" (2 Samuel 12:9, ESV). Nathan physically entering King David's space, accusing him of being horrible for taking what does not belong to him, and questioning his actions challenged King David's legitimacy and credibility (Janzen, 2012; Robbins, 1996).

King David's perception of Nathan's challenge. King David perceived Nathan's challenge to be a threat to his honor. As mentioned earlier, the social exchange of challenge-response was to only occur between individuals of the same social status (Neyrey, 1998; Robbins, 1996). King David was the King of Israel, and Nathan was not a king, so based on the differences in their social positions, King David and Nathan technically did not have the same social status. However, Nathan was a prophet and trusted advisor to King David (Stallard & Sanger, 2014). Nathan is a prophet sent by God and a trusted advisor to King David made their social statuses equal. Robbins (1996) claims that in ancient Mediterranean culture, to include ancient Israel, every social interaction that occurred outside of one's family or inner circle of friends was considered a challenge. Since Nathan was a trusted advisor to King David, Nathan was part of King David's inner circle (Stallard & Sanger, 2014). Therefore, Nathan was in the right social position to engage in a challenge-response exchange with King David (Neyrey, 1998; Robbins, 1996). Since Nathan was part of King David's inner circle, he considered it appropriate and allowed Nathan to enter his space and question his actions.

King David's reaction to Nathan's challenge. Nathan's use of the story regarding a selfish rich man taking a poor man's only lamb aligns with the definition of a juridical parable (Janzen, 2012). The purpose of juridical parable is to provide a realistic and relatable scenario to the intended receiver who committed a similar crime that results in the intended receiver to admit to their wrongdoings (Janzen, 2012). The story of the rich man and the poor man as a juridical parable worked because it caused King David to realize the consequences of his misconduct (Janzen, 2012). After King David heard Nathan's story, King David became angry and responded by stating that the rich man should die for the selfish and wicked action he did against the poor man (2 Samuel 12:5–6, ESV). At which point, Nathan informed King David that he was the wicked and selfish rich man when he had his affair with Bathsheba and murdered her husband Uriah (2 Samuel 12:8–9, ESV).

Since Nathan was a trusted advisor helps explain why King David allowed Nathan to speak so candidly and bluntly to him. Also, this may help explain why King David was so accepting of Nathan's criticism. After Nathan pointed out King David's misconducts and how his actions displeased God, King David responded stating, "I have sinned against the Lord" (2 Samuel 12:13, ESV). This statement further reinforces the assertion that King David perceived Nathan as a social equal and that they share a high level of trust and immediacy or closeness between each other. The next section discusses how Nathan's effective followership impacted King David's leader transparency.

## Nathan's Effective Followership Influencing King David's Transparency

Applying Robbins' (1996) social and cultural texture analysis to Nathan's rebuke of King David helped provide insight into the socially accepted conversionist worldview of ancient Israel, the concept of reciprocity through dyadic contracts, the importance of honor in ancient Israel's culture, and the effectiveness of the challenge-response social exchange. However, the social and cultural texture analysis challenge-response dynamic served as the most beneficial element to help explain Nathan's effective followership and how it inspired King David to engage in better leader transparency. Again, transparency becomes defined as the actions of an individual to ensure free-flowing communication and disclosure of timely, accurate, and trustworthy information that becomes perceived as valuable to both internal and external stakeholders who want to or have a right to know (Bennis et al., 2008; Das Neves & Vaccaro, 2013; Essandoh et al., 2017; Forssbaeck & Oxel, 2014). King David's affair with Bathsheba and the subsequent deceitful cover-up of his adultery through the killing of Bathsheba's husband highlights King David's lack of transparency.

However, Nathan serving as King David's follower and advisor, helped improve King David's leader transparency by engaging in effective followership. Nathan demonstrated the characteristics of effective followership by courageously, independently, and actively (Manning & Robertson, 2016) approaching King David with his concerns regarding King David's misconduct. Nathan's actions provided a model example of effective followership and managing upward (Kirchhubel, 2010) where Nathan used honest and open communication to point out King David's misgivings of having an affair with Bathsheba and his lack of transparency by trying to cover up his actions through the murder of Uriah and his marriage to Bathsheba. Through Nathan's effective followership of challenging King David, it resulted in King David honestly admitting to his crimes. Additionally, Nathan being an effective follower, reminded King David of the importance of transparency and the negative consequences of what happens when there is a lack of leader transparency, which is King David's case resulted in the death of his first-born son. Ultimately, Nathan's effective followership helped King David learn a valuable lesson regarding leader transparency and thus impacted King David's ability to engage in transparent leadership in the future.

## Conclusion

The continued occurrence of scandals, ethical lapses, and misconduct caused by both organizational leaders and followers (Bazerman & Tenbrunsel, 2011) highlights the need for transparent leadership. The improper disclosure by Boeing leadership to regulators and other stakeholders that contributed to the deadly plane crashes and the deaths of over 300 people (Gelles, 2019) illustrates the devasting and negative consequences associated when there is a lack of organizational transparency. To help organizational leaders engage in more transparent leadership, organizations must value the importance of its followers and their ability to positively impact leader transparency. Contemporary leaders can learn from the actions of the Biblical Prophet Nathan and his ability to improve King David's leader transparency through his effective followership. Therefore, it becomes recommended for today's leaders to cultivate and develop effective followers who are empowered to think critically and who can independently, actively, and courageously engage in open and honest communications and conversations with leaders to accomplish the organization's mission and goals.

## References

"Deloitte 2008 ethics & workplace survey finds transparency by leadership makes a positive impact on employee productivity". (2008, April 8). *PR Newswire*. Retrieved from http://eres.regent.edu:2048/login?url and https://search-proquest-com.ezproxy.regent.edu/docview/448669981?accountid=13479.

Agho, A. O. (2009). Perspectives of senior-level executives on effective followership and leadership. *Journal of Leadership & Organizational Studies, 16*(2), 159–166. https://doi.org/10.1177/1548051809335360.

Asacker, T. (2004). Ethics in the workplace: Start with honesty. *T+D, 58*(8), 42–44. Retrieved from http://eres.regent.edu:2048/login?url and https://search-proquest-com.ezproxy.regent.edu/docview/227012808?accountid=13479.

Aslani, S., Ramirez-Marin, J., Brett, J., Yao, J., Semnani-Azad, Z., Zhang, Z., ... Adair, W. (2016). Dignity, face, and honor cultures: A study of negotiation strategy and outcomes in three cultures. *Journal of Organizational Behavior, 37*(8), 1178–1201. https://doi.org/10.1002/job.2095.

Baum, H. (2005). Transparent leadership. *Leader to Leader, 2005*(37), 41–47. https://doi.org/10.1002/ltl.139.

Bazerman, M. H., & Tenbrunsel, A. E. (2011). Ethical breakdowns. *Harvard Business Review*. Retrieved from https://hbr.org/2011/04/ethicalbreakdowns.

Bennis, W. (2008). Transparent leaders. *Leadership Excellence, 25*(7), 19. Retrieved from http://eres.regent.edu:2048/login?url and https://search-proquest-com.ezproxy.regent.edu/docview/204516644?accountid=13479.

Bennis, W. (2009). New transparency. *Leadership Excellence, 26*(12), 7. Retrieved from http://eres.regent.edu:2048/login?url and https://search-proquest-com.ezproxy.regent.edu/docview/204637175?accountid=13479.

Bennis, W., Goleman, D., & O'Toole, J. (2008). Culture of candor. *Leadership Excellence, 25*(8), 4. Retrieved from http://eres.regent.edu:2048/login?url and https://search-proquest-com.ezproxy.regent.edu/docview/204626930?accountid=13479.

Berggren, E., & Bernshteyn, R. (2007). Organizational transparency drives company performance. *The Journal of Management Development, 26*(5), 411–417. http://dx.doi.org.ezproxy.regent.edu:2048/10.1108/02621710710748248.

Bernstein, E. (2015, February 23). The smart way to create a transparent workplace; openness can raise productivity–and undermine it: How to get the balance right. *Wall Street Journal* (Online) Retrieved from http://eres.regent.edu:2048/login?url and https://search-proquest-com.ezproxy.regent.edu/docview/1657252870?accountid=13479.

Buell, J. M. (2008). What it takes to be an authentic and transparent leader: Living the organization's mission, vision and values. *Healthcare Executive, 23*(6), 21–24. Retrieved from http://eres.regent.edu:2048/login?url and https://search-proquest-com.ezproxy.regent.edu/docview/200342303?accountid=13479.

Carmichael, C. (2008). Inheritance in biblical sources. *Law and Literature, 20*(2), 229–242. https://doi.org/10.1525/lal.2008.20.2.229.

Chaleff, I. (1996). Effective followership. *Executive Excellence, 13*(4), 16.

Cherrington, D. J., & Cherrington, J. O. (1993). Understanding honesty. *The Internal Auditor, 50*(6), 29. Retrieved from http://eres.regent.edu:2048/login?url and https://search-proquest-com.ezproxy.regent.edu/docview/202726216?accountid=13479.

Crumpton, M. A. (2011). The value of transparency. *The Bottom Line, 24*(2), 125–128. http://dx.doi.org.ezproxy.regent.edu:2048/10.1108/08880451111169188.

Currie, J. P. (2014). Complementing traditional leadership: The value of followership. *Reference & User Services Quarterly, 54*(2), 15–18. Retrieved from http://eres.regent.edu:2048/login?url and https://search-proquest-com.ezproxy.regent.edu/docview/1642547470?accountid=13479.

Das Neves, J. C., & Vaccaro, A. (2013). Corporate transparency: A perspective from thomas aquinas' summa theologiae. *Journal of Business Ethics, 113*(4), 639–648. http://dx.doi.org.ezproxy.regent.edu:2048/10.1007/s10551-013-1682-6.

Davis, A. K. (2008). Israel's inheritance: Birthright of the firstborn son. *CTS Journal, 13*, 79–94. Retrieved from http://chafer.nextmeta.com/files/v13n1_5davis_israel_s_inheritance_birthright_of_the_firstborn_son.pdf.

Ehret, M. G. (2016). *Common leadership strategies and practices among authentic senior leaders* (Order No. 10152947). Available from ProQuest Central; ProQuest Dissertations & Theses Global. (1816206631). Retrieved from http://eres.regent.edu:2048/login?url and https://search-proquest-com.ezproxy.regent.edu/docview/1816206631?accountid=13479.

Essandoh, M. K., Salani, R., Mendel, E., Brod, H. C., Koesters, S. C., & Satiani, B. (2017). Walking a tightrope of transparency. *Physician Leadership Journal, 4*(5), 49–51. Retrieved from http://eres.regent.edu:2048/login?url and https://search-proquest-com.ezproxy.regent.edu/docview/1933182090?accountid=13479.

Estlund, C. (2011). Just the facts: The case for workplace transparency. *Stanford Law Review, 63*(2), 351–407. Retrieved from http://eres.regent.edu:2048/login?url and https://search-proquest-com.ezproxy.regent.edu/docview/853266424?accountid=13479.

Forssbaeck, J., & Oxel, L. (2014). *The multi-faceted concept of transparency*. St. Louis: Federal Reserve Bank of St Louis. Retrieved from http://eres.regent.edu:2048/login?url and https://search-proquest-com.ezproxy.regent.edu/docview/1698462797?accountid=13479.

Gelles, D. (2019, October 29). Boeing 737 max: What's happened after the 2 deadly crashes. *The New York Times*. Retrieved from https://www.nytimes.com/interactive/2019/business/boeing-737-crashes.html.

Goldsmith, M., & Wheeler, P. (2007). Transparent leaders. *Leadership Excellence, 24*(11), 20. Retrieved from http://eres.regent.edu:2048/login?url and https://search-proquest-com.ezproxy.regent.edu/docview/204508448?accountid=13479.

Grover, S. L. (2014). Moral identity as a lens for interpreting honesty of indirect leaders. *Journal of Change Management, 14*(1), 48–65. https://doi.org/10.1080/14697017.2013.790836.

Ingram, H. J. (2009). *Organizational transparency, employee perceptions, and employee morale: A correlational study* (Order No. 3348676). Available from ProQuest Central; ProQuest Dissertations & Theses Global. (305125690). Retrieved from http://eres.regent.edu:2048/login?url and https://search-proquest-com.ezproxy.regent.edu/docview/305125690?accountid=13479.

Janzen, D. (2012). The condemnation of david's "taking in 2 samuel 12:1–14". *Journal of Biblical Literature, 131*(2), 209–220. Retrieved from http://eres.regent.edu:2048/login?url and https://search-proquest-com.ezproxy.regent.edu/docview/1636189037?accountid=13479.

Johnsson, R. B. & Schlangenstein, M. (2019, May 5). Boeing held off for months on disclosing faulty alert on 737 max. *Bloomberg*. Retrieved from https://www.bloomberg.com/news/articles/2019–05-05/boeing-left-airlines-faa-in-dark-on-737-alert-linked-to-crash.

Kerfoot, K. (2004). The transparent organization: Leadership in an open organization. *Nursing Economics, 22*(1), 33–4. Retrieved from http://eres.regent.edu:2048/login?url and https://search-proquest-com.ezproxy.regent.edu/docview/236936852?accountid=13479.

Kim, D., Fisher, D., & McCalman, D. (2009). Modernism, Christianity, and business ethics: a worldview perspective. *Journal of Business Ethics, 90*(1), 115–121. Retrieved from http://www.jstor.org.ezproxy.regent.edu:2048/stable/27735228.

Kirchhubel, D. (2010). Effective 'followership' how to manage upwards. *Manager*, 18. Retrieved from http://eres.regent.edu:2048/login?url and https://search-proquest-com.ezproxy.regent.edu/docview/1348903042?accountid=13479.

Krishner, T. (2019, July 31). *Watch: Senators clash with faa officials over boeing max oversight*. Associated Press. Retrieved from https://www.pbs.org/newshour/nation/senators-clash-with-faa-officials-over-boeing-max-oversight.

Krot, K., & Lewicka, D. (2012). The importance of trust in manager-employee relationships. *International Journal of Electronic Business Management, 10*(3), 224–233. Retrieved from http://eres.regent.edu:2048/login?url and https://search-proquest-com.ezproxy.regent.edu/docview/1240365052?accountid=13479.

Lowe, G. (2005). Want to reach staff? tell them a story. *Canadian HR Reporter, 18*(15), 16–16, 20. Retrieved from http://eres.regent.edu:2048/login?url and https://search-proquest-com.ezproxy.regent.edu/docview/220822209?accountid=13479.

Malamat, A. (2001). *History of biblical Israel: Major problems and minor issues.* Retrieved from https://ebookcentral-proquest-com.ezproxy.regent.edu.

Manning, T., & Robertson, B. (2016). A three-factor model of followership: Part 1—Introduction to followership, leadership and the three factor model of leadership. *Industrial and Commercial Training, 48*(6), 277–283. https://doi.org/10.1108/ICT-01-2016-0003.

Matthews, K. (2019, March 26). Boeing is handling the 737 max crisis all wrong. *Quartz.* Retrieved from https://qz.com/1581205/boeing-is-handling-the-737-max-crisis-all-wrong/.

McConkie, M. L., & Boss, R. W. (2001). David's rise to power–and the struggle to keep it: An examination of the change process. *Public Administration Quarterly, 25*(2), 190–228. Retrieved from http://eres.regent.edu:2048/login?url and https://search-proquest-com.ezproxy.regent.edu/docview/226976352?accountid=13479.

McGowan, I. (2009). *Perceptions about honesty* (Order No. 3388755). Available from ProQuest Central; ProQuest Dissertations & Theses Global; ProQuest One Academic. (305123128). Retrieved from http://eres.regent.edu:2048/login?url and https://search-proquest-com.ezproxy.regent.edu/docview/305123128?accountid=13479.

Molm, L. D. (2010). The structure of reciprocity. *Social Psychology Quarterly, 73*(2), 119–131. https://doi.org/10.1177/0190272510369079.

Neyrey, J. H. (1998). Questions, chreiai, and challenges to honor: The interface of rhetoric and culture in mark's gospel. *The Catholic Biblical Quarterly, 60*(4), 657–681. Retrieved from http://eres.regent.edu:2048/login?url and https://search-proquest-com.ezproxy.regent.edu/docview/220249833?accountid=13479.

Okaiwele, G. (2009). John 21: An exegetical study of leadership within Mediterranean context and the 21st century. *Emerging Leadership Journey, 2*(1), 43–53. Retrieved from https://www.regent.edu/acad/global/publications/elj/vol2iss1/Okaiwele_Greg_Final.pdf.

Parris, D. L., Dapko, J. L., Arnold, R. W., & Arnold, D. (2016). Exploring transparency: A new framework for responsible business management. *Management Decision, 54*(1), 222–247. http://dx.doi.org.ezproxy.regent.edu:2048/10.1108/MD-07-2015-0279.

Ramazzina, G. (2017). Don't forget the importance of followership. *TD Magazine, 71*(7), 70.

Riggio, R. E., Chaleff, I., & Lipman-Blumen, J. (2008). *The art of followership: How great followers create great leaders and organizations*. San Francisco, CA: Jossey-Bass.

Robbins, V. K. (1996). *Exploring the texture of texts: A guide to socio-rhetorical interpretation*. Harrisburg, PA: Trinity Press International.

Salvatico, R. (2006). Enabling transparent leadership: A small business manager's perspective. *The Journal of Management Development, 25*(10), 1018–1020. http://dx.doi.org.ezproxy.regent.edu:2048/10.1108/02621710610708658.

Scarnati, J. T. (1997). Beyond technical competence: Honesty and integrity. *Career Development International, 2*(1), 24–27. https://doi.org/10.1108/13620439710157452.

Schwarz, R. (2010). Transparent leadership. *Government Executive, 42*(4), 56. Retrieved from http://eres.regent.edu:2048/login?url and https://search-proquest-com.ezproxy.regent.edu/docview/204316765?accountid=13479.

Scott, M. (2016). Transparent leadership. *Smart Business Cleveland, 28*(4), 74. Retrieved from http://eres.regent.edu:2048/login?url and https://search-proquest-com.ezproxy.regent.edu/docview/1888660135?accountid=13479.

Shahzadi, G., John, A., Qadeer, F., & Mehnaz, S. (2017). Followership behavior and leaders' trust: Do political skills matter? *Pakistan Journal of Commerce and Social Sciences, 11*(2), 653–670.

Shum, C., Gatling, A., Book, L., & Bai, B. (2019). The moderating roles of follower conscientiousness and agreeableness on the relationship between peer transparency and follower transparency. *Journal of Business Ethics, 154*(2), 483–495. https://doi.org/10.1007/s10551-017-3471-0.

Stallard, D., & Sanger, K. (2014). The nathan solution to the bathsheba syndrome. *Marine Corps Gazette, 98*(4), 40–44. Retrieved from http://eres.regent.edu:2048/login?url and https://search-proquest-com.ezproxy.regent.edu/docview/1515632573?accountid=13479.

Strong, K. C., Ringer, R. C., & Taylor, S. A. (2001). THE rules of stakeholder satisfaction (timeliness, honesty, empathy). *Journal of Business Ethics, 32*(3), 219–230. https://doi.org/10.1023/A:1010714703936.

Uhl-Bien, M., Riggio, R. E., Lowe, K. B., & Carsten, M. K. (2014). Followership theory: A review and research agenda. *The Leadership Quarterly, 25*(1), 83–104. https://doi.org/10.1016/j.leaqua.2013.11.007.

Yukl, G. A. (2013). *Leadership in organizations* (8th ed.). Boston: Pearson.

CHAPTER 11

# To Reveal or to Conceal: Pertinent Sacred Considerations for Transparent Leaders in a Super-Intelligent World

*Sharon Hathaway Forrest*

## Introduction

Transparency has been described popularly as the "bedrock" (Stack, 2017) and the "currency" (Calvert, 2014) of trust in modern management media. Indeed, the decision to reveal or conceal information whether personal or professional is a foundational leadership function which when proper processes and procedures are lacking or ignored can make a leader vulnerable to public scrutiny and susceptible to reputation ruination (Schachter, 2013). As a case in point, the declaration of Boeing's soon-to-be ousted former CEO Dennis Muilenburg that "We own it" stressed the need to be more transparent in corporate operations as one of his last-ditch efforts to restore his and Boeing's credibility

S. H. Forrest (✉)
School of Business and Leadership, Regent University, Chesapeake, VA, USA
e-mail: sharfor@mail.regent.edu

Bellevue, WA, USA



B. E. Winston (eds.), *Transparent and Authentic Leadership*, Christian Faith Perspectives in Leadership and Business,
https://doi.org/10.1007/978-3-030-61996-1_11

with investors and the public at large after the downing of two 737 MAX Boeing planes and the deaths of 346 passengers due to a software failure (Sindreu, 2019). Then incoming CEO David Calhoun in his first email communication with employees reiterated the transparency agenda: "engaging one another and our stakeholders with greater transparency, holding ourselves accountable to the highest standards of safety and quality and incorporating outside-in perspective on what we do and how we do it" (Hames, 2019, paras. 4–5). Boeing's Board of Trustee's also released a public statement re-rehearsing the transparency mantra: "a change in leadership was necessary to restore confidence in the Company … Boeing will operate with a renewed commitment to full transparency, including effective and proactive communication with the FAA, other global regulators and its customers (Boeing Communications, 2019, paras. 3–4).

When making such consequential decisions within the contemporary context of synchronous communications and leadership in the digital era of social media, big data, virtual reality, advanced computational methods, and deep learning (Banks, Dionne, Sayama, Mast, 2019), leaders may resort to helpful guidance from the sacred scriptures. In conjunction with theoretical frameworks for post-heroic, skills, and entrepreneurial leadership eras (Clark & Harrison, 2018), spiritual, servant, ethical, authentic, transparent leadership paradigms have evolved (Hoch, Bommer, Dulebohn, & Wu, 2018) often from the moral underpinnings of the scriptures infused in Judeo-Christian cultures, which can provide entrepreneurial leaders confidence and assurance of good outcomes from transparent relations and conduct, including the respect of and performance from followers (Ilies, Morgeson, & Nahrgang, 2005). Concurrently, reaching beyond the predominant leadership studies paradigms of the past, whereby personality traits like honesty and openness persistently prevailed, new AI-enhanced tools like IBM Watson's content analysis can provide insights through the nonlinear and interaction effects unmasked through AI and machine learning capabilities (Spisak et al., 2019) for a more holistic, systems understanding of the role of individuals and their organizations in transparent leadership practices.

From public interest commercials addressing corporate malfeasance (govsingapore.com, 2018) to research from institutes on the future of humanity (https://www.fhi.ox.ac.uk/), a clarion call has been issued for transparent and authentic leaders in what has become a superintelligent world (Bostrom, 2014). Indeed, at the heart of numerous contemporary social, political, and business ethical controversies is a vital conflict over transparency or concealment. Representatively, remarking on the recently released Mueller Report, which was deemed a "transparency fight" (Shackford, 2019) with a resounding retort the *Washington Post* recorded: "Republicans trapped by transparency" (Downie, 2019). Accordingly, from within the environment of "silence and secrecy," Senate Majority Leader Mitch McConnell called for "transparency as the rules will allow" (CBS News, 2019). Then a media battle ensued with former White House Special Counsel Ken Starr stating that as a matter of law, which protects grand jury information, that only a compelling public interest would allow revealing the report legally (Fox Business Videos, 2019). Other reporters noted, "transparency is key" along with the cry "we need full transparency" (Downie, 2019). This media deluge on transparency likely even influenced a recent episode of *FBI*, an evening drama on CBS television which ended with "I appreciate your transparency…not a lot of that around here" (Wilder & de Segnozac, 2019).

Further, along with the paramount public interest in transparency, recognition of transparent leadership as a chief corporate commodity has become widespread. For instance, Timothy Dills, upon appointment as President and CEO to LinQuest, a technical solutions company to government security operations (located in Chantilly, VA), declared "I believe in transparent leadership fueled by honesty and trust" (Global Data Point, Executive Appointments Monitor, 2019). Another exemplary tech leader, Laurie Schrader, who as Chief Financial Officer of Faegre Baker Daniels, led a 70-member finance team to six consecutive years of revenue growth and profitability through implementing timely billing and collection fees with the adoption of mobile time-entry technology. Schrader was said to have "built a reputation for transparent leadership" ("Laurie Shrader," 2018). Indications are reputations rise or fall on followers' observations or perceptions of a leader's transparent behaviors or characteristics.

Thus, transparency is not just a public concern when governments are involved; corporations and non-profit organizations also bear responsibility in the public eye for being truthful themselves and even more importantly when engaged in elaborate multi-sector collaborations. Although the initial rise of multi-sector collaborations in the 1980s and 1990s through World Bank international development projects yielded a higher degree of scrutiny, the complexity of international development systems, including financial payments, makes transparency all the more critical to real progress.

## The Compelling Case for Transparent Leadership to Ensure Ethically-Aligned AI

Little wonder then that leadership guru Warren Bennis (2009) noted in the 20th anniversary of his best-selling book *On Becoming a Leader*, that a "new digital transparency" has emerged. This emergence Bennis along with colleagues Goleman, O'Toole, and Biederman (2008) observed historians place at or around 1998 along with the advent of social media blogs during the revelation of President Clinton's "dalliance" with a White House intern (p. 94). This digital transparency has coincided with the new interest in AI which came along with the capacity of advanced computing technologies and the promise of quantum computing to go even further to analyze Big Data. Indeed, in this author's analyses of the public statements of global tech leaders, transparency was a keyword and phrase (Forrest, 2018a, 2018b, 2018c, 2018d).

Such exemplary escalation in media attention of AI was apparent when the use of the keywords "artificial intelligence" were tracked in the global Factiva media database (January 1977–May 2019), which showed a phenomenal increase in the inclusion of "artificial intelligence" from 1.9K "hits" (includes mentions in news wires, publications, web news, blogs, pictures, and multimedia) in the decade 1977 to 1986 to over 422K "hits" in the past 29 months—January 2017 thru May 2019 (see Table 11.1). Additionally, media with the keywords "artificial intelligence" mentioned more than doubled from 2016 (45,853 "hits") to 2017 (111,102 "hits") such that the decade of 2007–2016 represented a 236.2% increase over the previous ten years 1997–2006. Further, with the number of documents having the mention of artificial intelligence climbing to 132,808 from January 1 to May 31, 2019, the current year (2019) is likely to far surpass previous annual records—even that of 178,078 in 2018. Likewise, on the day May 31, 2019, there were 994 hits in media mentioning AI in comparison to just 3 media in the Dow Jones Factiva database mentioning AI in all of 1977 (January 1–December 31, 1977). Also, of the 585,423 media "hits" which occurred over 1977 to May 31, 2019—almost 43 years, 72.1% occurred in less than the past 3 years.

**Table 11.1** Media with keywords "Artificial Intelligence" (Dow Jones Factiva, 2019)

| *All media from 1977 through May 2019 with Mention of "Artificial Intelligence"* | | | |
|---|---|---|---|
| *Years (ALL)* | *# of articles* | *% of total* | *% of increase over prior decade* |
| 1977–1986 | 1858 | 0.30 | |
| 1987–1996 | 12,629 | 2.20 | 579.7 |
| 1997–2006 | 34,143 | 5.80 | 170.4 |
| 2007–2016 | 114,805 | 19.60 | 236.2 |
| 2017 | 111,102 | 19.00 | |
| 2018 | 178,078 | 30.40 | |
| 2019 | 132,808 | 22.70 | |
| Total | 585,423 | | |

Even amongst engineers leading the development of AI, there is a clear call for ethical guidelines and professional codes of conduct. For instance, in March 2019, the Institute of Electrical and Electronics Engineers (IEEE) released a collaborative work of the IEEE Global Initiative on Ethics of Autonomous and Intelligent Systems "for the purposes of furthering public understanding of the importance of addressing ethical considerations in the design of autonomous and intelligent systems" (IEEE, 2019). The IEEE's initiative hopes for "values-driven, ethically aligned design for autonomous and intelligent systems now and in the future" (IEEE, 2019).

In step with technological advance in AI, Clark and Harrison (2018) defined eleven eras of leadership studies of which the "post-heroic era" was the ninth in the series and a definitive demarcation from the previous eight eras (p. 516). In explanation, Clark and Harrison mentioned transparent leadership in conjunction with ethical leadership as a primary reaction to failures of heroic leadership in the face of corporate scandals. During this defined "post-heroic" era, Clark and colleague also considered transparent leadership as a key leadership theory in this era along with authentic, entrepreneurial, distributive, servant and implicit leadership theories (p. 521).

Also, well beyond heroism, Chou (2019) recognized that although social, economic, and intellectual systems can process information more "effectively, efficiently, and precisely" (p. 107), there has also been a propensity to grow in the complexity such that "corrupt organizations and individuals can hide or disguise themselves" (p. 115) in the vast digital system. Further explicating the use of China's social credit system based on behavioral norms which can prevent access to credit for curtained undesirable "defined standards," Chou cautioned about "the complete and involuntary loss of privacy" (p. 116) of these new digitally transparent systems. Likewise, Trettel, Cherubino, Cartocci, Rossi, Modica, Maglione, & Babiloni (2017) in their research on transparency and reliability in the corporate use of neuroscience-based marketing methodologies replete with brain scans and neuroimaging, found confusion, miscommunication, and misinformation amongst corporate decision-makers and end-users regarding the use of these opaque marketing practices. Thus, transparent leadership is widely accepted as a necessary core leadership value, as well as, "a competitive tool" and "a critical business practice" (Baum, 2005, p. 1). Baum emphatically recognizes "transparency is the single biggest challenge facing corporate America today" (p. 1).

## Defining and Conceptualizing Transparent Leadership

Accordingly, Yi, Hao, Yang, and Liu (2017) define transparent leadership "as an important leadership style" and "as the relationship between leaders and followers that the leader proactively shares relevant information during interactions with followers, is open to give and receive feedback, and shows true personal feeling, emotion, strength, and weakness" (Yi, et al., p. 335, citing Norman, Avolio, & Luthans, 2010 and Vogelgesang & Lester, 2009). Some keywords used to describe transparency include accountable, artless, candid, direct, forthright, frank, guileless, honest, ingenuous, innocent, open, unreserved, plain-spoken, straight, straightforward, and upfront. Bing's online definition of transparency of an organization or its activities is "open to public scrutiny" (Bing, 2019).

### *Communicative Aspects of Transparent Leadership*

Understandably then, as the above media reports attest of the positive and negative communicative aspects of being transparent in a political context,

Anderson (2019) noted the benefits of communicating with employees includes an "ethical environment" with an increases in "productivity and employee happiness" (p. 21). In addition to noting transparency as a tool in human resource management, Anderson also found that despite regulatory guidelines, banks found they needed to "transform into trusting organizations" (p. 1) in order to increase transparency. Such a transformation meant a cultural change through "managerial leadership, performance rewards and punishments, and communication that recognizes and develops the bank's core values in employees' day to day performances (Xu, Loi & Ngo, 2016)" (Anderson, 2019, p. 1). Interestingly, Mark Zuckerberg found when testifying to Congress about Facebook's privacy policy that much of their discussion revolved around the use of "AI tools" (Forrest, 2018c, p. 9).

### *Transparent Leadership's Tie to AI-Enhanced HR Tools*

Thus, advanced communications are just the beginning of the transparency questions that the desire for transparency engenders. New AI-enhanced tools also bring about the question of privacy versus corporate privilege. Albinus (2018) in interviews of HR executives found that AI provided an innovative ability to assess issues transparently and quickly with "a new breed of apps that offer pulse surveys, open text feedback, sentiment analysis, and organizational network analysis' (paras. 1 and 6).

## Transparent Leadership's Tie to AI-Enhanced Governance

Further, in addition to human resource issues, AI can enhance corporate governance. Demonstrably, the recruitment brochure for SteadFin Uganda Sacco, a registered savings and credit cooperative in Uganda, lists transparency as a core value: "SteadFin values openness, communication, and accountability to our members and uphold that our actions should be scrupulous enough to bear public scrutiny" (SteadFin, n.d., available from https://steadfin.com/about-us). Notably, the public question and answer site, WhatIs.com states that transparency and accountability go hand in hand as "the two main pillars of good corporate governance" (WhatIs.com, n.d., available from https://whatis.techtarget.com/search/query?q=transparency). Accordingly, Bostrom and Yudkowsky (2011), officers in Oxford University's Future of Humanity

Institute, delineated the needed supports to ethical AI as responsibility, transparency, auditability, incorruptibility, and predictability—what sounds like a recipe for good old-fashioned corporate governance.

## Why Transparent Leadership for Ethically-Aligned AI

Further, Rossi (2019), in her depiction of "building trust in artificial intelligence" starts first and foremost with IBM's principles of trust and transparency, that is, that "AI should augment human intelligence rather than replace it, trust is key to adoption, and data policies should be transparent" (p. 128). In their description of AI, the IBM Watson sales-focused white paper for IBM supply chain management notes their AI-enhanced supply chain "elevates and optimizes the supply chain organization's existing systems and capabilities to provide greater visibility, transparency, and insight into supply chain data and processes" (IBM, 2018, p. 7). Bostrom and Yudkowsky (2011) also theorize that "when AI algorithms take on cognitive work with social dimensions—cognitive tasks previously performed by humans—the AI algorithm inherits the social requirements" (p. 2). Thus, Bostrom and colleague conclude that AI must be "transparent to inspection" (p. 2).

### *Transparency of Autonomous Systems*

Thus, Rossi (2019) calls also for leaders to provide "explainability" of AI systems: "Companies and users want AI systems that are transparent, explainable, ethical, properly trained with appropriate data, and free of bias" (p. 129). Chou (2019), in observation of this Fourth Industrial Revolution in China, notes that "digital foundation and innovation can take place at the same time" for "digital readiness" even on farm fields and construction sites equipped with AI to increase connectivity and transparency. Yet, Chou issues a warning on privacy and security: "Efforts must be made to ensure that our transition into the next stage of society is conducted in a safe and sound manner" (p. 118). Rossi also notes that: "Too often, commercially retrieved AI systems are an opaque black box, offering users scarce visibility about the underlying data, processes, and logic that lead to the system's decisions... This makes explainability an outstanding challenge..." (p. 129).

### *Scriptural Principles of Transparent Leadership*

So, what guidance do the sacred scriptures give to the moral and ethical considerations in the decision to reveal or to conceal? To be open and honest or secret and silent? To divulge corporate secrets or protect corporate proprietary information?

In a highly relevant and revealing essay, Tonstad (2017) illuminates the application of the New Testament book of Revelation to transparent leadership: "The working hypothesis is that the book of Revelation is committed to transparent leadership…With such a reading, Revelation strikes a blow to religious, political, and other institutions that thrive on secrecy and concealment" (pp. 1 and 64). Treating Revelation as "a revelatory, prophetic letter" (p. 64), Tonstad highlights God's desire for transparency and accountability with communication and access, for example, Apostle John's experience of an "open" heaven. From the Talmud, Cohen (1949) elaborated on the "virtues essential to Jewish culture": brotherly love, humility, charity, forgiveness, temperance, and honesty" (Winston & Ryan, 2008, p. 219). From the Beatitudes, Jesus's fifth statement of ***markaris*** (the timeless essence of being blessed) is applicable: "Blessed are the pure in heart" (Matthew 5:4, NIV). One mention of "transparency" from Ahl's review of Bailey's (2008) book, *Jesus Through Middle Eastern Eyes*, in reference to the sixth beatitude, Ahl (n.d.) notes that "The bless-ed exhibit purity in all aspects of their interior world: oneness of focus and vision, purity of thought, and transparency and openness" (paras. 14–15). Modern Christian television celebrity John Gray in promotion of his video series "Win from Within" (2019) carried forward the experiences of patriarchs Abraham, Joseph, and Jacob with the observation that transparent leadership is an inner work with outer manifestations: "If our leaders can't get transparent...If our leaders don't get honest with the places where they failed and where they have flaws and scars, then there is no hope for the people who are coming into the knowledge of the truth...An authentic encounter with Jesus changes everything."

As I have started a literature review of "transparent leadership," I have often found that in sources which mention or have a focus on transparency in leadership there is also mention or use of the words "open" and "honest" often in the same phrase, e.g., "open, honest and transparent leadership." Tellingly, Winston also in his description of the Beatitudes does not use the words "transparent" or "transparency" but does use the words "honest" (5 instances) and "open" (13 instances): "Employees and followers want leaders who are honest, open, and who keep the organization moving in a positive direction during both calm and stormy seas" (p. 9). Winston goes on to note that the Greek word in this beatitude, ***katharos***, meaning purity "speaks directly to the integrity of a leader" (p. 72). Although the words expressing the intent may be different, there is a tendency to associate openness, honesty, and transparency with having a "pure heart."

### *Transparent Leadership Situated in the Holy Spirit*

Transparent behavior and creativity like that found through Revelation's autopoietic (self-producing, self-healing) language (Leydesdorff, 2000; Luhmann, 1986) is "situated" in the revelatory powers of the Holy Spirit. Scriptures are replete with the need to warn and expose works of darkness:

> *Proverbs 3:11 – My son, do not reject the discipline of the LORD, or loathe His reproof, For whom the LORD loves He* ***reproves****, Even as a father corrects the son in whom he delights.* (NAS)

> *Ephesians 5:12 – Do not participate in the unfruitful deeds of darkness, but instead even* ***expose*** *them.* (NAS)

> *Proverbs 28:13 – Whoever* ***conceals*** *their sins does not prosper, but the one who confesses and renounces them finds mercy.* (NIV)

Yet, the spy Rahab was used to rescue Joshua and his men, who were themselves spies, with the reward of becoming a part of the lineage of Jesus (Joshua 2:1). Thus, the sacred scriptures are also replete with God's own created mysteries, concealment, and containment of the truth, which He wished to reveal.

> *Proverbs 25:2 – It is the glory of God* ***to conceal*** *a matter, the glory of kings to investigate a matter.* (ISV)

> *Ephesians 3:9–12 –* [9] *and* ***to make plain to everyone the administration of this mystery****, which for ages past* ***was kept hidden in God****, who created all things.*[10] *His intent was that now, through the church,* ***the manifold wisdom of God should be made known to the rulers and authorities in the heavenly realms****,*[11] *according to* ***his eternal purpose*** *that he accomplished in Christ*

*Jesus our Lord.*[12] ***In him and through faith in him we may approach God with freedom and confidence.*** (NIV)

In addition to Apostles Paul and John, even Jesus said that his parables were hard to be understood; yet, Jesus encouraged his disciples to understand. Clearly, as Paul stated in Ephesians above, freedom and confidence would come to those who in faith understood God's mysteries.

Further, Bennis and colleagues, in their discussion of transparency, made clear that candor and truth are must-haves for leaders. Leaders must be "transparent and honorable" (Bennis et al., 2008, p. 93). Dubbed the Father of Leadership, Warren Bennis (2009), in respect to an epilogue to the 20th anniversary edition of his best-selling book, *On Becoming a Leader*, said: "Opacity blocks the free flow of information, the sine qua non of informed decision making and organizational health. Without candor and transparency, organizations fail" (p. 207). Winston (2002, 2010) also states, both in his foundational work on love in the workplace and an accompanying leadership training video on the applications of the Beatitudes to workplace relationships, that in an *agapao* (loving) culture, the leader does "the right thing at the right time for the right reason" (p. 5). No wonder then that Yi et al. (2017) found that psychological safety and ability to focus attention mediated the positive relationship between leaders' transparent behavior and employee creativity.

### *Application of Scriptural Principles to Transparent Leadership of Ethically-Aligned AI*

The sacred scriptures, thus, would suggest that employee creativity through both affective and cognitive routes is empowered through revelation. The Apostle Paul wrote his letter to the Ephesians so that they would understand his insight into the mystery of Christ. Transparent leadership enables employees to approach leaders with freedom and confidence. Yi et al. (2017) define employee creativity as "the generation of novel and useful ideas of products, practices, services, and procedures in workplace" (p. 335, citing Amabile, 1996). Thus, through exploration of biblical codes and principles, leaders have a well-informed and biblical approach to cultivating transparent and authentic leadership in their organizations and the innovation and creativity which flourish as a result. Bennis et al. (2008) observed: "Candor and transparency become widespread only when leaders make it clear that openness is valued and will be rewarded. Openness happens only when leaders insist on it" (p. 8).

### *Transparent Leadership's Tie to Theories of Love, Service, and Other Compassions*

Yukl's (2013) review of situational leadership theory may provide a framework for the application of scripture as to when it is appropriate to reveal and when it is appropriate to conceal as a leader. That is, the transparent leadership problem has presented as one of situation. For example, van Dierendonck and Patterson (2015), in their review of the role of compassionate love in servant leadership, described compassionate love as: "valuing the other at a fundamental level, giving the other a free choice, a cognitive accurate understanding of the needs and feelings of another, being emotionally engaged and an attitude of openness and receptivity" (p. 122) as based on the foundational research of Underwood (2008) on compassionate love. Van Dierendonck and Patterson (2015) also found a tie from servant leadership to authentic leadership's transparency and openness: "an increased self-awareness, relational transparency, internalized transparency, an internalized moral perspective and balanced processing" (p. 126). Relational transparency, is, in turn, defined as the "the open and transparent manner with which authentic leaders share information about themselves to followers, including their personal values, weaknesses, and limitations" (Hoch et al., 2018, p. 506; Ilies et al., 2005). Sendjaya, Sarros, and Santora (2008) likewise note an application of authentic leadership and its differences to servant leadership when looking at the concept of transparency: "servant leadership emphasizes a spiritual orientation, which is not strongly highlighted in the authentic leadership model. We argue that spirituality is an important source of motivation for servant leaders" (pp. 403–404). Parris and Peachey (2013) in their comprehensive literature review also noted that servant leadership characteristics included honesty: "Russell and Stone's (2002) review revealed the following nine functional attributes, or operative qualities and distinctive characteristics of servant leaders: vision, honesty, integrity, trust, service, modeling, pioneering, appreciation of others, and empowerment" (p. 380). Thus, the development of a theory of transparent leadership would of necessity need to be analyzed in coordination with the overlap of other established leadership theories as exemplified in Table 11.2.

**Table 11.2** Keywords of transparency related to leadership styles

| *Keywords/phrases related to:* | *How used:* | *Leadership style:* | *Observed by:* |
|---|---|---|---|
| Transparent/transparency | "Transparency about their limitations" (leaders encourage followers) | Servant | Sendjaya et al. (2008) |
| Transparent/transparency | "relational transparency" | Authentic | Avolio and Gardner (2005) |
| Transparent/transparency | "internalized transparency" | Authentic | Avolio and Gardner (2005) |
| Honesty | "honesty" | Servant | Russell and Stone (2002) |
| Honesty | "honest about oneself" | Authentic | Van Dierendonck and Patterson (2015) |
| Openness | "open about inner thoughts and feelings" | Authentic | Van Dierendonck and Patterson (2015) |
| Openness | "an attitude of openness and receptivity" | Servant leadership—compassionate love | Van Dierendonck and Patterson (2015) |

## Further Research and Study with Application to Leadership Theories

Although there is an abundance of use of the word "transparency" as a desired attribute of leadership in global multi-modal media, there is a dearth of research and publications on transparent leadership as a recognized leadership style. Therefore, leadership theorists would be better served through utilization of IBM Watson Content Analysis enhanced with AI coding and natural language processing to review leadership studies for congruencies with the keywords and phrases known to "transparent leadership." Thus, in reference to the systematic literature review Parris and Peachey (2013) conducted on servant leadership, there is a compelling need for a systematic literature review for transparent leadership. Such a review would be significant step towards advancing a comprehensive understanding of transparent leadership as a leadership style. Also, a systematic literature review would result in a delineation between transparent leadership style's special characteristics and any overlap with other leadership styles. Of primary interest to researchers, the systematic literature review would assist in the development of a "working" theoretical definition of transparent leadership and help to identify the behaviors which express the attributes of transparent leadership most clearly. A concomitant review of the sacred scriptures would assist with the formation of new paradigms of transparent leadership. These informed theoretical constructions would help to guide discussions and additional research to help clarify practical considerations, especially in relation to principles of transparent leadership behaviors which would advance the design, development and use of ethically-aligned AI and other advanced technologies in a super-intelligent world, whose attention, as evidenced through a profusion of media communications, is focused on artificial intelligences.

## References

Ahl, D. (n.d.). *Wisdom of the Bible—The Beatitudes—Leader's guide*. Retrieved from http://www.swapmeetdave.com/Bible/Wisdom/Beatitudes-Leader.pdf. Accessed on 13 January 2019.

Albinus, P. (2018). Data analysis, AI will drive HR executives' toolkit. *Employee Benefit Adviser (Online)*. Retrieved from http://eres.regent.edu:2048/login?url/search-proquest-om.ezproxy.regent.edu/docview/1984579427?accountid=13479.

Amabile, T. M. (1996). *Creativity in context*. Boulder, CO: Westview Press.

Anderson, J. E. (2019). *Decreasing unethical behaviors in financial institutions* (Order No. 10976320). Retrieved from ProQuest Dissertations & Theses Global (2132484444). Retrieved from http://eres.regent.edu:2048/login?url/search-proquest-om.ezproxy.regent.edu/docview/2132484444?accountid=13479.

Avolio, B. J., & Gardner, W. L. (2005). Authentic leadership development: Getting to the root of positive forms of leadership. *The Leadership Quarterly, 16*, 315–338.

Bailey, K. E. (2008). *Jesus through Middle Eastern eyes: Cultural studies in the gospels*. Downers Grove, IL: IVP Academic.

Banks, G. C., Dionne, S. D., Sayama, H. & Mast, M. S. (Eds.) (2019). Leadership in the digital era: Social media, big data, virtual reality, computational methods, and deep learning. *The Leadership Quarterly, 30*(5), 101325. https://doi.org/10.1016/s1048-9843(19)30520-x.

Baum, H. (2005). Transparent leadership. *Leader to Leader, 37,* 41–47. https://doi.org/10.1002/ltl.139.

Bennis, W. G. (2009). *On becoming a leader* (20th anniversary ed.). New York: Basic Books.

Bennis, W. G., Goleman, D., O'Toole, J., & Biederman, P. (2008). *Transparency: How leaders create a culture of candor* (1st ed.). San Francisco, CA: Jossey-Bass.

Boeing Communications. (2019, December 23). *Boeing announces leadership changes*. PRNewswire. Retrieved from https://boeing.mediaroom.com/2019-12-23-Boeing-Announces-Leadership-Changes. Accessed on 29 April 2020.

Bostrom, N. (2014). *Superintelligence: Paths, dangers, strategies*. Oxford, UK: Oxford University Press.

Bostrom, N., & Yudkowsky, E. (2011). *The ethics of artificial intelligence* [Online article]. Berkeley, CA: Machine Intelligence Research Institute. Retrieved from https://nickbostrom.com/ethics/artificial-intelligence.pdf. Accessed on 17 February 2018.

Calvert, D. (2014, October 1). *Why being transparent is so important in leadership roles* [Online blog]. ManagingAmericans.com. Retrieved from http://www.managingamericans.com/BlogFeed/Leadership-Teambuilding/Why-Being-Transparent-Is-So-Important-in-Leadership-Roles.htm. Accessed on 12 August 2019.

CBS News. (2019, March 25). *The Mueller report: A turning point*. Retrieved from https://www.cbsnews.com/news/the-mueller-report-turning-point-cbs-news-special-watch-video-2019-03-25/. Accessed on 31 March 2019.

Chou, S. (2019). The fourth industrial revolution: Digital fusion with the internet of things. *Journal of International Affairs, 72*(1), 107–120. Retrieved from https://www-jstor-org.ezproxy.regent.edu/stable/26588346.

Clark, C. M., & Harrison, C. (2018). Leadership: The complexities and state of the field. *European Business Review, 30*(5), 514–528. https://doi.org/10.1108/EBR-07-2017-0139.

Cohen, A. (1949). *Everybody's talmud*. New York: Schocken Books.

Conley, C., & Wagner-Marsh, F. (1998). The integration of business ethics and spirituality in the workplace. In L. C. Spears (Ed.), *Insights on leadership: Service, stewardship, spirit, and servant leadership* (pp. 251–267). New York: Wiley.

De Pree, M. (2004). *Leadership is an art*. New York: Crown Business.

Dow Jones Factiva. (2019). *Search all dates all sources—"Artificial Intelligence"*. Retrieved from https://global-factiva-com.ezproxy.regent.edu/ha/default.aspx#./!?&_suid=155833117925105144837986550252.

Downie, J. (2019, March 24). Republicans trapped by transparency. *Washington Post*. Retrieved from https://www.bing.com/videos/search?q=Mueller+report+transparency&&view=detail&mid=95E4F9F77D51C6CC4DB295E4F9F77D51C6CC4DB2&&FORM=VRDGAR. Accessed on 31 March 2019.

Global Data Point, Executive Appointments Monitor. (2019, March 8). *Timothy Dills takes the helm as LinQuest president and CEO*. Amman: SyndiGate Media Inc. Retrieved from http://eres.regent.edu:2048/login?url/search-proquest-com.ezproxy.regent.edu/docview/2188841258?accountid=13479.

Farrell, M. (2016). Transparency. *Journal of Library Administration, 56*, 444–452. https://doi.org/10.1080/01930826.2016.1157426.

Forrest, S. H. (2018a). *The ethical development and use of artificial intelligence: Coding values and magnitudes in the interview of a technological leader* (Coursework for PhD, Organizational Leadership). Regent University. Retrieved from the author on request.

Forrest, S. H. (2018b). *Presidents Kennedy and Obama as technological leaders: Profiles through qualitative content analysis* (Coursework for PhD, Organizational Leadership). Regent University. Retrieved from the author on request.

Forrest, S. H. (2018c). *Shaping the debate on the ethics of artificial intelligence: Analysis of the public statements of global technology leaders* (Coursework for PhD, Organizational Leadership). Regent University. Retrieved from the author on request.

Forrest, S. H. (2018d). *Ethically developing artificial intelligence: The entrepreneurial leader's role in embedding empathy and the followers' emulation intention5* (Coursework for PhD, Organizational Leadership). Regent University. Retrieved from the author on request.

Fox Business Videos. (2019, March 26). *Full Mueller report shouldn't be public, but should be transparency, Ken Starr says* [Online news report]. Retrieved from https://finance.yahoo.com/video/full-mueller-report-shouldnt-public-162944293.html. Accessed on 28 March 2019.

Gray, J. (2019, March 18). *Praise*. Available from https://watch.tbn.org/videos/praise-375. Accessed on 12 November 2020.

Hames, A. (2019, December 16). *Learning from the Boeing tragedy—The importance of transparency and trust*. HR Technologist. Retrieved from https://www.hrtechnologist.com/articles/culture/learning-from-the-boeing-tragedy-the-importance-of-transparency-and-trust/. Accessed on 29 April 2020.

Hatch, M. J. (1993). The dynamics of organizational culture. *Academy of Management Review, 18*(4), 657–693.

Hoch, J. E., Bommer, W. H., Dulebohn, J. H., & Wu, D. (2018). Do ethical, authentic, and servant leadership explain variance above and beyond transformational leadership? A meta-analysiss. *Journal of Management, 44*(2), 501–529.

Houser, D., Levy, D. M., Padgitt, K., Peart, S. J., & Xiao, E. (2014). Raising the price of talk: An experimental analysis of transparent leadership. *Journal of Economic Behavior & Organization, 105,* 208–218.

IBM. (2018). *The AI revolution: Coming to transform your business network* [Online white paper]. Retrieved from https://www.techrepublic.com/resource-library/whitepapers/ibm-the-cognitive-revolution-coming-to-transform-your-business-network/. Accessed on 9 May 2019.

Ilies, R., Morgeson, F. P., & Nahrgang, J. D. (2005). Authentic leadership and eudaemonic well-being: Understanding leader–follower outcomes. *The Leadership Quarterly, 16,* 373–394.

Institute for Electricians and Electrical Engineers. (2019). *Ethically-Aligned Design* (1st ed.). The IEEE Global Initiative on Ethics of Autonomous and Intelligent Systems. Retrieved from https://ethicsinaction.ieee.org/?utm_medium=undefined&utm_source=undefined&utm_campaign=undefined&utm_content=undefined&utm_term=undefined. Accessed on 31 March 2019.

Laurie Schrader. (2018). *Indianapolis Business Journal, 39*(41) Retrieved from http://eres.regent.edu:2048/login?url/search-proquest-com.ezproxy.regent.edu/docview/2159925420?accountid=13479.

Leydesdorff, L. (2000). Luhmann, Habermas, and the theory of communication. *Systems Research and Behavioral Science, 17*(3), 273–288.

Loewenstein, G., Cain, D. M., & Sah, S. (2011). The limits of transparency: Pitfalls and potential of disclosing conflicts of interest. *The American Economic Review, 101,* 423–428. https://doi.org/10.1257/aer.101.3.423.

Luhmann, N. (1986). The autopoiesis of social systems. In Felix Geyer & Johannes van der Zouwen (Eds.), *Sociocybernetic Paradoxes* (pp. 172–192). London: Sage.

Norman, S. M., Avolio, B. J., & Luthans, F. (2010). The impact of positivity and transparency on trust in leaders and their perceived effectiveness. *Leadership Quarterly, 21,* 350–364.

Oster, G. (2011). *The light prize: Perspectives on Christian innovation.* Virginia Beach, VA: Positive Signs Media.

Parris, D. L., & Peachey, J. W. (2013). A systematic literature review of servant leadership theory in organizational contexts. *Journal of Business Ethics, 113*(3), 377–393. https://doi.org/10.1007/s10551-012-1322-6.

Rossi, F. (2019). Building trust in artificial intelligence. *Journal of International Affairs, 72*(1), 127–134. Retrieved from https://www-jstor-org.ezproxy.regent.edu/stable/26588348.

Russell, R., & Stone, A. G. (2002). A review of servant leadership attributes: Developing a practical model. *Leadership and Organizational Development Journal, 23*(3), 145–157.

Schachter, H. (2013, July 28). *Why it's better to reveal than conceal during a crisis* [Online newspaper]. Toronto: The Globe and Mail.

Sendjaya, S., Sarros, J. C., & Santora, J. C. (2008). Defining and measuring servant leadership behaviour in organizations. *Journal of Management Studies, 45*(2), 402–424. https://doi.org/10.1111/j.1467-6486.2007.00761.x.

Shackford, S. (2019, March 22). *As the Mueller report drops, a transparency fight begins: How much will we see of the special counsel's report? And when?* [Online blog]. Reason.com. Retrieved from https://reason.com/blog/2019/03/22/as-the-mueller-report-wraps-up-a-potenti. Accessed on 28 March 2019.

Sindreu, J. (2019, Apr 24). Why boeing needs to 'own' the 737 MAX debacle: Restoring the plane maker's reputation is a higher priority for chief executive dennis muilenburg than finding a quick fix for the grounded jet. *Wall Street Journal*. Retrieved from http://eres.regent.edu:2048/login?url=https://www-proquest-com.ezproxy.regent.edu/docview/2213247149?accountid=13479.

Spisak, B. R., van der Laken, P. A., & Doornenbal, B. M. (2019). Finding the right fuel for the analytical engine: Expanding the leader trait paradigm through machine learning? *The Leadership Quarterly, 30*, 417–426.

Stack, D. (2017). *How being transparent helps scale your company*. Entrepreneur.com. Retrieved from https://www.entrepreneur.com/article/276671. Accessed on 27 April 2020.

*SteadFin Uganda Sacco*. (n.d.). [Online brochure]. Retrieved from https://steadfin.com/sites/default/files/brochure.pdf. Accessed on 31 March 2019.

Tonstad, S. K. (2017). Transparency in leadership: The divine governance challenge from the apocalypse. *The Journal of Applied Christian Leadership, 11*(2), 64–75.

*Transparency*. (2018). [Online blog]. WhatIs.com. Retrieved from https://whatis.techtarget.com/definition/transparency. Accessed on 31 March 2019.

*Transparent*. (2019). [Online dictionary]. Bing.com. Retrieved from https://www.bing.com/search?q=transparent&qs=n&form=QBRE&sp=-1&pq=transparent&sc=9-11&sk=&cvid=38EAC656BF6C4E56BEC6E1493800D858. Accessed on 30 May 2019.

Trettel, A., Cherubino, P., Cartocci, G., Rossi, D., Modica, E., Maglione, A. G., … Babiloni, F. (2017). Transparency and reliability in neuromarketing research. *Ethics and Neuromarketing, 121,* 101–111. https://doi.org/10.1007/978-3-319-45609-6_6.

Underwood, L. G. (2008). Compassionate love: A framework for research. In B. Fehr, S. Sprecher, & L. G. Underwood (Eds.), *The science of compassionate love: Theory, research, and applications* (pp. 3–25). Malden, MA: Wiley-Blackwell.

van Dierendonck, D., & Patterson, K. (2015). Compassionate love as a cornerstone of servant leadership: An integration of previous theorizing and research. *Journal of Business Ethics, 128*(1), 119–131. https://doi.org/10.1007/s10551-014-2085-z.

Vogelgesang, G. R., & Lester, P. B. (2009). Transparency: How leaders can get results by laying it on the line. *Organizational Dynamics, 38,* 252–260.

Wilder, A. (Writer), & de Segnozac, J. (Director). (2019). Apex (Television series episode). In C. Turk (Executive Producer), *FBI.* Universal City, CA: Wolf Films.

Winston, B. (2002). *Be a leader for God's sake: From values to behaviors.* Virginia Beach, VA: Regent University.

Winston, B. (2010, August 4). Leading Biblically: Beatitudes in Business, Part 1—Whether you are at the top or bottom of the business ladder, Scripture lays out specific and practical principles on how to make the most of the workplace. Retrieved from https://www.boundless.org/adulthood/leading-biblically-beatitudes-in-business-part-1/. Accessed on 13 November 2020.

Winston, B., & Ryan, B. (2008). Servant leadership as a humane orientation: Using the GLOBE study construct of humane orientation to show that servant leadership is more global than western. *International Journal of Leadership Studies, 3*(2), 212–222.

Xu, A., Loi, R., & Ngo, H. (2016). Ethical leadership behavior and employee justice perceptions: The mediating role of trust in the organization. *Journal of Business Ethics, 134,* 493–504. https://doi.org/10.1007/s10551-014-2457-4.

Yi, H., Hao, P., Yang, B., & Liu, W. (2017). How leaders' transparent behavior influences employee creativity: The mediating roles of psychological safety and ability to focus attention. *Journal of Leadership & Organizational Studies, 24*(3), 335–344. https://doi.org/10.1177/1548051816670306.

Yukl, G. (2013). *Leadership in organizations* (8th ed.). Boston: Pearson.

CHAPTER 12

# Prostitutes and Promises: Multicultural Authentic Leadership

*Amy S. Hamilton*

## Introduction

The ancient city of Jericho destroyed by the Israelites may not be the most likely place to examine authentic leadership, but nevertheless, the story of Rahab and her authentic leadership traits are explored in this chapter. Authentic leaders are described by Luthans and Avolio (2003) "as confident, optimistic, and moral" it is the last trait that will be a focus of this chapter. Sidani and Rowe (2018) explain that the followers perceive leader authenticity when there is overlap between value systems, even when there are no clear moral standards.

Clapp-Smith, Vogelgesang, and Avey (2009) state that authentic leaders can distinguish between cultural morals and values and universal moral principles. Women are faced with double standards in many cultures where male values are viewed as desirable traits for leaders and feminine traits may be viewed as weaknesses (Hopkins & O'Neil, 2015). Kapasi,

A. S. Hamilton (✉)
Regent University–School of Business and Leadership, Arlington, VA, USA
e-mail: amyhami@mail.regent.edu



B. E. Winston (eds.), *Transparent and Authentic Leadership*, Christian Faith Perspectives in Leadership and Business,
https://doi.org/10.1007/978-3-030-61996-1_12

Sang, and Sitko (2016) argue that authentic leadership is based on being true to oneself, therefore gender bias should no longer be a discriminatory factor. Ngunjiri and Hernandez (2017) argue that minority and immigrant women are excluded from the mainstream and authentic leadership may be different for minority verses majority groups.

### *The Problem*

Authentic leadership is based on a concept of being true to oneself, but this lacks context (Ngunjiri & Hernandez, 2017). Different cultures have different values, and this may cause them to view authenticity through a unique lens, but the study did not support this hypothesis on authentic leaders from Romanian and the United States (Petan & Bocarnea, 2016). This leads to the question of whether those who practice activities that Christians or others consider to immoral, but are within their own cultural morals, authentic leaders?

This chapter explores that question through a socio-rhetorical analysis of Joshua and the character of Rahab. Rahab was a harlot in Jericho, a city known for bestiality and human sacrifices (McConkie, 2004). Hopkins and O'Neil (2015) explain that authentic leaders follow their own values instead of conforming to peer pressure and societal norms. Throughout the book of Joshua Rahab is faced with multiple situations where she must choose between her own genuine belief system and pressure to conform to include local authorities.

### *Authentic Leadership*

Study in authentic leadership has continued to increase as scandals involving top leadership in companies and corporate malfeasance has been on the rise (Cooper, Scandura, & Schriesheim, 2005). Authentic leadership has been recognized as a positive leadership style that charges leaders to lead with integrity, purpose, and values (Avolio & Gardner, 2005). The concept of authenticity comes from Greek philosophy and "to thine own self be true" (Avolio & Gardner, 2005). Women in leadership are often relationally focused and part of being authentic includes being supportive and nurturing of others (Hopkins & O'Neil, 2015).

Authentic leadership has been recognized as a positive leadership style that charges leaders to lead with integrity, purpose, and values (Avolio & Gardner, 2005). A key component of authentic leadership is the need for leaders to be self-aware (Avolio & Gardner, 2005). Positivity by authentic leaders is a key trait in developing trust with followers (Norman, Avolio, & Luthans, 2010).

Another critical component of authentic leadership is trust between the leader and followers (Clapp-Smith et al. 2009). Optimism and positivity are two traits identified in authentic leaders and when these traits are perceived by followers lead to higher team performance (Clapp-Smith et al. 2009). Authentic leaders must have strong integrity and these traits influence follower performance (Leroy, Palanski, & Simons, 2012). Kapasi et al. (2016) explain that women leaders often focus on relationships with followers to include trust and communications, which could lead to a higher perception of authentic leadership.

The case can be made that authentic leadership is not a style of leadership but instead a process that takes place between leaders and followers (Sidani & Rowe, 2018). Gardner, Avolio, Luthans, May and Walumbwa (2005) posited that the relationship and personal histories of the leaders and followers would be essential to the development of authentic followers by authentic leaders. The definition of leadership for this study will use Sidani and Rowe (2018):

> Authentic leadership represents legitimated follower perceptions of a leader's authenticity which are activated by moral judgements. (p. 623)

For those who have a social identity that sets them apart from society and the majority, there is a need to have a better understanding of the contextualization of authentic leadership (Ngunjiri & Hernandez, 2017). Often leadership has been defined in masculine terms and heroic actions by men, authentic leadership studies need to consider if authentic actions are taking place based on perceived relationships (Hopkins & O'Neil, 2015). Another aspect of authentic leadership perception is culture and research support that low-power distance cultures and high-power distance cultures do not perceive authentic leaders differently (Petan & Bocarnea, 2016).

### *The Book of Joshua*

The book of Joshua is the sixth book both in the Hebrew and Christian Bibles and is the first book of the Deuteronomistic history (Kuenen, 2005). The Law is the first five books and tell the tale of Moses and how the Israelites escaped Egypt to the wilderness, when Moses prepares for his end days, he turns the mantle of leadership to Joshua (Kuenen, 2005). The book is focused on the conquests of Joshua and the Israel people and there is some question to their historical accuracy and when they were written (Kuenen, 2005).

### *Socio-Rhetorical Criticism*

Socio-Rhetorical criticism is an approach to interpretive analytical understanding of the scriptures and uses multiple techniques to include literary, social cultural, and ideological interpretations (Robbins, 2002). There are five methods used in socio-rhetorical criticism: innertexture, intertexture, social and cultural texture, ideological texture, and sacred texture (Robbins, 2002). This study uses intertexture as the primary method because the objective is to have a better understanding of the text and how it interacts with the world outside (Robbins, 2002).

Intertexture involves the interpreter working between the author and the text, not the text and the reader (Robbins, 2002). The object of intertexture is to analyze the text using four techniques: oral-scribal intertexture, historical intertexture, social intertexture, and cultural intertexture (Robbins, 2002). It is not possible to exhaustive in intertexture analysis but instead the goal is to connect the scripture to the myriad of communications and networks in the world (Robbins, 2002). Social and Culture Texture is then used to develop further understanding of the text.

### *Intertextual Analysis of Joshua 2: 1–24*

#### *Rahab Is a Prostitute*

Joshua 2: 1 (NRSV) sets the scene with Joshua sending two spies into the city of Jericho where they stayed the night at the house of a prostitute. It is important to note that many versions of the Christian bible have changed the profession of Rahab to an innkeeper, but as it is stated that it was Raheb's house, not her husband or father, implies that even as an innkeeper she would also have been expected to perform as a prostitute in this historic period (McConkie, 2004). Another significant aspect is that the two spies are not named, but Rahab is named and a central figure of the story. Verse one in Joshua two makes it clear that Rahab is practicing a profession that is deemed immoral by the Israelites.

*Rahab Gains the Trust of the Spies*
Joshua 2: 2–7 (NRSV) tells the story of how the king of Jericho hear that there were guards dispatched to the house of Rahab to capture the spies. Rahab hid the spies under stalks of flax and told the guards that the men had already left. Rahab recognized the situation as dangerous and the spies trusted her to handle the situation with the guards (Joshua 2: 4 NRSV).

*Rahab Professes Her Beliefs in God*
In Joshua 2: 8 (NRSV) Rahab goes to the men she has hidden and explains her actions. Rahab has heard of the Lord and knows that he has given the land to the Israelites and those in her land should fear them (Joshua 2: 9, NRSV). Rahab is aware that their God dried the Red Sea so they could escape Egypt and that the Israelites gad defeated Sihon and Og (Joshua 2: 10, NRSV). Rahab next professes that the Judea-Christian God is the one true God of heaven and earth (Joshua 2: 11, NRSV). Next Rahab demands of the two spies whom she had just sheltered from the guards that the Israelites will be kind to her family, sparing her parents and siblings and demands a sign of good faith (Joshua 2: 12–13, NRSV). The men make a pact with Rahab and promise to be faithful to their promise to her (Joshua 2: 14, NRSV).

*Rahab Directs the Spies on How to Escape and Makes a Pact*
The spies escape the city by her window which is part of the city wall (Joshua 2: 15, NRSV). Having an abode on the outer wall was also an indicator of social status of Rahab, because the wealthy would be in the city center and the poorest and least desirable on the outer walls where they were least protected (Matties, 1995). Rahab directs the spies to stay hidden in the hills for three days (Joshua 2: 16, NRSV). The spies doubt Rahab and tell her repeatedly that if she breaks her oath that she and her family will be killed and that the only way for her family to be safe is to tie a crimson cord in her window and have her family there where she is promised no harm will come to them (Joshua 2: 17–20, NRSV). Rahab agrees with he spies and sends them away, tying the crimson cord around her window (Joshua 2: 21, NRSV).

*The Spies Report to Joshua*

The spies listened to Raheb's directions and stayed in the hills for three days and were not found (Joshua 2: 22, NRSV). The spies then reported to Joshua (2: 23 NRSV). The spies informed Joshua that the Lord had given them the land, having placed their trust in Rahab (Joshua 2: 24 NRSV).

## *Applying the Lessons from Rahab to Today*

Despite being of a profession that was morally against the beliefs of the spies, they place their trust in her. Another ethical concern regarding Rahab may be that she lies to the King's soldiers in Joshua 2: 4–5. Jerome (1995) theorizes that just as the Pharaoh's daughter and midwives protected and hid Moses for the greater moral right, that this is message regarding the need to do what is morally right.

Most leadership studies have focused on men and leaders to include studies on authentic leadership (Hopkins & O'Neil, 2015). Throughout the book of Joshua Raheb is the only female character in a book filled with men. Rahab is as honest as possible stating that the men had come to her house and in her profession, she most likely would not have asked every customer where they came from (Jerome, 1995). Rahab is a complex story of doing what is morally right on a universal level rather than a national or personal level a fundamental authentic leadership trait according to Clapp-Smith et al. (2009). The need to place the greater moral good over national and personal morals is an important aspect of authentic leadership that applies today.

Rahab clearly demonstrates that she is willing to do what she believes is right when she hides the spies, sends the guards away, professes that the Israeli God is the true God, makes a plea to protect her family, and finally sends the spies away with directions on how to avoid being captured by the guards. Kapasi et al. (2016) found that women who have been labeled by followers as authentic leaders have a strong sense of family. In Joshua 2: 17–20, Raheb demonstrates her love and need to protect her family from harm as an authentic leader. Luthans and Avolio (2003) state that authentic leaders are optimistic, confident, and moral. These traits demonstrated by Rahab continue to be needed in authentic leaders and have been a reason why authentic leadership continues to be a leadership style that is being researched at an increasing rate.

## Conclusion

Rahab is an example of a Biblical figure that placed the greater universal morals over her national morals and values, demonstrating the attributes of authentic leadership despite being in a morally questionable profession and committing the sin of lying. As asserted by Ngunjiri and Hernandez (2017) those that come from minority and fringe populations can still express authentic leadership. This analysis supports Hopkins and O'Neil's (2015) assertion that further studies need to explore authentic leadership factors of the true self in relationships to others. Rahab demonstrates both her leadership by hiding and providing instructions to the Israelite spies and by ensuring the security of her entire family.

There is a continuous need to reevaluate bias especially as they apply to other cultures and nationalities (Petan & Bocarnea, 2016). Rahab is a story that shows a leader who was willing to immediately make decisions and protect those who needed her protection, she is a clear example of a leader that "said what they did and did what they said". Rahab's demonstration of following her genuine beliefs to include hiding the spies when the authorities came to her home garnered the trust of foreign strangers and led to an open and honest exchange that protected her family from the invaders.

## References

Avolio, B. J., & Gardner, W. L. (2005). Authentic leadership development: Getting to the root of positive forms of leadership. *The Leadership Quarterly, 16,* 315–338.

Clapp-Smith, R., Vogelgesang, G. R., & Avey, J. B. (2009). Authentic leadership and positive psychological capital: The mediating role of trust at the group level of analysis. *Journal of Leadership & Organizational Studies, 15*(3), 227–240.

Cooper, C. D., Scandura, T. A., & Schriesheim, C. A. (2005). Looking forward but learning from our past: Potential challenges to developing authentic leadership theory and authentic leaders. *The Leadership Quarterly, 16*(3), 475–493.

Gardner, W. L., Avolio, B. J., Luthans, F., May, D. R., & Walumbwa, F. (2005). "Can you see the real me?" A self-based model of authentic leader and follower development. *The Leadership Quarterly, 16*(3), 343–372.

Hopkins, M. M., & O'Neil, D. A. (2015). Authentic leadership: Application to women leaders. *Frontiers in Psychology, 6,* 959.

Jerome, O. M. (1995). Rahab in the book of Joshua and other texts of the Bible. *Journal of Humanities and Social Science, 19*(3), 19–29.

Kapasi, I., Sang, K. J., & Sitko, R. (2016). Gender, authentic leadership and identity: Analysis of women leaders' autobiographies. *Gender in Management: an International Journal, 31*(5/6), 339–358.

Kuenen, A. (2005). *An historico-critical inquiry into the origin and composition of the hexateuch: Pentateuch and book of Joshua*. Wipf and Stock Publishers.

Leroy, H., Palanski, M. E., & Simons, T. (2012). Authentic leadership and behavioral integrity as drivers of follower commitment and performance. *Journal of Business Ethics, 107*(3), 255–264.

Luthans, F., & Avolio, B. J. (2003). Authentic leadership development. *Positive Organizational Scholarship, 241*, 258.

Matties, G. H. (1995). Reading Rahab's story: Beyond the moral of the story (Joshua 2). *Direction, 24*(1), 57–70.

McConkie, R. (2004). Rahab the Harlot: Her place in the Hebrew Bible. *Selections from the Religious Student Symposium, 2004*. Provo UT: Religious Studies Center, Brigham Young University.

Ngunjiri, F. W., & Hernandez, K. A. C. (2017). Problematizing authentic leadership: A collaborative autoethnography of immigrant women of color leaders in higher education. *Advances in Developing Human Resources, 19*(4), 393–406.

Norman, S. M., Avolio, B. J., & Luthans, F. (2010). The impact of positivity and transparency on trust in leaders and their perceived effectiveness. *The Leadership Quarterly, 21*(3), 350–364.

Petan, L., & Bocarnea, M. (2016). Follower perceptions of authentic leadership: A comparison between respondents from Romania and the United States. *Procedia-Social and Behavioral Sciences, 221*, 142–150.

Robbins, V. K. (2002). *The tapestry of early Christian discourse: Rhetoric, society and ideology*. Routledge.

Sidani, Y. M., & Rowe, W. G. (2018). A reconceptualization of authentic leadership: Leader legitimation via follower-centered assessment of the moral dimension. *The Leadership Quarterly, 29*(6), 623–636.

# Conclusion

## *Introduction*

This conclusion restates the main points from each chapter by unit. The focus here is to help the reader see the authentic and transparent leadership connections made by each author. The conclusion ends with a recommendation for additional study on the concepts of authentic and transparent leadership from a Christian perspective.

## *Unit One—Genuine Self-Concepts*

Kristan Price Mason's chapter provides the reader with the understanding that authentic leaders are self-aware and self-actualized. These two self-concepts enhance the leaders' abilities to approach problems and decisions with mindfulness about employees, stakeholders, and society as a whole.

Danica Myers then addresses how Web 2.0 communication technologies impact leaders' communication and enhance the leader's group-leadership and communication. Authentic leaders use digital communication methods to connect with and engage group members. Meyers points out that authentic leaders adapt to changes in the environment to build greater group cohesion and identity. Meyers stresses the desire of employees and stakeholders to seek leaders who are authentic, open, transparent, and moral.



B. E. Winston (eds.), *Transparent and Authentic Leadership*, Christian Faith Perspectives in Leadership and Business,
https://doi.org/10.1007/978-3-030-61996-1

Newcomb described female authentic leaders as being hopeful, optimistic, resilient, and transparent. Newcomb echoes Mason's understanding that authentic leaders are self-actualized and Myers' focus on authentic leaders as excellent communicators. Meyers posits that authentic leaders have the traits expressed by Northouse: (a) purposeful, (b) values-based, (c) trusting, (d) self-disciplined, and (e) purpose-driven. Newcomb adds that authentic leaders are hopeful and resilient. Newcomb illustrates her insights by examining the Biblical accounts of Deborah and Naomi.

Tim Gregory examines the eight leadership principles of King Josiah that enabled him to lead his nation in what could be considered one of the greatest reform movements to ever be successfully undertaken. According to Gregory, authentic leaders have moral integrity and set the moral standards of behavior. Authentic leaders value and esteem groups and teams. Gregory points out that authentic leaders are honest and transparent as demonstrated in the leaders' communication with followers. Authentic leaders are humble with regard to themselves and just in their treatment of others. According to Gregory, authentic leaders take the good path as they seek to achieve the organization's purpose and mission.

Julie Headley reviewed the lives of ancient Biblical leaders. Daniel, Joseph, and David as three exemplary leaders in the Old Testament that demonstrated the four components of authentic leadership: self-awareness, relational transparency, balanced processing, and internalized moral perspective. By applying the lives of these men to lessons of modern-day authentic leadership, current leaders can further develop their authentic leadership skills.

### *Unit Two—Honest Roles*

Unit two begins with Patrick Millsap's discussion of Balaam and his donkey, which is a story that reveals both authentic leadership and followership and inauthentic leadership and followership. The chapter includes applications for authentic leadership, authentic followership, and the possibility of authentic organizational context, or culture.

Daniel Holmquist presents a new model of judicious transparency. Judicious transparency refers to the wise, discerning, astute, and sensible use of transparency that seeks to build trust within organizations. This approach to transparency offers a more refined and robust understanding of the nature of transparency, a potentially stronger and more productive way of practicing transparency.

Andrew Morgan presents accounts of the disciple Peter's life from an intrapersonal and interpersonal perspective of authentic leadership. Peter's account offers an example of authentic and transparent leadership showing an honest focus on conviction and transparency of motive and interest. Morgan presented how Peter developed interpersonal relationships using the authentic leadership dimensions of self-awareness, moral perspective, and balanced processing.

### *Unit Three—Ethical Leadership*

Alicia Peltier discussed leaders use of social media and how transparency and authenticity should be demonstrated. Ethical-based leadership supports how leaders cultivate authentic relationships with stakeholders. Peltier included the concept of *Agapao* (love) in describing authentic leaders' relationship with followers. Agapao, as presented by Peltier, is the base of the beatitudes that can, and should, guide our behavior toward others.

Emmanuel Mamaril examined the Prophet Nathan's rebuke of King David which offers contemporary leaders and followers the power of effective followership and its impact in improving leader transparency. Mamaril, used the case example of Boeing and the 737 Max aircraft as a platform to discuss ethical transparent communication.

Sharon Hathaway Forest examines what transparent leadership behaviors are most likely to ensure ethically aligned design and use of AI, the Internet of Things (IoT), blockchain, and cloud services. Her chapter looks at how the rapidity of advanced communications and pervasiveness of social media influence a new digital transparency in leadership along with heightened concerns for privacy and security. Leaders who desire to guide their organizations in the ethical design, development, and use of artificial intelligence and other advanced technologies will find the chapter highlights illuminative strategies for transparent actions and communications.

Amy S. Hamilton examined Rahab's traits and authentic leadership behaviors through a socio-rhetorical analysis of the book of Joshua. Hamilton's chapter explores the question of whether a person who behaves in ways that align with his/her culture but are not aligned with other cultures can be authentic. Hamilton illustrates the concept of 'to thine own self be true.'

### *Conclusion*

Future research might look at case studies of contemporary authentic and transparent leaders with a focus on deeper understanding of the Biblical principles associated with authentic and transparent leadership. Operationalized statements of Biblically based authentic and transparent leadership may pave the way for new measures that include Biblical principles. Case studies of contemporary employees that experienced positive outcomes through the interaction with authentic and transparent leaders may help scholars understand additional benefits of practicing authenticity and transparency.

# Index





B. E. Winston (eds.), *Transparent and Authentic Leadership*, Christian Faith Perspectives in Leadership and Business,
https://doi.org/10.1007/978-3-030-61996-1

The manufacturer's authorised representative in the EU is Springer Nature Customer Service Centre GmbH, Europaplatz 3, 69115 Heidelberg, Germany. If you have any concerns regarding our products, please contact ProductSafety@springernature.com

Printed and bound by CPI Group (UK) Ltd, Croydon, CR0 4YY

30/09/2026

02225702-0004